BREAKTHROUGH

BREAKTHROUGH

The Struggles and Secret Talks that Brought Apartheid South Africa to the Negotiating Table

MAC MAHARAJ AND Z. PALLO JORDAN

PENGUIN BOOKS

Published by Penguin Books
an imprint of Penguin Random House South Africa (Pty) Ltd
Reg. No. 1953/000441/07
The Estuaries No. 4, Oxbow Crescent, Century Avenue, Century City, 7441
PO Box 1144, Cape Town, 8000, South Africa
www.penguinrandomhouse.co.za

Penguin
Random House
South Africa

First published 2021
Reprinted in 2021 (twice)

3 5 7 9 10 8 6 4

Publication © Penguin Random House 2021
Text © Mac Maharaj and Z. Pallo Jordan 2021

Cover images: Oliver Tambo: © Marc Hutten/AFP via Getty Images;
P.W. Botha: © Gallo Images; Nelson Mandela and
F.W. de Klerk: © Louise Gubb/CORBIS SABA/Corbis via Getty Images

PUBLISHER: Marlene Fryer
MANAGING EDITOR: Robert Plummer
EDITOR: Bronwen Maynier
PROOFREADER: Alice Inggs
COVER DESIGNER: Ryan Africa
TYPESETTER: Monique van den Berg
INDEXER: Sanet le Roux

Set in 11.5 pt on 16.5 pt Adobe Garamond

Printed by **novus print**, a division of Novus Holdings

MIX
Paper from
responsible sources
FSC
www.fsc.org   FSC® C022948

ISBN 978 1 77609 647 3 (print)
ISBN 978 1 77609 648 0 (ePub)

Contents

Foreword vii

Chronology of Events, 1980–1990 ix

Abbreviations xxiii

1. Breakthrough 1

2. The Imprisoned Society 7

3. The Landscape Is Reconfigured 15

4. Apartheid Bows, But Does Not Bend 25

5. The Gathering Storm 35

6. State Terrorism 51

7. The White Laager Wavers 63

8. Botha Trips Himself 71

9. Shaping Setbacks into Opportunities 97

10. Seizing the Initiative 119

11. Botha in a Bind 147

12. New Terrain, New Challenges 167

Annexures

A. Memo from Nelson Mandela to P.W. Botha 181

B. Constitutional Guidelines for a Democratic South Africa 193

C. Harare Declaration 199

Bibliography 207

About the Authors 213

Index 215

Foreword

Why and how South Africa moved from the certainty of the abyss into which apartheid had propelled it to the promise of a non-racial, non-sexist democracy buttressed by an ambitious Constitution are essential questions, not only to understand the past but also to come to terms with the present and embrace the future.

Several publications have claimed that one or other person, generally someone with some connection to the *ancien régime*, was the key to the dramatic changes that occurred in the early nineties. But a sustained analysis by key ANC figures in the move towards constitutional democracy has not been available until the authors of this work, Mac Maharaj and Pallo Jordan, set pen to paper. Both have much to offer in search of answers. They did not simply sit in the grandstand observing proceedings. They were on the field of play, buttressed by the struggle of the millions who bore the brunt of an inhuman system, seeking with their comrades to replace racist authoritarianism with non-racial democracy.

This book crisply and incisively documents the often slow but nevertheless inexorable political process by which the ANC gained the upper hand in its bitter contest with the National Party government. With no more room for manoeuvre other than to enter negotiations with the very organisation that it had sought to destroy over a period of more than forty years, the apartheid regime buckled.

The authors' understanding of the relationship between the balance of political forces and the importance of the internal struggle – led with increasing intensity and success by the independent trade union movement and the United Democratic Front, and combined with the moral authority of the ANC in the eyes of the majority of South Africans – produces a book of nuanced analysis and a narrative that has not been available to the public until now. Although the desperate attempts by P.W. Botha and his securocrat minions to divide their opposition are set out luminously, as are the strategies adopted by the ANC, the unbending moral conduct of Nelson Mandela in placing the interests of the nation above his personal liberty and the astute leadership of the ANC by Oliver Tambo are not forgotten; the roles of these two giants of the liberation movement are discussed in fitting detail.

The book also provides a ringside seat to the deliberations within the ANC as the movement began to translate the principles of the Freedom Charter into a justiciable Constitution. In this respect, the role of Pallo Jordan in pushing for consideration of a Bill of Rights as the ANC sought to negotiate the setback caused by the signing of the Nkomati Accord between South Africa and Mozambique in 1984, together with the work of the ANC Constitutional Committee constituted after the publication of the Jordan document, will be of great interest to constitutional scholars. It will also serve to debunk the claim of a constitutional 'sell out' so prevalent among contemporary populists.

Reading this book, I could not help but think of the enormous sacrifices that were made by millions to finally defeat apartheid and which this work consistently recognises. But it also serves to remind South Africa of the astute leadership of Mandela, Tambo and others who were deeply committed to a democracy based on freedom, equality and dignity for all. We are fortunate that Mac Maharaj and Pallo Jordan, who have lived that very commitment, have provided answers to our past in a way that should help guide us through present attacks on the very fabric of the constitutional enterprise.

DENNIS DAVIS
RETIRED JUDGE PRESIDENT
COMPETITION APPEAL COURT

Chronology of Events, 1980–1990

1980
---

8 January	African National Congress (ANC) annual January 8 statement declares 1980 'the Year of the Freedom Charter'.
4 April	Booysens Police Station is attacked by G5 unit of uMkhonto weSizwe (MK), which includes Petrus Jabane and Anthony 'Bobby' Tsotsobe.
18 April	Zimbabwe becomes independent.
June	Tennyson Makiwane is killed in the Transkei.
1 June	Sasol I at Sasolburg and Sasol II at Secunda are attacked.
12 June	Major General J.R. Roux profiles Nelson Mandela.
July	Percy Qoboza of the *Sunday Post* launches renewed campaign for the release of Nelson Mandela.
14 September	Council of Unions of South Africa is launched.
October	Chief Gatsha Buthelezi appoints the Buthelezi Commission to propose a regional constitutional dispensation for Natal, including KwaZulu.
21 November	Surrounded in a house in Chiawelo by the South African Police (SAP), Petrus Jabane fights back until he is killed (he is hence known as the Lion of Chiawelo).
28 November	Oliver Tambo signs declaration of adherence to the Geneva Conventions of 1949 and their Protocol I of 1977.

1981

According to the South African Institute of Race Relations (SAIRR), between January and October 1981 there are at least forty ANC guerrilla attacks in urban areas; there are seventeen between July 1979 and June 1980.

30 January	South African Defence Force (SADF) raid Matola, Maputo, killing sixteen South Africans and one Mozambican.
April	United Women's Organisation is launched.
May	Month set aside for the twentieth Republic Day celebrations.
31 July	Joe Gqabi is assassinated in Harare.
10 August	SADF military headquarters at Voortrekkerhoogte is attacked.
September	Detainees' Parents Support Committee is launched.

1982

According to the SAIRR, there are at least twenty-six sabotage attacks by the ANC between December 1981 and November 1982; thirteen suspected ANC cadres are killed in shoot-outs with the SAP. According to the SAP, there are thirty-nine acts of insurgency in 1982.

8 January	ANC declares 1982 'the Year of Unity in Action'.
February	South Africa and Swaziland enter into secret non-aggression and land deals.
5 February	Dr Neil Aggett, a trade unionist, is killed in detention.
14 March	ANC headquarters in London is bombed.
April	Mandela and four others are moved from Robben Island to Pollsmoor Prison.
3 May	P.W. Botha asks State Security Council (SSC) for advice regarding Mandela.
25 May	SSC submits document by Lieutenant General J.F. Otto providing this strategic advice.
June	SSC discusses the strategic advice and concludes that Mandela cannot be released and that the matter will be reviewed annually.
4 June	Petrus and Jabulile Nyawose are killed in Swaziland.

August	World Alliance of Reformed Churches declares apartheid a heresy and suspends membership of the Nederduitse Gereformeerde Kerk and Nederduitsch Hervormde Kerk.
17 August	Ruth First is killed by a parcel bomb in Maputo.
9 December	SADF raids Maseru, massacring forty-two people.
18 December	Koeberg nuclear power plant is attacked.

1983

	Revolutionary Council is replaced by Politico-Military Council.
	J.P. de Lange is elected chair of the Broederbond.
	Dr Wouter Basson is authorised to set up Project Coast devoted to the development and use of chemical and biological weapons.
23 January	Reverend Allan Boesak suggests idea of a united democratic front at a conference of the Transvaal Anti-South African Indian Council Committee.
20 May	Car bomb explodes near the South African Air Force (SAAF) headquarters in Church Street, Pretoria, prematurely at 16:30, killing nineteen people, of whom at least eleven are SAAF officers.
June	Azanian People's Organisation, Azanian Students' Movement, Action Youth, Cape Action League and other organisations launch the National Forum.
20 August	United Democratic Front (UDF) is launched. Delegates from 565 organisations participate in the launch at the Rocklands Community Hall in Mitchells Plain.
22 September	Tricameral dispensation becomes law.
2 November	Referendum approves Botha's tricameral constitutional proposals.
6 December	SADF launches Operation Askari in Angola.

1984

	SADF troops deployed in townships.
	SADF raid into Botswana kills three people execution-style.
	Tambo sets up a committee convened by Pallo Jordan to investigate the feasibility of negotiations.
3 January	Twenty-one members of the SADF are killed during operation Askari in clash with Cuban/Angolan forces at Cuvelai.
February	Stuart Commission investigates unrest in the MK camps in Angola.
16 February	Angola, Cuba and South Africa sign Lusaka Accord establishing a no-man's land in southern Angola.
16 March	Botha and Samora Machel sign the Nkomati Accord.
29 May	Botha sets out on eight-nation European tour.
27 June	Cradock Four are murdered by a hit squad.
28 June	Parcel bomb kills Jeanette Schoon and her six-year-old daughter, Katryn, in Lubango, Angola.
August	Professor H.W. van der Merwe meets Alfred Nzo and Thabo Mbeki in Lusaka.
	South African team headed by Niël Barnard meet Soviet team in Vienna, Austria.
	Effective boycott of elections for the tricameral Coloured and Indian chambers.
15 September	Botha is inaugurated state president.
December	Dr Piet Muller of *Beeld* publishes report-based interview with Thabo Mbeki.

1985

According to the Institute for Strategic Studies, Pretoria, there are 136 MK attacks during this year, a 209 per cent increase compared with figures for 1984.

Popo Molefe, Terror Lekota and twenty others on trial at Delmas for treason.

	Military Intelligence commence Operation Marion to provide Chief Buthelezi with paramilitary capability to take on the ANC/UDF.
	Forty ANC/MK cadres suffer from poisoning at a transit camp in Chelston, Lusaka.
20 January	Lord Bethell visits Mandela at Pollsmoor Prison.
23 January	Professor Samuel Dash visits Mandela.
31 January	Botha offers to release Mandela if he renounces violence.
10 February	Mandela's response read out by Zindzi Mandela at Jabulani Stadium, Soweto.
13 February	Mandela and his colleagues write to Botha rejecting his offer.
April	*Leadership* editor Hugh Murray meets Thabo Mbeki and proposes an ANC/business meeting.
15 May	Brakpan Commissioners Court and offices of the Messenger of the Court in Brakpan are attacked on the morning of the funeral of Andries Raditsela, who died in detention.
June	Klaas de Jonge escapes detention and takes refuge in the Netherlands embassy in Pretoria.
	From mid-June, a range of paramilitary and 'vigilante' groups appear in the townships.
14 June	Operation Plecksy: fifty members of the SADF raid Botswana; twelve people are killed and six injured; eight houses and two offices are destroyed.
16 June	ANC Consultative Conference is held in Kabwe, Zambia.
26 June	Eight activists killed and seven wounded by booby-trapped hand grenades provided by apartheid agent Joe Mamasela.
July	Soweto 'Suicide Squad' attacks homes of two Soweto policemen.
20 July	Partial state of emergency covering thirty-four districts is declared.
	Maki Skosana is murdered at a Duduza rally in the first 'necklace' killing due to a rumour planted by Joe Mamasela that she was an informer.

31 July	Chase Manhattan Bank announces it will no longer roll over credits and grant new loans to South Africa.
15 August	Botha delivers his 'Rubicon' speech at the National Party (NP) congress in Durban.
September	Buthelezi and Frederik van Zyl Slabbert launch the National Convention Alliance.
2 September	Botha regime imposes a four-month freeze on the repayment of debts because its foreign exchange reserves are under pressure.
14 September	ANC and a business delegation led by Gavin Relly meet at Mfuwe, Zambia.
October	Special meeting of the SSC Coordinating Intelligence Committee discusses whether it is possible to avoid a settlement with the ANC.
12 October	ANC and the Progressive Federal Party (PFP) meet in Lusaka, Zambia.
15 October	Three youth killed by Security Branch in 'Trojan horse massacre' in Cape Town.
16 October	Commonwealth Conference establishes the Eminent Persons Group (EPG).
18 October	Malesela Benjamin Moloise executed despite calls for clemency.
31 October	Margaret Thatcher writes a letter to Botha about the Commonwealth Conference.
November	Minister of constitutional development Chris Heunis announces creation of 5 000 municipal police known as *kitskonstabels*.
	Four people, including SAP officer, his wife, and railways police, killed in Cape Town in various hand-grenade attacks. Twenty such attacks are recorded by this time according to the SAP.
	Sasol II and III attacked; three cadres killed by SAP.
	Anti-tank mine in Soutpansberg area injures four SADF members and four civilians.

3 November	Mandela hospitalised at Volks Hospital.
3/4 November	Kobie Coetsee visits Mandela at Volks Hospital.
4 November	*Cape Times* editor Tony Heard publishes an interview with Tambo.
23 November	Mandela discharged from Volks Hospital. On return to prison, he is separated from his colleagues at Pollsmoor.
27 November	ANC subcommittee headed by Pallo Jordan submits paper titled 'A submission on the question of negotiations'.
December	National Education Crisis Committee meets ANC in Lusaka.
1 December	Launch of the Congress of South African Trade Unions (COSATU) consisting of thirty-three unions representing 460 000 organised workers.
13 December	One soldier is killed when SADF troop carrier explodes anti-tank mine.
14 December	One cadre killed in stand-off in Chiawelo.
20 December	SADF launches attacks in Botswana, Zambia and Zimbabwe; nine killed in Botswana and three in Zimbabwe.
20 December	Six killed in Messina by anti-tank mine.

1986

	Samuel Phinda and Themba Ngesi die from poisoning in separate incidents in Mozambique.
January	UDF delegation led by Arnold Stofile meets ANC in Sweden.
8 January	ANC Constitutional Committee meets on 8–12 and 14 January 1986. ANC January 8 statement calls on people to make apartheid unworkable and South Africa ungovernable.
February	Mandela sends George Bizos to brief Tambo.

February	Van Zyl Slabbert resigns from parliament and leadership of the PFP.
	EPG makes its first visit to South Africa.
28 February	Olof Palme, prime minister of Sweden, is assassinated.
March	Joint alliance/COSATU communiqué notes that 'lasting solutions can only emerge from the national liberation movement, headed by the ANC, and the entire democratic forces of our country, of which COSATU is an important and integral part'.
3 March	Gugulethu Seven led into ambush and killed by Security Branch.
14 March	Coetsee confirms with Botha that he will continue his talks with Mandela while a team headed by Barnard meets with Mandela separately.
April	ANC considers EPG proposal.
	Coetsee commissions the South African Law Reform Commission to look into the definition and protection of group rights.
May	Mbeki meets De Lange, chair of the Broederbond, at a conference on education organised by the Ford Foundation.
16 May	EPG puts its proposal to Mandela.
19 May	EPG meets Botha's cabinet committee.
20 May	SADF air strikes on Gaborone, Harare and Lusaka end EPG initiative.
June	Broederbond discusses position paper, 'Basic political policy conditions for the survival of the Afrikaner', which advocates consultations beyond the ranks of collaborators.
	Mandela meets General Willemse, who arranges a meeting between Mandela and Coetsee at the latter's residence.
12 June	Countrywide state of emergency imposed.
14 June	Car bomb outside Magoo's and the Why Not bars in Durban kills three and injures sixty-nine.
24 June	Tambo meets businessmen in London, including Michael Young of Consolidated Gold Fields.

25 June	Two car bomb attacks in Johannesburg.
July	After a two-hour gun battle, SAP kill one cadre.
30 July	Three SAP officers and four civilians killed, and seven SAP injured in attack on Umtata police station.
9 August	Lieutenant Victor Raju killed in grenade attack on his home in Durban.
16 August	Anti-tank mine kills five and injures two civilians in Eastern Transvaal.
22 August	Grenade attack on Winnington Sabelo of Inkatha kills his wife, Evelyn, and injures their three children.
September	British foreign secretary Geoffrey Howe meets Tambo.
2 October	Comprehensive Anti-Apartheid Act of 1986, first introduced in 1985, passed by US Congress.
6 October	Anti-tank mine injures six SADF members in Mbuzini, near Mozambique.
10 November	Two bombs explode at Newcastle Magistrate's Court, injuring twenty-four people, including the magistrate and prosecutor.
December	Mandela taken on sightseeing trip of Cape Town.

1987

	Mandela and Coetsee hold three meetings; between 1985 and December 1989 they meet at least fifteen times.
8 January	ANC statement commits to Bill of Rights and multiparty democracy.
20 January	KwaMakhutha massacre: twelve women and children killed by men trained under Operation Marion.
29 January	Tambo meets George Schultz, the US secretary of state.
February	Adriaan Vlok refuses to disclose to parliament the number and nature of sabotage, armed attacks and explosions that occurred during 1986. The Institute for Strategic Studies states there were 230 incidents of insurgency, a 69.1 per cent increase over the 136 incidents in 1985.

28 May	In his Canon Collins Memorial Lecture, Tambo draws attention to an alternative democratic power emerging in the country that needs to be supported while maintaining the isolation of apartheid South Africa.
9 July	Job Tabane (aka Cassius Maake) and Peter Sello Motau (aka Paul Dikeledi) are assassinated in Swaziland by apartheid security forces.
	Dakar Conference organised by the Institute for Democratic Alternatives in South Africa begins with sixty-one people from South Africa attending.
14 July	National Union of Mineworkers conference adopts the Freedom Charter.
30 July	Car bomb outside Witwatersrand Command kills one SADF member and injures sixty-eight military personnel and civilians.
30 August	Grenade thrown at soldiers at military barracks in Dobsonville kills or injures an estimated eight SADF members.
September	Marble Hall commander of KwaNdebele National Guard and his son (an SAP officer) found killed by AK-47.
7 September	Prisoner exchange involving 133 Angolan soldiers, two Frenchmen and Klaas de Jonge for Captain Wynand du Toit and the remains of two South African Special Forces soldiers killed in Cabinda takes place in Maputo.
6 October	Mandela and Coetsee meet at the Pollsmoor Prison guesthouse.
7 October	First of eight Mells Park talks takes place between ANC and a group led by Willie Esterhuyse.
9 October	ANC National Executive Committee (NEC) issues statement titled 'The question of negotiations'.
5 November	Govan Mbeki and Harry Gwala released from prison.
1 December	ANC International Solidarity Conference begins in Arusha, Tanzania.

December   Culture in Another South Africa, held in Amsterdam, adopts a nuanced policy on sport and cultural boycotts.

1988

      Detentions, trials, press censorship and military occupation of townships take their toll; UDF immobilised and COSATU taking strain.

February   Crackdown in the form of regulations in terms of the state of emergency restrict the UDF and sixteen other organisations as well as individuals and the press.

22 February   Second Mells Park meeting, with Mbeki leading the ANC team.

23 March   End of the battle of Cuito Cuanavale in Angola.

29 March   Dulcie September is assassinated in Paris.

25 May   First meeting between Mandela and the team led by Barnard. By December 1989, they will have met forty-eight times.

11 July   Nelson Mandela 70th Birthday Tribute concert at Wembley Stadium.

August   ANC publishes 'Constitutional Guidelines for a Democratic South Africa' for public discussion.

12 August   Mandela is admitted to Tygerberg Hospital.

21 August   Third Mells Park meeting.

October   ANC and South African Rugby Board meet in Harare.

December   Fourth Mells Park meeting.

      Operation Vula enables Mandela and Tambo to communicate secretly.

22 December   New York Accord between Angola, Cuba and South Africa signed and to be implemented on 1 April 1989; independence for Namibia; withdrawal of Cuban forces from Angola.

1989

January	Botha suffers a stroke.
February	Botha relinquishes NP leadership but remains president of South Africa; F.W. de Klerk becomes new leader of the NP.
23 February	ANC, International Campaign Against Apartheid Sport and South African Non-Racial Olympic Committee meet in Lusaka.
April	During April, Mandela and Coetsee meet three times; Mandela gives Coetsee the letter to Botha and Operation Vula sends the text to Tambo.
21 April	Fifth Mells Park meeting.
May	Tambo informs Mac Maharaj of need to develop a kind of '435' position to be formulated by the ANC and adopted by the Frontline States and Organisation of African Unity (OAU).
6 June	UDF/COSATU delegation briefed by ANC on above developments and their views solicited.
16 June	Tambo asks Operation Vula for inputs from selected individuals, including Mandela.
26 June	Programme of defiant action discussed at ANC/UDF/COSATU meeting.
July	Maharaj meets Tambo, Joe Slovo and Ivan Pillay in Moscow.
5 July	Botha meets Mandela at Tuynhuys.
26 July	Mass Democratic Movement and COSATU announce national defiance campaign.
July	End of July, Mandela gives Barnard a copy of his letter to Botha that he delivered through Coetsee in April.
8 August	ANC finalises position on draft that later becomes the Harare Declaration; that evening, Tambo suffers a stroke.
15 August	Botha gives up the presidency. To defuse the defiance campaign, De Klerk announces he will repeal Separate Amenities Act, etc.

21 August	Harare Declaration adopted by the OAU Ad-hoc Committee on Southern Africa.
September	ANC NEC meets and considers Mandela's letter to Botha.
3 September	Twenty-three people killed by police in different parts of the country.
6 September	NP wins general election, but with reduced majority.
12 September	First direct ANC and National Intelligence Service (NIS) talks take place in Lucerne, Switzerland.
13 September	De Klerk allows a march in Cape Town of 50 000 people led by Archbishop Desmond Tutu and Reverend Boesak.
14 September	De Klerk inaugurated president of South Africa.
29 September	Sixth Mells Park meeting; Tony Trew records that an element of 'talks about talks' has become evident.
10 October	Coetsee and Gerrit Viljoen meet Mandela.
15 October	Rivonia trialists are released, along with the ANC's Wilton Mkwayi and Oscar Mpetha, and Jafta Masemola of the Pan Africanist Congress.
November	Mandela writes to De Klerk concerning the need to create a climate of understanding so that negotiations can take place.
1 November	Mandela and Coetsee meet.
5 November	Mandela and Coetsee meet.
3 December	De Klerk holds cabinet bosberaad.
8 December	Mike Louw of the NIS sends Coetsee a memo. Conference for a Democratic South Africa held in Johannesburg, attended by 4 600 delegates.

1990

29 January	Three-ministers committee asks for recommendation concerning the release question and related matters, including amnesty.
2 February	De Klerk announces changes that enable progress to be made towards negotiations.

9 February   De Klerk and Mandela meet.
              Seventh Mells Park meeting.

11 February   Mandela, on the day of his release from Victor Verster Prison, addresses a mass rally from the balcony of Cape Town City Hall.

20 March   Gibson Njenje, Jacob Zuma, Mathews Phosa and Penuell Maduna arrive in South Africa to attend to logistics of a government and ANC meeting.

2 May   Government and ANC meet at Groote Schuur.

Abbreviations

ANC: African National Congress
AZAPO: Azanian People's Organisation
COSATU: Congress of South African Trade Unions
CUSA: Council of Unions of South Africa
EPG: Eminent Persons Group
FLS: Frontline States
FOSATU: Federation of South African Trade Unions
FRELIMO: Mozambique Liberation Front
IDASA: Institute for Democratic Alternatives in South Africa
IFP: Inkatha Freedom Party
IPRD: Internal Political and Reconstruction Department
JMC: Joint Management Centre
MDM: Mass Democratic Movement
MK: uMkhonto weSizwe
MPLA: People's Movement for the Liberation of Angola
NEC: National Executive Committee
NIS: National Intelligence Service
NP: National Party
NSC: National Statutory Council
NSMS: National Security Management System
NUM: National Union of Mineworkers
NWC: National Working Committee
OAU: Organisation of African Unity
PAC: Pan Africanist Congress
PFP: Progressive Federal Party
PMC: Politico-Military Council

RC: Revolutionary Council
RENAMO: Mozambican National Resistance
SACC: South African Council of Churches
SACOS: South African Council on Sport
SACP: South African Communist Party
SACTU: South African Congress of Trade Unions
SADC: Southern African Development Community
SADF: South African Defence Force
SAIRR: South African Institute of Race Relations
SANROC: South African Non-Racial Olympic Committee
SAP: South African Police
SARB: South African Rugby Board
SARU: South African Rugby Union
SSC: State Security Council
STRATCOM: Strategy Planning, Strategic Communications
SWAPO: South West Africa People's Organisation
TRC: Truth and Reconciliation Commission
UDF: United Democratic Front
UN: United Nations
UNITA: National Union for the Total Independence of Angola
ZANLA: Zimbabwe African National Liberation Army
ZANU: Zimbabwe African National Union
ZAPU: Zimbabwe African People's Union
ZIPRA: Zimbabwe People's Revolutionary Army

1

Breakthrough

It is Wednesday, 2 May 1990. The venue: Groote Schuur, Cape Town.[1]

For the first time in the forty-two-year history of apartheid rule, the National Party (NP) government is holding an official meeting with a delegation of the African National Congress (ANC).

President F.W. de Klerk is heading the government delegation. As president of the country and leader of the National Party, he is hosting the meeting at his official residence. Seated opposite him is Nelson Mandela, deputy president of the ANC, first commander-in-chief of its military wing uMkhonto weSizwe (MK),[2] arch adversary of apartheid and champion of a united, non-racial and non-sexist South Africa. The serving president of the ANC, Oliver Tambo, suffered a debilitating stroke in exile on 8 August 1989. In his absence, Nelson Mandela, who was released on 11 February 1990 after being imprisoned for twenty-seven years, is leading the ANC team.

Mandela is flanked by Walter Sisulu, Joe Slovo, Alfred Nzo, Thabo Mbeki, Ahmed Kathrada, Joe Modise, Ruth Mompati, Archie Gumede, Reverend Beyers Naudé and Cheryl Carolus. De Klerk's team includes ministers Gerrit Viljoen, Pik Botha, Dawie de Villiers, Kobie Coetsee, Barend du Plessis, Adriaan Vlok, Stoffel van der Merwe and Roelf Meyer – all white Afrikaners and not a woman among them.

---

1. Groote Schuur was the name of the official residence of President F.W. de Klerk. When Nelson Mandela became president in 1994, De Klerk, who was one of the two deputy presidents in the democratic government, requested that he continue living at Groote Schuur. President Mandela therefore occupied Westbrooke, changing its name to Genadendal. Since that time, the latter has been the official residence of the president of the Republic of South Africa.
2. uMkhonto weSizwe means 'The Spear of the Nation'.

The talks at Groote Schuur marked the end of skirmishing in the shadows and the beginning of formal negotiations. A long and torturous road lay ahead. It would be another four years and eight days before Mandela became the president of a democratic South Africa. During this period the country would swing wildly between high expectations and dashed hopes and see the senseless slaughter of thousands of black people. In the end, however, the country was able, through dialogue, to transition from apartheid to democracy.

How did South Africa arrive at this moment when negotiations were about to begin?

F.W. de Klerk had spent his political life consumed with the task of managing the implementation of apartheid. He had built his career on ensuring that such a moment never arrived. His father, Jan de Klerk, had been among the architects of one of the world's most reviled social, political and economic systems founded on institutionalised racism.

Then, on 2 February 1990, in a thirty-five-minute address to parliament, De Klerk announced a package of measures that amounted to an about-turn. These included the immediate lifting of the ban on the liberation organisations, the impending release of Nelson Mandela and hundreds of other political prisoners, a moratorium on executions, and a declaration of his readiness to engage in dialogue about the future of South Africa. During an occasion carefully choreographed to draw the world's attention, De Klerk opened the sluice gates to make a settlement of the South African conflict through negotiations possible.

The ANC had sought such a pathway to peace on many occasions. In 1952, before the launch of the Defiance Campaign, the then president of the ANC, Dr James Moroka, wrote to Prime Minister D.F. Malan. He informed the government of the ANC's decision and gave Malan a deadline by which to repeal six unjust laws, considered emblematic of apartheid.[3] Malan's private secretary cursorily dismissed the demands and

---

3. The six laws were the Suppression of Communism Act, the Group Areas Act, the Separate Representation of Voters Act, the Bantu Authorities Act, the pass laws and the stock limitation laws.

ended his letter with the threat that the government would not hesitate to make full use of its power to quell any disturbances. The campaign went ahead on 26 June 1952. In all, more than 8 500 volunteers served prison terms for defying the unjust laws.

In 1955, the ANC and its allies organised the Congress of the People with the slogan 'Let the People Speak'. They canvassed the views of people across all walks of life about their vision of a future South Africa. They aimed at making the campaign an inclusive exercise to ensure that the resultant Freedom Charter would genuinely reflect the interests and aspirations of the South African people.[4] The organisers issued an open invitation to all South Africans and all political parties to take part in drafting the Charter. The parties represented in the all-white parliament ignored the invitation. In the subsequent 1956 Treason Trial, the Freedom Charter became the centrepiece of the state's case of a so-called communist-led plot to overthrow the government. After a four-year-long trial, the court, presided over by three judges, acquitted all the accused.

In December 1960, shortly after a whites-only referendum decided that South Africa would become a republic, a Consultative Conference of African Leaders was convened in Orlando, Johannesburg, to consider the republic referendum, among other matters. The Consultative Conference decided to call an All-in African Conference in March 1961. Attended by 1 400 delegates drawn from 145 different organisations, the conference demanded that the government convene a National Convention so that all South Africans could determine the country's constitutional future. If the government did not accede to this demand, the ANC would organise a three-day national stay-at-home protest beginning on 31 May, the date on which South Africa was to become a republic. Mandela, on behalf of the Action Committee, wrote to the prime

---

4. The ANC, the South African Indian Congress, the Coloured People's Congress, the South African Congress of Trade Unions and the Congress of Democrats constituted the National Action Council. The Liberal Party, formed in 1953, which opposed apartheid but did not support universal franchise at the time, agreed to co-sponsor the campaign. It withdrew before the Congress of the People was held.

minister, Dr Hendrik Verwoerd, explaining the call for a National Convention. Verwoerd later told parliament: 'A letter was received, signed by N R Mandela, in arrogant terms, to which no reply has been given.'[5] Mandela also wrote to the leader of the opposition United Party, Sir De Villiers Graaff, who simply ignored the letter.

In yet another instance, in its manifesto issued on 16 December 1961 to coincide with acts of sabotage carried out that day, MK explicitly reiterated this search for a non-violent solution:

> We of Umkhonto weSizwe have always sought – as the liberation movement has sought – to achieve liberation without bloodshed and civil clash. We do so still. We hope – even at this late hour – that our first actions will awaken everyone to the realisation of the disastrous situation to which the Nationalist policy is leading. We hope that we will bring the government and its supporters to their senses before it is too late ...[6]

By now, the ANC and practically all organised liberation formations believed it was time to go to war to find peace. During the next three decades, a bitter struggle ensued.

Twenty-nine years later, the two sides were meeting. During the intervening period, apartheid destroyed thousands of lives and tore apart countless families. The blood-drenched streets of the townships were patrolled day and night by armed police. At Groote Schuur, the NP government and the ANC pledged that there was a future beyond the bloodletting.

Mandela and De Klerk eyed each other across the table, poker-faced, determined neither by choice of word nor demeanour to allow a glimpse

---

5. Quoted in Anthony Sampson, *Mandela: The Authorised Biography* (London: HarperCollins, 1999), p. 146.
6. O'Malley Archive, 'Manifesto of Umkhonto we Sizwe', available at https://omalley .nelsonmandela.org/omalley/index.php/site/q/03lv02424/04lv02730/05lv02918/ 06lv02950.htm (last accessed 5 March 2021).

into their thoughts and emotions at this historic event. It was lawyer facing lawyer, politician squaring off against politician. De Klerk, straining to keep his nervousness in check, was determined to outfox his adversary. Mandela, eyelids drooping, stony-faced, his back ramrod straight, was unshakeable in his resolve to ensure dialogue would bring democracy and peace to a South Africa cursed with the plague of racism.

Mandela took the initiative. He remarked that the meeting represented not only what the ANC had been seeking for such a long time, but also an end to the master–servant relationship that characterised black and white relations in South Africa. 'We had come to the meeting not as suppliants or petitioners,' Mandela later wrote, 'but as fellow South Africans who merited an equal place at the table.'[7]

In measured tones, Mandela explained that, from its inception in 1912, the ANC had sought ways to resolve the South African problem through non-violent means. He also sketched an outline of history that covered the hardships the Afrikaner had endured – the Anglo-Boer War and concentration camps, and their subsequent humiliation, oppression and poverty.

According to foreign affairs minister Pik Botha, Mandela remarked that 'it had been a puzzle to him … why the Afrikaner, who had had to endure so much trauma, misery and humiliation, had never reached out to his black compatriots, who had also had to bear the yoke of poverty and been deprived of education.'[8]

'This idea that he expressed in his opening speech affected me deeply,' Botha later acknowledged. 'Because we did not really have a proper answer. And at that time we were not in a position to give a reasoned explanation. Because why didn't the Afrikaner do this? One had to try to find the answer for oneself: why did our history take this particular course?'[9]

---

7. Nelson Mandela, *Long Walk to Freedom* (Johannesburg: Macdonald Purnell, 1994), p. 507.
8. Theresa Papenfus, *Pik Botha and His Times* (Pretoria: Litera, 2010), pp. 648–9.
9. Ibid., p. 649.

What was De Klerk's game plan when he opened the sluice gates on 2 February 1990? Before we delve into this question, let us consider the context.

2

The Imprisoned Society

From the time the NP ascended to power in 1948, Pretoria ruthlessly suppressed all organised efforts to pressure it to change course. Colonialism provided the foundations for apartheid. The dominant white minority exercised the political rights and privileges typical of citizens of a colonial power, while the black majority were governed as rightless subjects. In essence, it was a white autocracy in which the majority were held down by force.

In 1963, the regime passed a law permitting the police to detain anyone for questioning for 90 days without charge. In 1965, this was extended to 180 days. In 1967, the Terrorism Act extended the detention to an indefinite period. The legislation enabled the Security Branch to use systematic torture of detainees, leading at times to death. Shielded by this law, inquests into deaths in detention consistently found them to be self-inflicted by the detainee. However, even under the watchful eyes of the police state, some kept searching for ways to resist.

Repression forced the ANC into exile. In 1967, it entered into a military alliance with the Zimbabwe African People's Union (ZAPU) and a combined guerrilla force entered Rhodesia (now Zimbabwe) 'on a common route, each bound for its destination'.[1] A group of about eighty crossed the Zambezi River into Rhodesia on 30–31 July 1967, in what became known as the Wankie (Hwange) Campaign.[2] To honour Chief

1. Vladimir Shubin, *ANC: A View from Moscow* (Cape Town: Mayibuye Books, UWC, nd.), p. 78, quotes the Joint Communiqué issued on 19 August 1967 by Tambo and James Chikerema, the vice president of ZAPU.
2. 'Wankie' was the European corruption of 'Hwange'.

Albert Luthuli, who had died under mysterious circumstances less than two weeks earlier, Oliver Tambo, who succeeded him as acting ANC president, christened them the Luthuli Detachment.

Towards the end of 1967, preparations were made to attack the enemy in Rhodesia from the east, towards Sipolilo. The Pyramid Detachment – made up of seventy-four Zimbabwe People's Revolutionary Army (ZIPRA)[3] fighters and twenty-six MK fighters, under the command of ZIPRA's Moffat Hadebe – crossed into Rhodesia on the night of 29 December 1967. A further hundred guerrillas joined the operation in February 1968 and a third group of ninety-one followed in July.

An ANC submission to the Truth and Reconciliation Commission (TRC) recorded that twenty-five MK combatants lost their lives during the Wankie Campaign and at least twenty-three died in the Sipolilo Campaign. ZIPRA launched both campaigns with the aim of establishing bases within Rhodesia, while MK sought to carve a path into South Africa for its combatants. Both guerrilla forces failed to realise their objectives. Their achievement, however, overshadowed their failure. Those in power in Pretoria and Salisbury (now Harare) came to fear the fighting prowess of the MK combatants, while the black masses drew inspiration from their courageous exploits and determination. The embers of resistance were being fanned.

How widespread were underground activities within South Africa at the time? Historian Gregory Houston writes:

During the second half of the 1960s, political activity in South Africa was heavily shackled by state repression ... Underground work nevertheless continued during this period and from mid-1965 to the end of 1969, at least 452 people were convicted under the Suppression of Communism Act, 245 under the Unlawful Organisations Act, 54 under the Terrorism Act (from 1968 only), and 80 of sabotage

---

3. ZIPRA was the military wing of ZAPU.

under Section 21 of the General Law Amendment Act of 1962. Repeated efforts were made during this period to revive local, regional and national underground networks.[4]

Despite the regime's determination to keep the public in the dark, the media covered a number of court cases relating to the liberation struggle.

In February/March 1969, Dorothy Nyembe and eleven others appeared in the Pietermaritzburg Supreme Court, charged under the Terrorism and the Suppression of Communism Acts. Among the accused were several trained guerrillas, including some who had fought in the Wankie Campaign. Many black people did not see the trial as a setback for the struggle; instead, they viewed the prosecution as evidence that the struggle was continuing. It gave them courage and was proof that things were happening.

Evidence in the trial of Samson Ndou and twenty-one others who appeared in court on 1 December 1969 revealed that Winnie Mandela and a few colleagues with a long history of ANC membership had begun to reconstitute the organisation as far back as 1966. The trial of Ndou and his co-accused went on until 16 February 1970, when the state withdrew the charges. The state had unintentionally handed the ANC a propaganda coup. Realising their error, they charged Ndou and his comrades once again. This time the case collapsed.

Another case that enhanced the image of the ANC and MK was the trial of the 'Pretoria Six', in which Alex Moumbaris featured prominently. They were charged under the Terrorism Act, found guilty and sentenced to a total of seventy-seven years' imprisonment in 1973. Moumbaris was sentenced to twelve years but escaped from Pretoria Central Prison together with Tim Jenkin and Stephen Lee in 1979.[5]

---

4. South African Democracy Education Trust (SADET), *The Road to Democracy in South Africa*, vol. 1, *1960–1970* (Pretoria: UNISA Press, 2014), pp. 639–40.
5. See also Tim Jenkin, *Inside Out: Escape from Pretoria Prison* (Johannesburg: Jacana, 2003).

During this time, underground activists smuggled propaganda produced in London into South Africa, which supplemented the hope generated by these trials. As Houston notes:

> On 14 November 1969, tape recordings of ANC and MK propaganda were played at various places in Johannesburg, Cape Town, Kimberley and Port Elizabeth … In the 1970 operation, activists placed 12 'bucketbombs' at various places in Johannesburg, Cape Town, Durban, Port Elizabeth and East London within a 48-hour period.[6]

Apartheid survives

The Western powers continued providing Pretoria with strong economic and political support. They did so despite the Sharpeville massacre in 1960, the sentencing of the Rivonia trialists to life terms in 1964, and the repeated torture and killing of detainees.[7] During the 1960s, the economy grew at an average rate of 6.1 per cent per year, with manufacturing the fastest-growing sector.

In the late sixties, Prime Minister John Vorster initiated an effort to promote friendly relations with independent African states. This so-called outward-looking policy of détente enjoyed some success and raised the prospect of undermining efforts to isolate South Africa and thus outmanoeuvre the exiled liberation movements. The Fifth Summit Conference of East and Central African States held in Lusaka in 1969 adopted the Lusaka Manifesto urging a negotiated solution in South Africa. While the Organisation of African Unity (OAU) endorsed it, both the ANC and the Pan Africanist Congress (PAC), who believed that any negotiated solution at that time would be overwhelmingly on Pretoria's terms, rejected it. Vorster was so confident of the success of his outward-looking

---

6. SADET, *The Road to Democracy in South Africa*, vol. 1, p. 637.
7. Solwandle Looksmart Ngudle, a member of the ANC underground, was the first ninety-day detainee to die in police custody, in September 1963. His death was described as 'suicide' by the authorities.

policy that in a confidential conversation with journalist Tony Heard on 14 February 1975, he predicted that he would address the OAU by the end of the year.[8]

The apartheid regime believed that by eliminating instability and dissent, it would be able to install collaborationist black leaders over the country's black population.

The Broederbond, an exclusively white Afrikaner male secret society, had been the driving force behind the National Party's ascent to power in the 1948 whites-only election. It saw its role as the think tank in the creation, legitimisation and maintenance of apartheid. By dint of the systematic capture of several Afrikaner cultural and non-governmental organisations, it became the strategising centre of Afrikaner ethnic nationalism. Once the NP had captured political power in the name of Afrikanerdom, it set about using that power to refine the colonial character of the state by eliminating the inconsistencies in its practice.[9]

The NP government promoted Afrikaners into the civil service and the security forces as a means of enhancing its control. Employment in state-owned institutions like the railways, harbours and other enterprises helped to eradicate the poor-white problem and consolidate their support behind the NP. By deliberately favouring Afrikaner-owned enterprises, the NP leveraged the entry of Afrikaners into the ranks of the capitalist class. After the 1953 elections and the opening of the goldfields in the Free State, for example, the Anglo American Corporation unbundled some of its mining interests to the Afrikaner-controlled General Mining Corporation.

The Broederbond remained a significant strategising body and successive prime ministers maintained a close relationship with it. In 1963,

8. O'Malley Archive, 'Chronology of some pointers to the history of the media in South Africa', available at https://omalley.nelsonmandela.org/omalley/index.php/site/q/03lv02167/04lv02264/05lv02303/06lv02329/07lv02330.htm (last accessed 24 May 2021).
9. Owing to the survival of elements of Cape liberalism, African and Coloured property owners had the vote in the Cape and Natal until 1935 and 1955 respectively.

internal documents of this secret society revealed something about its operations and brought to light debates and dissent within its ranks. The case of Reverend Beyers Naudé was evidence of the disputes.

In 1961, Verwoerd and the Broederbond had ensured that the Dutch Reformed Church withdrew from the World Council of Churches. The withdrawal caused much disquiet in Reverend Naudé, who had joined the Broederbond in 1936 and risen steadily in its ranks to become the moderator of the Southern Transvaal Synod of the church by 1963. Together with a small group of colleagues, in 1962 he had begun the monthly publication *Pro Veritate* to stimulate discussion about racial issues. In 1963, the Christian Institute of Southern Africa was launched to unite South African Christians against apartheid, and Naudé was appointed director. When the Dutch Reformed Church and the Broederbond subsequently forced him to choose between his role as a minister and the Christian Institute, he resigned his church post. Naudé and his family were banished to the wilderness by most of the Afrikaner community.[10]

Another breach in the ranks of Afrikanerdom came from a group of influential dissident Afrikaner writers called the Sestigers. Some of them had studied abroad, mostly in France, where they came under the influence of existentialism. Many of their novels and poems focused on apartheid and race relations, and they began to challenge the status quo in their literature. The emergence of the Sestigers was another signal that there were dissident voices inside the laager of Afrikanerdom willing to ask difficult questions in the public arena.

Beyers Naudé went on to play an essential role in the struggle against apartheid, while the Sestigers significantly influenced the development of Afrikaans literature. However, neither Naudé's breakaway from the Broederbond nor the emergence of the Sestigers made a significant impact on the unity of Afrikanerdom and the enormous influence of the Broederbond.

---

10. Colleen Gaye Ryan Clur, 'From acquiescence to dissent – Beyers Naude 1915–1977', MA thesis, UNISA, June 1997.

By the end of the 1960s, developments in the field of sports told a different story. Sport, like religion, is deeply embedded in the South African psyche. Apartheid South Africa was becoming a pariah in the world sporting community. First, the country was denied participation in the 1968 Summer Olympics in Mexico. Next came its expulsion from the International Olympic Committee. Anti-apartheid demonstrators dramatically disrupted the 1969–70 Springbok rugby tour of Britain, leading to the cancellation of a cricket tour to that country. White South Africans were dismayed and wounded by the sports boycott. The Vorster regime therefore felt compelled to find ways to amend its sporting codes to circumvent isolation in sports. In 1970, the Vorster-led NP government, in an effort to prevent further isolation, allowed the presence of Māori players and spectators during the New Zealand national rugby union tour of South Africa. Despite these significant setbacks, white South Africans bought into the propaganda that their security depended on the perpetuation of white minority rule, and they continued to stand behind the apartheid regime.

When the Vorster government began to adjust its sports policy to counter isolation, it was concerned that this should not cause discord within the sports fraternity and among white South Africans. The Broederbond played a critical role in ensuring maximum unity, while the regime made adjustments to its policy and practice. To this end, write Robert M. Price and Carl Gustav Rosberg, 'the Bond brought members serving in sports-controlling bodies from all over the country together for a secret top-level discussion. The proposals emanating from this meeting were discussed by the Executive Council [of the Broederbond] and submitted to the political leadership. With consensus established among the leading sports administrators, the cabinet could move ahead; in the meantime, all Bond members were assured that the formulations of the Executive Council will be reflected in official Government statements.'[11]

---

11. Robert M. Price and Carl Gustav Rosberg, eds, *The Apartheid Regime: Political Power and Racial Domination* (Berkeley: Institute of International Studies, 1980), p. 41.

While there had been a crisis of confidence among the Western allies of apartheid because of the Sharpeville massacre, it was short-lived. The governments in the West resumed their support and multinational companies stepped up participation in the economy. Loans continued and funds flowed back into South Africa. The economy was booming. Under these conditions, the influence of Afrikaner capitalists matured and the authority of business within the NP and the Broederbond became increasingly pronounced. Efforts to revive the struggle against apartheid from within South Africa and from exile seemed doomed to fail. The white laager drawn together by Afrikaner nationalism stayed intact, confident that its future was secure. But beneath the surface, discontent among the oppressed was growing. The inherent injustice and contradictions of the system of white minority rule made this inevitable.

3

The Landscape Is Reconfigured

The period 1973 to 1979 is one of the most seminal in the history of the liberation struggle. A spate of strikes in South Africa's Durban-Pinetown industrial complex shattered the pall of fear fostered by rampant repression. Black Consciousness emerged as the catalyst of the protests that rocked the tribal and ethnic-based secondary and tertiary education institutions. Apartheid had designed these institutions to indoctrinate and co-opt black students. African high-school students, encouraged by the assertive outlook of Black Consciousness and enraged by conditions in their schools, marched into the lead of a fourteen-month revolt. Their assertiveness emerged at a time when the ANC and the PAC had been immobilised within the country for almost a decade. These groundbreaking events reconfigured the political landscape.

After the Wankie and Sipolilo campaigns, the ANC met in a consultative conference in June 1969. The movement emerged from that conference with a refined strategy that saw mass mobilisation as the foundation for the armed struggle. The 'four pillars of struggle', which gained prominence in the early 1980s, refined this approach. The first of these, the reconstruction of an effective underground organisation inside the country, would be responsible for stimulating and organising mass political action. Mass mobilisation would create the political environment for the armed struggle to take root. All three would be sustained through international solidarity to support the liberation movement while isolating the apartheid regime.

The architecture of these mutually constitutive pillars of struggle began to take shape during this period. The leadership role of the ANC was the

15

outcome of its ability to identify these four pillars, understand their strengths and ensure they reinforced one another by enhancing their complementarity. Gradually, the presence of the ANC began to be felt in each arena, and its guiding hand became manifest as the struggle intensified.

Migrant workers, whose labour power built the economy, struck the first blows in the 1970s. On 9 January 1973, about 2 000 migrant workers at the Coronation Brick and Tile factory in Durban went on strike for higher wages. Between January and the end of March, the Durban area experienced 146 strikes involving 61 410 workers. The strikes brought South Africa's second most important industrial complex to a standstill. Workers on the factory floor led the strikes and the regime was unable to find evidence of a leadership that was in overall charge.[1]

The strikes initiated a new phase in industrial relations and in the rebuilding of the trade union movement. They were 'the pivotal event around which black worker organisations [were] constituted, a pivot created by black workers themselves'.[2]

The fundamentals of 'grand apartheid' were premised on so-called independent black homelands. Connie Mulder, the minister of plural relations, claimed in January 1978 that 'there will not be one black man with South African citizenship' in South Africa.[3] In the meantime, growth and developments in the economy were accelerating the urbanisation of Africans.

P.W. Botha, the previous defence minister who succeeded Vorster as prime minister in 1978, responded to these challenges by resorting to

---

1. There were also stirrings of Black Consciousness–inspired student activity, though there is no evidence of any link between them. See David Lewis, 'Black workers and trade unions', in Thomas G. Karis and Gail M. Gerhart, eds, *From Protest to Challenge: A Documentary History of African Politics in South Africa, 1882–1990*, vol. 5: *Nadir and Resurgence, 1964–1979* (Bloomington: Indiana University Press, 1997), pp. 197 and 201.
2. Karis and Gerhart, *From Protest to Challenge*, vol. 5, p. 190.
3. Ibid., p. 311. The idea that urban Africans were a permanent part of South Africa and not 'temporary sojourners' in 'white' South Africa was an issue that the Broederbond, even when it acknowledged the unworkability of the apartheid system, could not find a way around.

the twin strategies of repression and reform. The reforms were in part an attempt to take into account the changes in the economy, the increasing demand for skilled labour and rapid urbanisation. The reform measures also sought to cultivate and co-opt sections of the black population as well as forestall the unity of forces for freedom.

This twin-track strategy, however, brought to the surface internal divisions within the ruling party. And some of the measures, such as granting nominal independence to Transkei in October 1976, failed to garner recognition from the international community.[4] Reforms based on the recommendation of the Wiehahn Commission that African workers be permitted to join registered unions, thereby incorporating them into the industrial bargaining system, would lead to the emergence of the Congress of South African Trade Unions (COSATU) in the frontline of the Mass Democratic Movement (MDM).

The Unholy Alliance collapses

An important blow against the regime was the collapse of the 'Unholy Alliance' between Portugal, South Africa and Rhodesia. The alliance had been stitched together under the leadership of John Vorster after Rhodesian prime minister Ian Smith's declaration of unilateral independence in 1965, in order to emasculate the liberation struggle. The 1974 coup in Portugal precipitated the independence of Mozambique, Angola and Guinea-Bissau. In October 1975, the South African Defence Force (SADF), with the backing of the USA and Zaire (now the Democratic Republic of Congo), launched a military incursion codenamed Operation Savannah into Angola. The aim was to prevent the installation of a government led by the People's Movement for the Liberation of Angola (MPLA) in Luanda, and to back its rivals, the National Front for the

---

4. The United Nations regarded Transkei's independence as a 'sham'. While self-government and independence for some of the bantustans raised debate about the appropriate tactics to be used, the prospect of 'independence' did not change the strategic goal.

Liberation of Angola (FNLA) and the National Union for the Total Independence of Angola (UNITA). The regime kept this wanton act of war secret even from parliament. The SADF soldiers did not wear their regular uniforms or insignia. Parliament and the public were left to piece together information from rumours and oblique messages in the press. The parents of the first white South African soldier killed in Angola were not allowed to announce the cause of his death; the funeral notices stated that Chris Robins had died in a fatal accident.[5]

In response to an appeal from the MPLA in November that year, Cuba launched a large-scale military intervention to repel the apartheid regime's forces. The SADF had no option but to withdraw from Angola in August 1976. In the larger scheme of global politics, the apartheid regime saw the US renege on its promised support for South Africa's military adventure.

Angola's independence would continue to be destabilised by apartheid South Africa's military support for rebel movement UNITA. However, the vesting of power in the MPLA led by Agostinho Neto boosted the prospects of independence for Namibia. The South West Africa People's Organisation (SWAPO) and its armed wing, the People's Liberation Army of Namibia (PLAN), consequently acquired base facilities in a country that shared a long border with Namibia. The MPLA government also allowed the ANC and ZAPU to set up military camps in the north and central regions of Angola.

Alongside these developments, in 1975 independent Mozambique allowed the Zimbabwe African National Union (ZANU) and its armed wing, the Zimbabwe African National Liberation Army (ZANLA), to establish bases in Mozambique from which they were able to step up the war in Rhodesia. The new Mozambique Liberation Front (FRELIMO) government also granted the ANC and MK limited facilities. Mozam-

---

5. O'Malley Archive, 'Chronology of some pointers to the history of the media in South Africa'.

bique shared a long border with South Africa, but given its support for ZANLA against the Smith regime, it could not afford to provoke South Africa overtly and find itself in a war on two fronts. Mozambique and the ANC agreed that MK cadres and underground operatives would not cross directly from Mozambique into South Africa; they would cross from Mozambique into Swaziland, from where they would move into South Africa.

The facilities made available to the ANC by Angola and Mozambique could not have come at a better time. Hundreds of youths were fleeing South Africa in the wake of the 1976 Soweto Uprising in the hope of joining the armed struggle.

The withdrawal of the SADF and the installation of an MPLA government in Angola, and a FRELIMO government in Mozambique, meant that the Unholy Alliance and Vorster's outward-looking diplomacy were shredded and consigned to the dustbin of history.

The objectives of his policy of détente would later be realised by other means, however, when the military capacity of the SADF became the lynchpin of an aggressive strategy to subvert governments in the independent states of southern Africa. Under Botha, the SADF's engagement in the war in Angola escalated, with the intent to overthrow the MPLA government and install Jonas Savimbi's UNITA.

By the late 1970s, spending on internal and external security had increased by leaps and bounds. Every white male over the age of eighteen underwent two years' compulsory military service. Seventeen thousand permanent members, of whom about 5 000 were black, and a separate contingent of 38 000 white conscripts now made up the SADF. There were 255 000 white citizen reserve personnel. Besides, there was the South African Police with 37 000 members, of whom 55 per cent were white, and 31 000 reservists, a sophisticated Security Branch and the Bureau of State Security (BOSS), the civilian intelligence agency.[6]

---

6. O'Malley Archive, 'Historical background: "Total Onslaught"', available at https://omalley.nelsonmandela.org/omalley/index.php/site/q/03lv00017/04lv01495/05lv01506.htm (last accessed 24 May 2021).

Bantu Education upended

The apartheid regime had lost legitimacy among the African people during the 1960s as a result of the Sharpeville massacre, but by recourse to mass repression, support from its Western allies and the relative weakness of the liberation forces, it had won a temporary respite. The blows struck by the students in 1976 stripped apartheid of all vestiges of legitimacy. Side by side with the changing face of industrial relations, equally significant consequences were emerging from the imposition of an ethnic-based education system. The system condemned Africans to be 'hewers of wood and drawers of water', the aim being to dissuade them from aspiring to rise in the professions. Instead, both secondary and tertiary levels of Bantu Education became the hothouse where political activism emerged on a scale never experienced before among black students. The inspiration for this revival of mass resistance was the Black Consciousness Movement.

What began on 16 June 1976 as a one-day protest demonstration against Afrikaans as a medium of instruction in the African high schools in Soweto spiralled into a nationwide revolt.[7] The police opened fire on the crowd, killing twelve-year-old Zolile Hector Pieterson. This uncapped the fury of the marching students. By evening, Soweto had become a battle zone. The uprising spread to Krugersdorp and downtown Johannesburg. Soon the flames of revolt engulfed all four provinces of South Africa, and more than a hundred urban areas were affected.[8]

The Bantu Education system and the government's regional administration boards, as well as black collaborators in the Urban Bantu Councils and the bantustan governments, became the principal targets. The students tried a variety of tactics, from strikes and stayaways to the

---

7. The protest had been ongoing since April 1976. On 16 June, the students took to the streets.
8. See Nozipho T. Diseko, 'The origins and development of the South African Students' Movement (SASM)', *Journal of Southern African Studies*, 18 (1), March 1992, pp. 40–62 for a discussion of the conditions that generated the revolt and the role of the SASM and the Soweto Students' Representative Council.

destruction of buildings, liquor outlets and beer halls, as well as consumer boycotts.[9]

By the end of February 1977, the official death toll stood at 575, of whom 494 were African, 75 Coloured, two White and one Indian.[10] The final count, though not conclusively established, would turn out to be much higher.

The world was shocked at this carnage. But the global outcry at the death in detention on the night of 12 September 1977 of Steve Biko, the charismatic proponent of Black Consciousness that unlocked the courage and daring of the youth, failed to deter the regime from its path of using brute force, intimidation and terror to bludgeon this generation into submission. On 19 October 1977, the South African Student Organisation, the Black People's Convention, the Black Community Programmes, the South African Students' Movement, the Soweto Students' Representative Council and almost every organisation linked to Black Consciousness, as well as *The World* newspaper and the Christian Institute, were declared unlawful. The regime detained a dozen individuals who were banned and more than fifty leaders of the organisations that were prohibited.

The state deployed the full might of the repressive arsenal it had developed in the late fifties and early sixties. Firepower against demonstrations, indiscriminate arrests, indefinite detention without trial, torture in detention leading to death and court trials leading to imprisonment became routine. Mass arrests reinforced these techniques. On a single

---

9. See Karis and Gerhart, *From Protest to Challenge*, vol. 5, pp. 169–78 for a discussion of the tactics used by the students and the regime.
10. An enraged mob of hostel dwellers from Mzimhlophe hostel in Meadowlands stormed the adjacent Soweto townships on 24 August 1976. For more than a week, residents and hostel dwellers were locked in street battles while the police looked on or steered clear of these areas. This was the beginning of 'black-on-black' violence, which obscured the role of the police and the covert arms of the apartheid state in the conflict. See also Nicholas Haysom, 'Mabangalala: The rise of right-wing vigilantes', Occasional paper no. 10, Centre for Applied Legal Studies, University of the Witwatersrand, 1986.

day in September 1976, 200 people were arrested in African and Coloured townships in the Eastern Cape. The arrests of more than 800 people in a house-to-house sweep in Alexandra township in Johannesburg broke the back of that community's support for the three-day stay-at-home in September 1976.

The uprisings petered out by the end of 1977. The students and youth, by dint of fearlessness and daring, had forced themselves into the frontline of the struggle. Through their actions they had shown that 'despite the ruthless counter-measures taken by the enemy, it is still possible to form a legal organisation inside the country auxiliary to our underground work', wrote Nelson Mandela from prison.[11] How the Black Consciousness Movement responded to the challenge of illegality and whether it found ways to link up with the workers' struggles would determine its future path. The workers' strikes and the students' revolt had stripped apartheid of all pretensions of legitimacy. White South Africans remained trapped in denial despite the jolt to their confidence, yet the country would never be the same again.

The world rejects apartheid

Shunned by the world's religious bodies and wounded by the escalating sports boycotts, apartheid South Africa began to feel the sharp end of international sanctions against its policies and practices. After the 1973 workers' strikes, international anti-apartheid solidarity, including that from the International Confederation of Free Trade Unions and the World Federation of Trade Unions, brought disinvestment and trade sanctions against South Africa into sharp focus. Solidarity with the struggles of South African workers became an inextricable part of the international anti-apartheid campaign.

---

11. Nelson Mandela, 'Whither Black Consciousness', written in prison in 1978, is reproduced in Mac Maharaj, *Reflections in Prison*, pp. 21–64. How and why the Black Consciousness Movement withered away organisationally is a question deserving of a separate study.

At a meeting held during March 1975, the National Executive Committee (NEC) of the ANC resolved to consolidate its status as the 'undisputed leader of the people's revolutionary onslaught against apartheid oppression'.[12] The ANC mobilised the Anti-Apartheid Movement, the World Peace Council, the Women's International Democratic Federation, the Pan African Youth Movement and the World Federation of Democratic Youth to attend the Ninth Extraordinary Session of the Council of Ministers of the Organisation of African Unity in Dar es Salaam in April 1975. They pressured the session to strengthen the call for economic sanctions and the international isolation of South Africa.

The Council of Ministers, meeting a month later, unanimously adopted the Dar es Salaam Declaration urging the OAU and the United Nations (UN) to work together for the total isolation of the apartheid regime. The ministers committed all African states to remain united 'in the policy of isolating South Africa and ostracising the apartheid regime'.[13]

The suppression of the uprisings of 1976–77 and the murder of Biko fuelled the campaign to isolate apartheid South Africa. Years of patient work began to yield concrete results. In the early 1970s, a small union in the US comprising mainly African American workers had gone on strike to protest the participation of the Polaroid Corporation in the administration of South Africa's pass laws by producing the passbook photos, and as a result Polaroid banned all sales to the South African government. In March 1977, pressure from their workers persuaded eleven US multinationals that had operations in South Africa to announce the adoption of the Sullivan Code, which demanded the equal treatment of employees regardless of race. On 4 November 1977, the UN Security Council declared arms trade with South Africa a 'threat to peace' and pressure for an oil embargo began to grow. In 1979, the US Congress

---

12. SADET, *The Road to Democracy in South Africa*, vol. 2, *1970–1980* (Pretoria: UNISA Press, 2014), p. 627.
13. Ibid., p. 629.

passed legislation codifying the prohibition of Eximbank loans to South African government firms, as well as firms that did not adhere to the Sullivan Code. That same year, Norway and the UK banned the sale of North Sea oil to South Africa, and Sweden prohibited Swedish companies from investing in any new business ventures in South Africa and Namibia.

The campaign to ostracise apartheid South Africa was reaching every area of activity. In the field of sport, the British Commonwealth of Nations adopted the Gleneagles Agreement in 1977 calling for a ban on sports contact with South Africa. It carried the message that apartheid South Africa could no longer take for granted the sympathy of member states like Britain, Australia, Canada and New Zealand.[14] Six months later, the UN agreed to a similar boycott of South Africa in the sports arena. Its effects gave impetus to moves to intensify the cultural and economic isolation of apartheid.

---

14. James Callaghan, the Labour leader, was prime minister of Britain at the time.

4

Apartheid Bows, But Does Not Bend

During the mid-1970s, insecurity began to seep into influential circles in the white community. Apartheid faced a hostile oppressed majority simmering with discontent and rebelliousness; beyond its borders, the *cordon sanitaire* that had made South Africa practically immune to attack from the 'terrorists' was disintegrating.

Vorster, the then prime minister, capitalised on white voters' fear of 'black power' and resentment at the world's condemnation evoked by the Soweto revolt and the killing of Biko. The state's disinformation and insidious propaganda campaigns were taking effect. The white electorate rallied to the side of the ruling National Party in the elections of November 1976. They voted for repression.

The spectre of the Soweto Uprising remained. Vorster, who had maintained close relations with the Broederbond, fell back on the time-worn tactic of divide and rule. In 1977, he floated the idea of constitutional changes aimed at an intensified attempt to co-opt Coloureds and Indians as junior partners. His proposal entailed establishing two additional houses in parliament – one for Coloureds and one for Indians, with a president's council, constituted in a way that would ensure that white control remained firmly in place. He also suggested a change from the existing system of a prime minister as the head of government and a president as the ceremonial head of state to an executive president. His manoeuvre was a transparent attempt to wean away Coloureds and Indians from the militancy and revolt promised by the workers' strikes and the Soweto Uprising. He was not able to pursue his idea. It was, however, something that resonated with the thinking of Gerrit Viljoen, chairman of the Broederbond at the time.[1]

When the NP won political office in May 1948, the outcome owed much to the 1902 Treaty of Vereeniging and the 1908–9 South African National Convention. By mutual agreement, rural constituencies were weighted at the expense of urban ones by a factor of 3:1. Consequently, though the NP did not command the majority of white votes cast in the 1948 general election, it won the majority of constituencies. And so, while the NP had a majority of seats in parliament, that did not reflect popular support among the white population, even among Afrikaners.

The achievement of a republic in 1961 marked the triumph of Afrikaner nationalism. With its base secure, it was time to speak for all whites. Through the leverage of political power, Afrikaner business had developed and begun to find common ground with English capital.

The mining sector dominated the economy and the country depended on earnings from the export of primary products. It was a sector dependent on migrant labour drawn from within the country as well as from the southern African region. During the Second World War, the manufacturing industry grew. However, its growth was constrained by the country's geographical location and the size of its internal market, made up mainly of the white minority. By the 1970s, monopolies and conglomerates had come to dominate the economy. They were increasingly aware of the need for a permanent labour force and the shortage of skilled and semi-skilled labour. The system of repressive control of the workforce had broken down. Capital-intensive processes were replacing labour-intensive production methods. Their interests dictated that there be structural changes to the economy, and they were keen to carve out the African market as their 'natural' market.

Bowing to the concerns of business, in 1977 Vorster appointed the

---

1. Karis and Gerhart, *From Protest to Challenge*, vol. 5, p. 242.

Wiehahn Commission to look into the industrial relations system and the Riekert Commission to address the issue of manpower utilisation. Both reported back in 1978, and the new prime minister P.W. Botha accepted their recommendations. While business welcomed this development, trade unionists were able to exploit this to their advantage, as we shall see when we address developments at the level of unionism.

The shifts in the body politic and the economy gave rise to different perspectives from which the regime and business sought to address the crisis thrust upon them by labour restiveness and the Soweto Uprising. But the main objective of the proposed changes to the external features of the system of apartheid was the perpetuation of white minority domination.

In 1978, Vorster resigned as prime minister and took up the ceremonial position of state president. However, he was forced to step down when he became implicated in the abuse of state funds and corruption around what was dubbed the Information Scandal. In 1973, Vorster had agreed to minister of information Connie Mulder's plan to shift about R64 million from the defence budget to undertake a series of propaganda projects. Plans included bribing international news agencies and the purchase of the *Washington Star* newspaper. Those implicated included Vorster, Mulder, BOSS head General Hendrik van den Bergh, and Dr Eschel Rhoodie, the secretary of the Department of Information.

The scandal was a reflection of the concern and the stresses caused by the international campaign to impose sanctions on South Africa. It also spoke to the desperate measures apartheid was prepared to take to forestall their imposition. The Vorster–Mulder machinations sought to prevent the USA in particular from joining the sanctions campaign.

Vorster was later also implicated in the use of a secret slush fund to establish *The Citizen*, the only major English-language newspaper that was well disposed towards the National Party, fronted by Louis Luyt. A commission of inquiry concluded in mid-1979 that Vorster 'knew everything' about the corruption. He resigned from the presidency in disgrace after only eight months in office.

Botha, the iron-fisted 'reformer'

After P.W. Botha took over as prime minister from Vorster, the sense of siege became the excuse to depict the developments inside and outside the country as a 'total onslaught' requiring a 'total strategy' in response. 'The resolution of the conflict in the times in which we now live,' he explained, 'demands inter-dependent and coordinated action in all fields: military, psychological, economic, political, sociological, technological, diplomatic, ideological, cultural, etcetera. We are today involved in a war whether we like it or not. It is therefore essential that a total national strategy [is] formulated at the highest level.'[2]

What was needed was a policy that combined repression and reform. Botha marketed this twin strategy as division of power, while others talked of power-sharing. Dressed this way, he believed he could win the favour of South Africa's allies in the West and the hearts and minds of black South Africans.

In his various capacities as minister of defence, prime minister and later state president, Botha, along with General Magnus Malan, who served as chief of the SADF from 1976 to 1980 and as minister of defence from 1980 to 1991, was the principal architect of this strategy. Malan was inspired by Andre Beaufré, the French Army officer and military strategist on whose theories the right-wing Organisation de l'Armée Secrète built its terror campaign in the early 1960s against the movement for the independence of Algeria. Botha and Malan also consulted other counter-insurgency experts, such as Colonel J.J. McCuen, the American Vietnam veteran and author of *The Art of Counter-Revolutionary War*, and Samuel Huntington, a political strategist from Harvard University.

Power unconstrained

A key element in their strategy was the establishment and operational-ising in 1979 of the National Security Management System (NSMS),

---

2. Republic of South Africa, Department of Defence, White Paper on Defence and Armaments Supply, 1977, p. 5, quoted in Padraig O'Malley, *Shades of Difference: Mac Maharaj and the Struggle for South Africa* (New York: Penguin, 2007), p. 199.

presided over by the State Security Council (SSC). Formed in 1972 as one of twenty cabinet committees, the SSC's function was to advise the government on formulating and executing national security policy. Under Botha, it became the nerve centre for coordinating the police, the army and intelligence, as well as critical civilian departments, including foreign affairs, information, and cooperation and development (previously Bantu administration and development).

Chaired by Botha, the SSC was at the apex of the newly established NSMS, which 'subsumed and co-opted existing structures, both public and private, in a comprehensive security apparatus' aimed at protecting the state.[3]

The core of the implementation of the NSMS was a network of regional, district and local committees called Joint Management Centres (JMCs) that reported on the activities and whereabouts of political activists so as to form an overall security profile, thus enabling the SSC to make decisions on security action.[4]

The SSC had four divisions or branches: Strategy Planning, Strategic Communications (STRATCOM), National Intelligence Interpretation and Administration. Ultimate control was vested in Botha himself.

STRATCOM was responsible for developing a package of strategy alternatives in response to requests coming in from ministries, government departments and JMCs. Nothing could happen in the townships – not even the provision of services – without harnessing the action to the task of winning hearts and minds. Implementation was either carried out at the level of STRATCOM or sent down the NSMS chain. Every government department had its 'stratcom' committee.

The SSC reached into every part of the country. It identified anti-apartheid activities and activists, formulated a continuous national security profile, and made decisions about what action had to be carried

---

3. Chapter 5: National Security, in Rita M. Byrnes, ed., *South Africa: A Country Study* (Washington, DC: Federal Research Division, Library of Congress, 1997), p. 340.
4. M. Coleman, 'State violence: A study in repression', paper presented at the Centre for the Study of Violence and Reconciliation, University of the Witwatersrand, 1990.

out at central, local and even international level. Formal law enforcement and other structures were responsible for covertly implementing the SSC's decisions. By 1979, the SSC was operating outside of the law and beyond the reach of the executive and parliament. The police state had become a lawless police state.

By mid-1986, the SSC and the National Joint Management Centre, chaired by the deputy minister of law and order and 'tasked with the executive co-ordination of the implementation of SSC decisions' relating to the 1985 state of emergency,[5] formed the apex of state power and the vanguard of state action.[6]

White power dressed-up as power-sharing

A firm grip on the situation through the NSMS was a crucial part of any reforms directed at the oppressed. Huntington, who first visited South Africa in 1974, urged 'intense attention' to the strategy and tactics of reform, which should 'be introduced from positions of relative strength when the government can still dictate the terms'.[7] It was a position that Botha found attractive. Botha was, by nature, a streetfighter. Streetfighters do not respect rules or boundaries created in the name of law or morality. *Kragdadigheid* (a predilection to use force or repression; uncompromising autocracy) was his forte, and Huntington urged that repression and reform worked in tandem.

Any long-term strategy for a minority to oppress a majority needs a credible segment of the oppressed to collaborate with the oppressor.

---

5. In 1985 the regime imposed a state of emergency affecting thirty-four magisterial districts in an effort to crush the unrest and uprisings. It did not cover the entire country.

6. ANC submissions to the TRC: (1) 'ANC statement to the Truth and Reconciliation Commission', dated August 1996; (2) 'Umkhonto we Sizwe operations report' in 'Further submissions and responses by the ANC to questions raised by the Commission for Truth and Reconciliation', dated 12 May 1997. These are essential reading for anyone who seeks to understand the nature of the war and the extent of the apartheid state's disregard for international law, rules and norms, as well as the challenges this posed for the national liberation struggle.

7. Z. Pallo Jordan, *Letters to My Comrades* (Auckland Park: Jacana, 2017), p. 59.

Apartheid's forays in this direction had so far failed. It was necessary to embark on a new initiative. Botha's reforms sought to blunt the edge of black opposition through various stratagems of co-option and the tactics of divide and rule. Alongside the ethnic-based bantustans, premised on the fanciful notion that these could become economically viable and politically sovereign entities, came a flurry of proposals designed to give Coloured and Indian communities, and eventually a section of urbanised Africans, a subordinate role in the apartheid system. The co-option strategy was at the heart of the proposed tricameral system, capped by an executive president, and the Urban Bantu Councils. The latter were intended to provide a forum for local-level African representation that would produce a pool of credible collaborators.

To get the white community and parliament to support these constitutional changes, Botha played the apartheid stock-in-trade tactic of invoking and pandering to white fears. He claimed that his reforms were the only way forward. South Africa 'had to adapt ... otherwise we die'.[8] Fear of the future was his way of easing their present insecurities.

In a referendum in 1983, the white electorate endorsed Botha's tricameral constitutional reform proposal, which called for the implementation of 'power-sharing' between the white, Coloured and Indian communities. The effect was to further entrench white control.

As mentioned previously, Botha had by now accepted the reform proposals that flowed from the Wiehahn and Riekert Commissions. They were necessary because a chronic shortage of skills and rigidities in the mobility of African labour were stifling economic growth.[9] The average

---

8. Hermann Giliomee, *The Last Afrikaner Leaders* (Cape Town: Tafelberg, 2012), p. 141.
9. Various laws made it impossible to respond to the demands of industry for skilled African workers in trades required by an expanding economy. Effectively, they imposed a host of restrictions on both the 'pass-bearing Bantu' and potential employers. The laws included the pass laws that controlled the movement of Africans; the Mines and Works Act, which defined what jobs Africans could do; the Natives Land Act, which set aside 87 per cent of the land exclusively for whites; and the Native Administration Act of 1927, which declared that every African, irrespective of domicile or preference, was the subject of a 'chief'.

31

annual growth rate had fallen to 3.4 per cent by the end of the seventies and a full-blown recession was to follow. A capitalist segment within Afrikanerdom had matured. The time had arrived for English and Afrikaner capitalists to work together in an alliance. Monopolies and conglomerates had begun to dominate the economy, and the interests of business had come to dominate the thinking in the NP and the Broederbond. As a result, the hegemony of the NP as the authentic voice of all Afrikaners had fractured.

The NP came to power in 1948 on the basis that it represented the Afrikaner workers, middle class and emergent capitalists – the Afrikaner *volk*. During the sixties and seventies, Afrikaner capitalists became more influential in the NP and the Broederbond. By the late 1970s, their interests coincided particularly with elements among the monopolies and conglomerates that now dominated the economy. Together they wanted reforms that would ease the constraints on labour organisation, mobility and the development of a black middle class. The NP's attempts, under Botha's leadership, to effect reform had the support of an alliance of Afrikaner and English-speaking capitalists.

With the hold of the NP over the Afrikaners fracturing, Botha made strenuous efforts to woo and consolidate a partnership with business under the banner of an NP government.[10] On 22 November 1979, he organised a conference of business leaders at Carlton Centre in Johannesburg, where he announced plans to launch the Constellation of Southern African States, a programme to establish the regional dominance of South Africa and its big business partners. Two years later, he repeated the exercise with the Good Hope Conference held in Cape Town.

The rewards of this were evident in the results of the 1983 referendum concerning his proposed constitutional changes. One significant

---

10. According to Giliomee, the proportion of Afrikaners supporting the NP dropped from more than 80 per cent in the 1977 election to just over 60 per cent in the early 1980s (*The Last Afrikaner Leaders*, p. 145).

measure was the support for a 'yes' vote from English-language news-papers such as the *Sunday Times, Sunday Express, Daily Dispatch, Friend, Natal Mercury, Financial Mail* and *Finance Week*.[11]

Botha bowed to the interests of business but remained unbending to the demands of black workers and the people politicised by the Soweto Uprising. A few intellectuals and sections of the business community questioned whether his reforms were sufficient to diffuse a revolt of the masses. It soon became apparent that Botha had not reckoned with the power of a risen people.

---

11. David Shandler, 'Structural crisis and liberalism: A history of the Progressive Federal Party 1981–1989', MA thesis, UCT, 1990, p. 70.

5

The Gathering Storm

Two developments in the arena of overt struggle played a critical role in tilting the balance of power in favour of the democratic forces: the launch of the United Democratic Front (UDF) on 20 August 1983 and that of the Congress of South African Trade Unions in November 1985. Both put the masses centre stage in a manner that the regime was never quite able to suppress. They would provide renewed impulse to the international sanctions campaign and exert pressure on South Africa's allies. Once activists in the African American community came out in support of the anti-apartheid cause in the late 1970s, the US government found it difficult to resist the demands of its citizens.

During the late seventies and early eighties, there was a mushrooming of localised grassroots community and youth organisations, as well as unions. The renewed clampdown on political activity in October 1977 failed to prevent the setting up of new organisations. The revived Natal Indian Congress and the campaign against the collaborationist and toothless South African Indian Council encouraged the development of local and civic organisations.[1] The Azanian People's Organisation (AZAPO) entered the field in 1979 to keep the Black Consciousness Movement alive. The same year saw the birth of the Congress of South African Students, which was inclined towards the Freedom Charter; the launch of the Release Mandela Committee in Natal; and the founding of the Azanian Students' Organisation, which was also Black Consciousness

---

1. The Natal Indian Congress was revived in 1971. Its activities became more pronounced in the post-1977 period.

oriented. Notable too among the community-based organisations was the Soweto Civic Association, also founded in 1979.

By that time, community organisations were becoming active in different parts of the country. They included the Soweto Action Committee established in November 1977, the Phoenix Working Committee, the Durban Housing Action Committee and the Port Elizabeth Black Civic Organisation.

The Release Mandela Campaign fired the people's imagination in 1980, both within the country and across the world. The non-racial Detainees' Parents Support Committee launched in 1981 soon burgeoned into a powerful national organisation. The revival of the Federation of South African Women in the Transvaal and the founding of the United Women's Organisation in the Cape strengthened the crucial role of women in the struggle.

In contrast, relations between the ANC and Inkatha, led by Chief Mangosuthu Buthelezi, were headed for a rupture. The Inkatha National Cultural Freedom Movement, as it was known then, was not prepared to work with the ANC in a manner that their actions complemented and strengthened the overall struggle to overthrow apartheid. Buthelezi would also find himself at loggerheads with the mass democratic movement, as well as the trade unions. Inkatha was preoccupied within the country and abroad with condemning the armed struggle and the international campaign to impose sanctions against apartheid South Africa. This position aligned more with the interests of the regime than with those of the liberation struggle. Most commentators believed that Buthelezi was obsessed with being the leader rather than with bringing down apartheid.[2]

The resurgence in mass activity brought new challenges. Its power depended on acting together. A united force required a shared set of objectives. The localised and sectional grievances found common ground in the

2. See Mzala, *Gatsha Buthelezi: Chief with a Double Agenda* (London: Zed Books, 1988).

overall struggle against apartheid, but they had to ensure that their unity did not stifle their autonomy and initiative. The space for mass action that had been forced open despite repression had to be deepened and guarded.

An important consideration was how best to ensure that the linkage with the overall anti-apartheid struggle, which involved the relationship between legal and illegal work, did not jeopardise the continuation and growth of forms of struggle within the legal spaces, no matter how restricted these were. Safeguarding the division between legal and illegal work was a necessity imposed by the repression. At the same time, maintaining the interconnection and complementarity between legal and illegal work was a condition for the victory of the liberation struggle.[3]

Tactical imperatives demanded the separation of the legal and the illegal, whereas strategy required a combination of the two. This relationship was a continuing challenge that entailed ongoing adaptations at the practical level as the struggle developed. The characterisation of the 'four pillars of struggle' by the ANC in the early eighties encapsulated this perspective. It inspired activists inside and outside the country. They realised that they were not alone. They felt the power that belonged to the indivisibility of the struggle.

Cooperation and unity among likeminded organisations soon began to find expression in some tentative moves on the ground. The Durban Housing Action Committee, which had drawn together about twenty Indian civic organisations, merged with the African township-based associations to form the Joint Rent Action Committee. Some Africans joined the Natal Indian Congress and the Transvaal Indian Congress. In the Cape Province, some community and civic organisations, together with adherents of the Unity Movement, launched the Cape Action League in 1983.

---

3. This issue was given much attention in 1979 when the ANC adopted the 'Report of the Politico-military Strategy Commission to the ANC NEC' (referred to as the Green Book). The Green Book emphasised the need to avoid compromising the limited legal space within which the community, mass-based organisations and the trade unions were operating.

The path to cooperation and unity was not an easy one. There were many obstacles: the confinement to race-based ghettoes, physical separation through the provision of separate amenities and the differential treatment accorded to different population groups that made up the black community, to mention but a few. Differences in organisational approaches and ideology among the oppressed added to the complexity.

The UDF Unites, Apartheid Divides

There was a growing need to establish an agency at the national level, a mechanism that would address these challenges. On 23 January 1983, at a conference of the Transvaal Anti-South African Indian Council Committee, Reverend Allan Boesak, leader of the separate Coloured branch of the Dutch Reformed Church, called for a united democratic front to be established.[4] The call culminated in the launch of the UDF in August 1983.

Parallel to this and due to ideological differences manifest in the resurgence of overt struggle, AZAPO initiated a conference called the National Forum. Held in June 1983, it was attended by some 200 organisations. The Forum sought to bring together those adherents of Black Consciousness who remained sceptical of the ANC,[5] Africanists inclined towards the PAC, and followers of the ultra-left Unity Movement tradition. Though the Forum sought to carve out a position to the left of the

---

4. Boesak was involved in the World Alliance of Reformed Churches, which declared apartheid a heresy and expelled the Dutch Reformed Church from the world body.
5. Their antipathy towards the ANC was out of sync with the positions that Biko and some of his key colleagues had reached. In his political report to the Kabwe Conference in 1985, Oliver Tambo disclosed that the ANC and the Black Consciousness Movement had reached agreement and arrangements were being made for a meeting between him and Steve Biko. Tambo explained that 'by this time Steve and his colleagues had arrived at the following positions: (a) that the ANC is the leader of the revolution; (b) that the Black People's Convention (BPC) should concentrate on mass mobilization; (c) that the BPC should function within the context of the broad strategy of our movement; and (d) that a meeting between the leadership of the BPC and ourselves was necessary'. See also Thabo Mbeki, 'Steve Biko: 30 years after', in Chris van Wyk, ed., *We Write What We Like* (Johannesburg: Wits University Press, 2007), pp. 21–41.

UDF, the glue that held it together was a shared anti-ANC stance. Such a platform could not hold for long. When the National Forum met again in July 1984, a number of the groups present at its first meeting stayed away. By the late eighties, it had ceased to exist.

Delegates from 565 organisations participated in the launch of the UDF held at the Rocklands Community Hall in Mitchells Plain, Cape Town, on 20 August 1983. The UDF elected three presidents, all with impeccable ANC credentials – Albertina Sisulu, Oscar Mpetha and Archie Gumede. Initially, the UDF limited its task to coordinating opposition to the introduction of a tricameral parliament, which provided for racially segregated representation for Coloured and Indian communities in the central government in a manner that would ensure white domination. The African majority was excluded from this arrangement and was to be accommodated only in segregated local government institutions. The UDF denounced these apartheid-designed 'reforms' and led the opposition to the tricameral parliament. It mobilised the boycott of elections to the House of Representatives for Coloureds and the House of Delegates for Indians in August 1984. Seventy-seven per cent of eligible Coloured voters and 80 per cent of Indian voters boycotted the elections for the respective Houses.

Within days of the successful boycott, the Vaal Triangle and the East Rand were engulfed in uprisings, which spread to the Witwatersrand, the eastern Transvaal, the northern Free State, and the eastern and western Cape over the following two years.

The uprisings were the product of discontent over local issues, such as rent and bus fare increases, the raising of rates and service charges, and the demolition of shacks. The bantustan policies and the state's dispensation for urban African people were the focus of these civic grievances. The township councillors and the bantustan authorities who were cooperating with the regime bore the brunt of the people's anger.

While neither the UDF nor the ANC played a direct role in the township struggles of 1983–84, they influenced and stimulated the activists who were leading the civic protests. These included the inspiration they drew from the actions of MK, the increasing availability of ANC and South African Communist Party (SACP) literature both in print and in Radio Freedom broadcasts, the resistance to elections to the tricameral parliament and the Urban Bantu Councils, as well as the spread of resistance to other parts of the country. Funerals of leaders and activists, and especially those killed in detention or by the security forces, became occasions to challenge the fiat of the state and demonstrate support for the ANC, MK and the SACP.

Most of the organisations involved in the township revolts regarded themselves as UDF affiliates. The protests soon adopted the banner of the UDF and pressured the UDF to develop a more aggressive and militant approach.

The UDF had to evolve an organisational structure that would allow for innovation and initiatives by communities. It had to ensure a shared vision that would give a measure of cohesion and combined thrust to the plethora of community, sports, cultural, youth and student organisations involved in the uprisings that were sweeping the country. The differences among mass organisations centred on tactics and the degree to which the UDF identified with the ANC, rather than principles.

In its January 8 statement of 1985, the ANC called on the people to make apartheid institutions unworkable and to render South Africa ungovernable. The emergence of the UDF, the uprisings that began in the Vaal Triangle, the rejection of the tricameral system and the growing militancy among the workers resonated with the ANC's call.

Dynamics within the churches gave these developments a further boost. The South African Council of Churches (SACC) and the Institute for Contextual Theology began to play a more active anti-apartheid role. The 'Kairos Document' issued by a group of theologians that year provoked a vigorous debate. Partly influenced by liberation theology in Latin America, twenty-nine theologians, mostly based in the black township of Soweto, challenged the churches' response to the policies of apartheid.

They affirmed that 'the most loving thing we can do for both the oppressed and for our enemies who are oppressors is to eliminate the oppression, remove the tyrants from power and establish a just government for the common good of all the people'.[6]

A giant stirs

The task of establishing a trade union movement, which would represent the interests of workers and ensure their organised participation in the struggle for national liberation, was long and complicated.

Trade union organisers exploited the space that arose from the legalisation of African trade unions based on the Wiehahn Commission recommendations. During the early 1980s, there were several attempts to build unifying trade union structures.

The diverse traditions that attended the development of unions from the days of gold and diamond mining were part of the fabric of trade unionism in South Africa, and they impacted on the task of bringing together the unions into a single federation. They took organisational root during the revival of the trade unions and were an element of contestation within and among the trade unions. Differences manifested around several practical issues: whether African unions should register; how to reconcile unions organised on an industry basis with general workers' unions whose members spanned industries; whether workers' organisations have a role in community struggles and the national struggle for liberation; and whether black leadership ought to be prioritised over the view that unions and union leadership should be colour-blind.

Three main groupings emerged in the post-Wiehahn period.

April 1979 saw the launch of the Federation of South African Trade Unions (FOSATU), with a membership of about 45 000. The General

---

6. Kairos Document, 'Challenge to the church: A theological comment on the political crisis in South Africa', dated 25 September 1985, available at https://www.sahistory.org .za/archive/challenge-church-theological-comment-political-crisis-south-africa-kairos -document-1985 (last accessed 25 May 2021).

Workers Union, the Food and Canning Workers' Union and the Cape Town Municipal Workers' Association stayed out.[7] FOSATU chose the path of registration and it gained union recognition in many factories in the early 1980s.

The FOSATU leadership stressed working-class autonomy and was opposed to any alliance with the UDF. It frowned upon 'popular politics' as being 'petty bourgeois'.[8] The reality was that African unionists faced enormous hardships both in the workplace and at community level. Growing numbers of FOSATU members and officials wanted their unions to be engaged with the community and in township mobilisation. Around 1982, the federation yielded, somewhat cautiously and sporadically, to growing pressure to be involved in struggles beyond the factory gates.

FOSATU's emphasis on worker autonomy was in sharp contrast to the life of a black worker, an issue which became prominent in the 1979 wage dispute at the Belville plant of Fatti's & Moni's. The company vigorously resisted demands for wage negotiations by the Food and Canning Workers' Union. The union had little leverage, but pressure from the community changed the balance when the Western Cape Traders Association called for a boycott of Fatti's & Moni's products.[9] The boycott snowballed as teachers, students, the South African Council on Sport (SACOS), churches and women's organisations, among many others, took up the matter. The boycott spread to Johannesburg and Durban and seemed set to take on a national dimension. The campaign lasted for almost the whole of the second half of 1979. Ultimately, Fatti's and Moni's negotiated a settlement with the union. The community

---

7. Karis and Gerhart, *From Protest to Challenge*, vol. 5, p. 217.
8. Jeremy Baskin, *Striking Back: A History of COSATU* (Johannesburg: Ravan Press, 1991), p. 49.
9. The Western Cape Traders Association was made up of Indian traders. There were very few Coloured and African traders and they were not affiliated to it.
   Nevertheless, the consumer boycotts enjoyed the support of the Coloured and African townships.

action highlighted the fact that the lives of workers were determined both in the factory and at community level, and that the majority were black and disenfranchised.[10]

The Council of Unions of South Africa (CUSA), which originated from the Urban Training Project and the Consultative Committee of Black Trade Unions, entered the field in 1980 with a membership of about 30 000. The philosophy of Black Consciousness influenced most of its unions, which emphasised self-reliance and rejected the idea of white officials. By 1983–84, the National Union of Mineworkers (NUM) had become its biggest affiliate. Initially, CUSA unions avoided political involvement. CUSA's stance was weakened, however, when an affiliate, the Black Allied Workers' Union, had to endure the breakaway of two strong community-linked unions, the South African Allied Workers Union and the General and Allied Workers Union.[11]

The Vaal Uprising of 1984 triggered upheavals in townships throughout the country. It was now no longer tenable for FOSATU and CUSA to avoid involvement in community struggles and engagement with community and youth organisations.

By 1984, NUM, under the leadership of Cyril Ramaphosa and James Motlatsi, had a membership of 100 000 mineworkers. It was increasingly unhappy with the stance of its fellow unions in CUSA. Similarly, while it was impressed with the militancy and effectiveness of FOSATU, it had reservations about FOSATU's reluctance to be involved in the community and national struggle. NUM was ready to break ranks with CUSA, and it geared itself to play its part in the creation of a new federation that would accord with the challenges of the time. It also became

10. James Leatt, 'Fattis and Monis dispute: A case study of the role of pressure groups in labour relations' (First presented at the Unit for Futures Research Seminar, Stellenbosch, September 1980), *Reality* 13 (5), September 1981, pp. 13–17.
11. See the South African Labour Bulletin for the views of FOSATU general secretary Joe Foster (1982), the Food and Canning Workers' Union (1982), the General Workers Union (1983), and South African Allied Workers Union general secretary Sisa Njikelana (1984).

the first union to adopt the Freedom Charter and elect Nelson Mandela as its honorary life president.

The Congress of South African Trade Unions was born during the 1985 state of emergency in a climate of popular uprisings and ruthless repression. In November 1985, 760 delegates from thirty-three unions representing 460 000 organised workers launched COSATU in Durban. After its launch, at least twelve regional strikes took place during the period from November 1985 to February 1986. The founding congress elected Elijah Barayi as president and Jay Naidoo as general secretary.[12] The policies adopted at the founding congress placed it firmly in the camp of the democratic forces determined to bring an end to apartheid. The convenor of the congress, Cyril Ramaphosa, set the tone in his opening remarks when he proclaimed, 'a giant has risen and will confront all that stand in its way'.[13]

Apartheid's total onslaught strategy was a policy that licensed a dirty war. This war recognised neither international law nor state boundaries and operated beyond the reach of South African law even inside the country. Combined with the spaces for mass mobilisation inadvertently opened by Botha's reforms, this dirty war was the defining condition of the struggle during the eighties.

The ANC and its allies were best positioned to engage with the challenges arising from community militancy, as well as the development of trade unions searching for ways to aggregate their strength and find common ground with community struggles.

In 1955, the South African Congress of Trade Unions (SACTU) had emerged as the fifth wheel in the Congress Alliance, and the resolutions adopted on strategy and tactics at the ANC's Morogoro Conference in 1969 carried this forward in recognising the central role of the working

---

12. Barayi was vice president of NUM. In 1952, he joined the ANC and took part in the Defiance Campaign. He served a one-month prison sentence. For the different tendencies that were present in COSATU, see Baskin, who identifies eight tendencies (*Striking Back*, p. 54).
13. Baskin, *Striking Back*, p. 54.

people in the liberation struggle. The ANC, the SACP and SACTU redoubled their efforts to support and engage with developments within the country.

The ANC constructively engaged with the Black Consciousness Movement and the participants in the Soweto Uprising of 1976. Over the years, the ANC had grappled with issues of identity and militancy under colonialism and apartheid. The ANC was able to empathise with mainstream Black Consciousness, in which it recognised its own evolution of an African nationalism that was militant, progressive and inclusive. Above all, it was a process that entailed welcoming supporters of Black Consciousness into its ranks and interacting with some of their leaders, including Steve Biko, who understood the need for and the relationship between mass mobilisation and the armed struggle.

In late 1977, the ANC had created the Internal Political and Reconstruction Department (IPRD) within the Revolutionary Council, which would focus, among other tasks, on assisting and mobilising the masses into united action.[14] This focus was present in its propaganda, especially in the form of Radio Freedom broadcasts beamed to South Africa from stations in five African countries.

The annual January 8 statement delivered by the president of the ANC on behalf of the NEC became an essential mobilising medium for activists. It helped them to stay focused as well as attend to the tasks for the coming year. The centrality of mass action was at the forefront of every call.

The NEC set the strategic line to be followed by the ANC and its allies at its meeting in August 1979, which endorsed the recommendations contained in the 'Report of the Politico-Military Strategy Commission to the ANC NEC', usually referred to as the Green Book.

---

14. The tasks of the IPRD were to (1) establish and maintain a political underground within South Africa, (2) ensure the mass mobilisation of the people into political action, (3) conduct propaganda work inside the country, and (4) recruit members for MK and create facilities for returning MK combatants.

These were:

- to 'work unceasingly to reinforce and extend our underground presence in every part of our land';
- to 'work for the political mobilisation and organisation of the masses of our people into active struggle';
- to 'help organise genuine mass organisations among all sections of our people and establish contact with and provide guidance to those which have been formed through the initiative of others';
- to 'provide, either directly or indirectly, the main campaign slogans and issues around which the people can be mobilised to organise and act at national and regional levels';
- to 'work for the strengthening of a Trade Union movement which will genuinely represent the interest of the working class and ensure their organised participation in the struggle for national liberation';
- to 'work for the creation of a widespread network of nuclei among the people which can undertake military and para-military activities'; and
- to 'maintain our independence as the vanguard of our revolution and win growing acceptance for our long-term programme, strategy and tactics'.[15]

The IPRD, as well as Radio Freedom and other propaganda tools such as the publications *Mayibuye, Sechaba, Dawn,* the *African Communist* and *Umsebenzi,* made sure that this approach was at the forefront of their activities. The contents of the annual January 8 statement became the subject of intense study by increasing numbers of activists. The underground structures of the ANC charged with organising within the country used them extensively. Tambo and other leaders of the movement also kept them in mind in discussions and meetings with leading persons from

---

15. See Annexure B 'Summarized theses on our strategic line', point 8 'What is our principal immediate strategic line of struggle?' in the Green Book, available at https://www.sahistory.org.za/sites/default/files/GREEN%20BOOK%2C%20August%201979.doc.pdf (last accessed 25 May 2021).

South Africa.[16] The more the January 8 statement resonated with the issues on the ground with which activists in the country could identify, the more the people turned to it for guidance. In this way, the external/internal barriers imposed by repression were gradually whittled away.

Within this framework, the activities of MK inside South Africa drew sustenance from the resurgence of worker militancy and community resistance, and its exploits, in turn, stirred the imagination and inspired all who found a place in the struggle. MK's deeds were testimony to the daring, resourcefulness and courage that were so necessary to defeat apartheid.

MK, no target is beyond its reach

Red flames more than a hundred metres high pierced the late-night winter sky of the Orange Free State province on 1 June 1980, exactly nineteen years and one day since Verwoerd declared South Africa a republic. The fire burned for three days. During the daylight hours, clouds of thick black smoke mushroomed above the gold and red flames. Limpet mines packed with thermite had penetrated the Sasol I oil storage tanks in Sasolburg and set off an inferno that was visible from hundreds of kilometres away. The acrid smell of burning oil lingered in the air for days.

On the same night at the same time, more than 300 kilometres away, storage tanks at Sasol II in Secunda in the eastern Transvaal were blown up. Because the tanks were empty, there were no plumes of fire and smoke. The damage was nonetheless extensive.

---

16. The exchange of views extended to many prominent and influential persons during their travels abroad. Tambo and other leading members never missed an opportunity to engage such persons. They included Archbishop Desmond Tutu, Reverend Allan Boesak, Reverend Beyers Naudé of the Christian Institute, Albertina Sisulu, Jessie Duarte, Popo Molefe of the UDF, Billy Nair, Reverend Arnold Stofile, Smangaliso Mkhatshwa of the Institute of Contextual Theology, Reverend Frank Chikane of the SACC, COSATU general secretary Jay Naidoo, NUM general secretary Cyril Ramaphosa, COSATU assistant general secretary Sydney Mufamadi, Raymond Suttner, Sister Bernard Ncube, Cas Saloojee, Dr Jerry Coovadia, Zak Yacoob, Dr Essop Jassat, Pravin Gordhan, Thumba Pillay, Ismail Meer, Joe Foster of FOSATU, Jakes Gerwel, Peter Mokaba and Rapu Molekane, to name but a few from a long list.

Panic struck the white community, while Black South Africans, including peace-loving men and women of the cloth, intoned prayers of thanks to MK.

The simultaneous attacks on Sasolburg and Secunda marked the birth of uMkhonto weSizwe's Special Operations Unit.[17] In 1979, Oliver Tambo had obtained a mandate from the NEC to establish a team to attack key strategic targets that would hurt the economy and inspire the oppressed. The unit would report directly to Tambo, who took political responsibility for their actions. The founding Special Operations Command consisted of Joe Slovo, Montsho Mokgabudi (aka Obadi) and Aboobaker Ismail (aka Rashid).

A 1978 visit to Vietnam had impressed on the ANC delegation the role and significant impact of armed propaganda on the morale of the people. Tambo and Slovo designed Special Ops to meet this need. It struck the Sasol plant at Secunda on three subsequent occasions. On 21 July 1981, Special Ops attacked the power station at Arnot, and later targeted the Delmas and Camden power stations.

One of the spectacular coups of Special Ops was when they used the Grad-P rocket launcher, with its 2.54-metre-long barrel and a range of 11 kilometres, to attack the military headquarters of the SADF, located at Voortrekkerhoogte near Pretoria, on 12 August 1981. Mere days before, at the funeral of former Robben Island prisoner Joe Gqabi, whom apartheid's killers had gunned down at his home in Ashdown, Harare, Tambo promised: 'Today, over the heroic corpse of Joe Gqabi, I want to declare on behalf of the ANC that it was Matola[18] yesterday, it is Ash-

---

17. Barney Molokoane was the commander of the unit that attacked Secunda as well as the SADF headquarters at Voortrekkerhoogte. Victor Khayiyana commanded the unit that attacked Sasolburg. Molokoane and Khayiyana were killed in a skirmish with the SADF and the South African Police on the Swazi border in 1985.
18. This was a reference to the SADF raid on the suburb of Matola, Maputo, on 30 January 1981, when sixteen South Africans and one Portuguese national were murdered. They included the first operational commander of Special Ops, Obadi Mokgabudi.

down in Salisbury today, but tomorrow it will be Pretoria.'[19] Through the action of Special Ops on 12 August 1981, Tambo was telling both the regime and the oppressed that he never spoke an idle word.

By the time four blasts struck the Koeberg nuclear power station near Cape Town on 18 December 1982,[20] MK occupied a proud place in the minds of all engaged in the struggle against apartheid. No one any longer questioned the ability of MK to penetrate any target anywhere in South Africa.

The apartheid regime launched indiscriminate attacks on neighbouring states, which violated international norms. On 30 January 1981, the SADF carried out a military attack on several sites in Matola, near the Mozambican capital Maputo, killing twelve and abducting three people in what has been called the Matola Raid. On 9 December 1982, the SADF inflicted forty-two deaths in an attack on Maseru, Lesotho. An air attack on Mozambique claimed six lives, while the South African security forces killed three people execution-style in Botswana.[21] In response to such actions by the apartheid security forces, attacks on military personnel became part of the mandate of Special Ops. One such operation was the detonation of a car bomb at the South African Air Force headquarters in Church Street in the heart of Pretoria's business district on 20 May 1983.[22]

Parallel to these actions by Special Ops, there was a steady increase in

19. Speech by Oliver Tambo at the funeral of Joe Gqabi, Harare, 9 August 1981, available at https://www.sahistory.org.za/archive/speech-oliver-tambo-funeral-joe -gqabi-harare-9-august-1981 (last accessed 25 May 2021).
20. Rodney Wilkinson and his partner, Heather Gray, carried out the attack. The commissioning of the plant was delayed by twelve months at a cost of R500 million, according to Eskom estimates.
21. A list of SADF raids into neighbouring countries is available at https://www.sahis tory.org.za/article/list-sadf-raids-neigbouring-countries (last accessed 25 May 2021).
22. The car bomb exploded at 16.30, killing nineteen people, of whom at least eleven were Air Force officers. Over 200 people were injured, of whom over seventy were members or employees of the South African armed forces. The bomb went off prematurely. Both cadres involved in the attack were killed in the explosion. The attack was aimed at a military target and was not intended to incur civilian casualties.

the number of operations carried out by other MK units from Botswana, Mozambique, Lesotho, Swaziland and Zimbabwe.

As we have seen, the tricameral system failed to co-opt the Coloured and Indian communities. On the contrary, it provided the focal point for the UDF to mobilise rejection and expand this into resistance against the bantustans and local authority structures based on the so-called separate development system.

Botha's way forward was to rely on his abilities as a streetfighter, the best of whom is always calculating. And the best, according to their books, survive because they do not consider themselves bound by any rules.

6

State Terrorism

Botha steadfastly pursued the goal of building a formidable military capability. In 1977, when he was minister of defence, apartheid began its secret nuclear weapons programme. Prime Minister Vorster had approved the plan in 1974. One may well ask: Nuclear weapons to fight insurgency? One never carries a loaded pistol if one does not intend to use it. The programme was secretly shut down by De Klerk in 1989. It appears that the regime and its allies did not want nuclear weapons to fall into the hands of a democratically elected government in which blacks would be the majority.[1] While some in the regime have since claimed, somewhat implausibly, that they never intended to use the bombs, P.W. Botha never made this claim.

The package devised by the JMCs included such tactics as assassinations, attacks on neighbouring countries, economic sabotage and campaigns of character defamation. They disseminated false information aimed at discrediting the ANC and fomenting dissent within the ranks of the liberation movement. They set up front companies to hide their dirty war. The JMCs helped identify local activists who were then detained without trial by the Security Branch or physically eliminated by its hit squads. Those who gave the orders sought to absolve themselves of responsibility for these murders by hiding behind the terminology of 'permanent removal'. Most detainees belonged to affiliates of the ANC-aligned UDF. By 1984, SADF troops were occupying the townships,

---

1. Satellite photographs enabled Soviet Intelligence to detect the construction of a test site. Despite this exposure, the programme continued. When it was shut down in 1989, six nuclear bombs were dismantled.

with uniformed and gun-toting soldiers even having to serve as teachers in township classrooms.

In its submission to the Truth and Reconciliation Commission dated August 1996, the ANC provided examples of the state's tactics. Included among them was the establishment of a network of state agents in the media, and the deliberate diversion of trade union subscription payments into a private bank account to disrupt the activities of the union and sow suspicion among members and the leadership. A bomb placed by apartheid security agents exploded outside a cinema showing the film *Cry Freedom*, about Steve Biko, for which agents in the media sought to implicate the far-right Afrikaner Weerstandsbeweging (AWB). More elaborate operations transgressed international borders.

The arsenal of dirty tricks included the setting up of 'hit squads' to conduct extra-legal terror and assassinations. The so-called Civil Cooperation Bureau and the counter-insurgency unit at Vlakplaas had links with many such units. By June 1985, the UDF listed at least twenty-seven people as missing and another twelve as victims of assassinations. Hit squads were responsible for the murders of the 'Cradock Four' – Matthew Goniwe, Sparrow Mkonto, Fort Calata and Sicelo Mhlauli. In the KwaMakhutha massacre of 21 January 1987, men secretly trained in the Caprivi Strip by the SADF in line with Operation Marion killed twelve women and children.[2]

ANC leaders Joe Gqabi (in Harare, Zimbabwe); Dulcie September (in Paris, France); Job Shimankana Tabane, aka Cassius Make, and Peter Sello Motau, aka Paul Dikeledi (in Swaziland); Ruth First (in Maputo, Mozambique); and Patrick and Jabu Nyawose (in Swaziland) were all assassinated, along with many others in exile and inside the country.

---

2. The aim of Operation Marion was to 'limit UDF/ANC intimidation ... by means of Inkatha', to 'establish Inkatha as a more effective organization against the ANC/UDF' and to 'use Inkatha's intelligence potential to maximum effect for the RSA'. See 'ANC statement to the Truth and Reconciliation Commission', dated August 1996, pp. 30–35.

The regime also resorted to poison in attempts to murder its opponents and used chemical weapons in attacks on neighbouring states.

The SADF, through its medical division, the South African Medical Service, had been researching and producing chemical weapons for use in war. This activity soon extended to chemical and biological weapons for offensive purposes. In 1981, P.W. Botha authorised the development of technology for use against those engaged in the struggle. The South African Medical Service hired Dr Wouter Basson, a cardiologist, to drive the initiative. In 1983, Basson motivated for and headed a programme codenamed Project Coast. At least four front companies were set up to conceal its activities.[3] The resultant extrajudicial assassinations carried out within and beyond the borders of South Africa with the aid of science and medicine constituted a crime against humanity and highlighted the moral and ethical deficit of the regime.

Project Coast remains shrouded in secrecy, any knowledge limited to the testimony of a few who were involved. Basson and his co-conspirators produced a large variety of lethal offensive chemical and biological weapons that were used to eliminate individuals, as well as groups of freedom fighters. One of the front companies of Project Coast paid considerable attention to identifying substances that could kill without leaving any trace. They even tried to develop biological weapons that could be customised to kill only black people.

Several instances of the use of such substances have come to light. In September 1977, South African police agents who had infiltrated MK attempted to wipe out some 500 MK cadres undergoing training at the Nova Catengue camp in Angola by poisoning their food. Fortunately there were no deaths. In another incident, in 1985, about forty cadres in the ANC transit camp in Chelston, Lusaka, took ill from poisoning. In 1986, Samuel Phina and Themba Ngesi died from poisoning in

---

3. The four front companies were Delta G Scientific, Roodeplaat Research Laboratories, Protechnik and Infladel.

Mozambique. The following year, Petrus Lubane was given a drink laced with sleeping tablets and murdered by members of the Northern Transvaal Security Branch. They then detonated explosives strapped to his corpse to get rid of his body. In 1987, Gibson Mondlane (aka Gibson Ncube) was poisoned in Maputo, while four people at Dakawa, Tanzania, suffered the same fate.[4]

Between 1979 and 1988, many members of SWAPO were killed by SADF Special Forces assassin Johan Theron, using a lethal injection of muscle relaxants. Their bodies were then thrown from aircraft into the sea or dumped in the mountains. About 200 people lost their lives in this way. Theron alleged that he and Basson gave five prisoners sleeping pills and then injected them with a lethal dose of muscle relaxants, a claim Basson denied.

Dirk Coetzee, the co-founder and commander of the notorious covert Security Branch hit squad based at Vlakplaas, poisoned, tortured and killed activist Selby Mavuso and askari Peter Dlamini.[5] In 1981, Brigadier Jan du Preez and Colonel Nic van Rensburg ordered the murder of Eastern Cape student activist Siphiwo Mthimkhulu. Shortly before his release from detention in Port Elizabeth, Mthimkhulu was administered a rare poison. He was later hospitalised, where he was found to be suffering from thallium poisoning. When he sought to sue the police, he and his friend Topsy Madaka disappeared.[6]

In 1987, ten youths from Mamelodi between the ages of fifteen and twenty-two were lured by askari Joe Mamasela under the false pretence

4. 'ANC statement to the Truth and Reconciliation Commission', dated August 1996, pp. 33–5, has a list of some of the cadres killed by poisoning and other means.
5. During the period of the European colonial empires in Africa, locally recruited soldiers designated as askaris were employed by the Italian, British, Portuguese, German and Belgian colonial armies. In South Africa, the term refers to former members of the liberation movements who defected or were forced to serve the apartheid government security forces.
6. The poisoning of Mthimkhulu is dealt with in Janet Cherry, 'No easy road to truth: The TRC in the Eastern Cape', Paper presented at the Wits History Workshop – The TRC: Commissioning the Past, 11–14 June 1999.

that they would be going outside the country to join the ANC. They were given laced drinks and the Security Branch used explosives to blow up the kombi containing their unconscious bodies. In that same year, assassins twice attempted to poison Conny Braam, the secretary of the Dutch Anti-Apartheid Movement. She survived with severe damage to her health. In the case of Klaas de Jonge, another Dutch civil rights activist, the poison was administered by application to his clothes in April 1988. He survived but lost an eye. Two unsuccessful attempts were made on the life of Reverend Frank Chikane by secretly applying organophosphates to the underwear in his travel bag.

At the trial of Wouter Basson, SADF military intelligence member Jan Anton Nieuwoudt testified that in 1989 he used an operative to give ANC member Enoch Dlamini a poisoned beer in Swaziland. Dlamini became ill and died in hospital.[7]

We will never know precisely the extent of the use of chemical agents to kill activists within the country and abroad. What is clear, however, is that there was a systematic attempt to research, produce and use these weapons from as early as 1981. It was an undertaking sanctioned at the highest level. No one has been brought to book for this nefarious programme. It remains a testimony to the depravity of the regime and the degradation of all those who participated in it, including the scientists.

The government continuously devised more means to augment its capacity to terrorise the masses. In 1980, it set up paramilitary units called Home Guards. They were established ostensibly to protect bantustan leaders. In reality, they were instruments for intimidating the population. From around mid-1985, a range of paramilitary anti-ANC/UDF/COSATU groups began popping up across the country and various vigilante and pseudo-revolutionary groups appeared in many townships.

---

7. These and many other instances featured in an exhibition titled *Poisoned Pasts: Legacies of South Africa's Chemical and Biological Warfare Programme*, curated by Kathryn Smith, Chandré Gould and Brian Rappert, which was on show at the Nelson Mandela Foundation in Johannesburg in November 2016.

In November 1985, Chris Heunis, the minister of constitutional development, announced that at least 5 000 mostly black 'special constables', also known as *kitskonstabels*, would be trained over the next six months.[8] The state deployed these *kitskonstabels* to crush anti-apartheid forces in the townships and then used its agents in the media to create the impression that this was 'black-on-black violence'.[9] Other state-sponsored formations violently attacked members of pro-democracy groups and sought to bolster unpopular community councillors. These nefarious apartheid-survival schemes would linger into the nineties, wreaking havoc on black lives.

The system of repression and extra-legal and extra-territorial terror of the 1980s was premised on the need to meet total onslaught with total war in an arena where the frontlines were fluid. The apartheid forces ruthlessly hounded and eliminated their opponents, be it inside the country, in the states of southern Africa, or even in the European capitals of London, Stockholm and Paris.[10]

Southern Africa, too, was subject to a policy of unrelenting destabilisation. Pretoria resorted to overt military action right up to the late eighties. Most countries in the Southern African Development Community (SADC) region have their own story to tell in this regard.

The Botha regime never gave up on overthrowing the government

---

8. *Kitskonstabel* means 'instant constable' in Afrikaans, as in instant coffee.
9. Among the more notorious was the creation of the AmaAfrika National Front led by Ebenezer Maqina, which adopted 'Black Consciousness' positions and was later linked to and then expelled from AZAPO. See 'ANC statement to the Truth and Reconciliation Commission', dated August 1996, pp. 30–35.
10. Johann Coetzee, Craig Williamson, John McPherson, Roger Raven, Wybrand du Toit, John Adam, James Taylor and Eugene de Kock were granted amnesty by the TRC for bombing the ANC's London headquarters on 14 March 1982. Olof Palme, the prime minister of Sweden and a staunch supporter of the ANC, was assassinated on 28 February 1986 in Stockholm. It was suspected that South Africa had a hand in his murder. On 29 March 1988, Dulcie September was assassinated outside the Paris office of the ANC. She was shot five times from behind with a silenced .22-calibre firearm. It has been suggested she was investigating weapons trade between France and South Africa. See Evelyn Groenink, *Incorruptible: The Story of the Murders of Dulcie September, Anton Lubowski and Chris Hani* (Johannesburg: Jacana, 2018).

of Angola, which provided facilities for the Namibian and South African liberation movements. The SADF funded, provisioned and militarily intervened in support of Jonas Savimbi's UNITA, and only withdrew after failing to capture the southern Angolan town of Cuito Cuanavale in a protracted battle that ended in March 1988. A May 1978 airborne assault led by General Constand Viljoen had set the pattern for operations. The raid on a SWAPO refugee camp at Cassinga, Angola, commenced with carpet-bombing, followed by a ground attack by paratroopers armed with assault rifles. Viljoen and his men killed more than 600 people at Cassinga, of whom 167 were women and 298 teenagers and children. This and subsequent operations were described by apartheid military strategists as 'pre-emptive' strikes at SWAPO deep inside Angola.

In 1982, the Botha regime entered into a deal in terms of which it promised to cede approximately 10 000 square kilometres of South Africa to Swaziland. The cession included the bantustan of KaNgwane, as well as the Ingwavuma district, which was part of Natal. The rationale behind this seeming generosity was to secure a secret non-aggression pact between South Africa and Swaziland, entered into in February 1982. In terms of the agreement, Swaziland would cooperate in intercepting ANC fighters trying to enter South Africa from Mozambique. The land deal never went through. Nevertheless, Swaziland assumed a position of hostility towards the ANC from the time of the agreement's signing.[11]

After Zimbabwe won its independence in 1980, South Africa assumed full control (which it had formerly shared with Smith's Rhodesia) of funding, resourcing and supporting the Mozambican National Resistance (RENAMO) led by Afonso Dhlakama to overthrow the FRELIMO government of Samora Machel. Support for the rebel RENAMO, military

---

11. King Sobhuza II, who owed his position to tradition, was a lifelong supporter of the ANC. Ironically, despite the monarch's historical attitude, his prime minister and ministers who had received modern education succumbed to pressures from the apartheid regime and collaborated with it. In 1975, King Sobhuza II refused to hand over Thabo Mbeki and Albert Dlomo to Pretoria. He asked South Africa, 'Why do you want to kill my children?'

incursions and air raids into Mozambique, and the country's economic vulnerability, took their toll. On 16 March 1984, at Komatipoort on the South African side of the border, President Samora Machel and Prime Minister Botha signed the 'Agreement on Non-Aggression and Good Neighbourliness between Mozambique and South Africa', which came to be known as the Nkomati Accord.

In terms of the agreement, the Botha regime undertook to stop supporting RENAMO. In return, Mozambique would not allow the ANC to establish bases in or transport arms and personnel through its territory. Since its independence, Mozambique had been crucial to the ongoing efforts of MK to carry the war into South Africa. While Mozambique kept to the terms of the Accord, the SADF continued to provide support to RENAMO clandestinely. When this came to light, the Accord was severely shaken.

The Nkomati Accord was a massive setback for the ANC, made even more significant because it came at a time of sustained upsurge in mass political activity within South Africa. At the same time, however, this latter development was conducive for the ANC to root itself within the country. The regime would soon find that there were limits to how far it could rule by intimidation and force. Every action has a reaction.

Africa stiffens its resolve

Despite the independence of Angola and Mozambique in 1975 and the independence of Zimbabwe in 1980, South Africa's neighbouring states could not render the kind of assistance to the South African liberation struggle that they would have liked. Their geographical location, their dependence on the South African economy, and the fact that they could neither individually nor collectively match the military might of the apartheid state, made it difficult for them to enforce sanctions and isolate the country. They could not afford to provide direct and overt assistance to the liberation forces. In the meantime, they suffered numerous punitive military raids. South Africa used its military to coerce them to submit to its dictates and will. The apartheid regime was also engaged in fomenting civil war in Mozambique through the provision of weapons and logistical support to the rebel RENAMO movement, and it conducted repeated and continuing incursions to overthrow the MPLA government in Angola by helping UNITA prosecute a prolonged civil war.

At the same time, many of these states could not countenance living side by side with apartheid South Africa. Nor could they wash their hands of the plight of its people. In 1980, they met in Lusaka and established the Southern African Development Coordination Conference (SADCC) with the intention of rendering themselves less dependent on apartheid South Africa and to facilitate joint economic development.[12]

Angola, Mozambique, Zambia, Zimbabwe and Tanzania began to coordinate their positions concerning apartheid and develop a shared policy towards the apartheid government and the liberation movements. They came to be known as the Frontline States (FLS) and their role in the defeat of apartheid gained significance, so much so that in 1989, the Harare Declaration, adopted in the capital of Zimbabwe, became the road map for negotiations in South Africa.

The ANC's approach took into account the Namibian experience. South Africa had administered Namibia in terms of a League of Nations mandate since 1920. The United Nations assumed these responsibilities after 1946. After the UN Security Council adopted Resolution 435 in 1978, which unequivocally called for an end to South African occupation of Namibia, a group of Western states, including the US, UK, France, Canada and the Federal Republic of Germany, had constituted what was called a 'contact group' with the aim of steering the implementation of Resolution 435. The ANC sought to develop a position on negotiations that would enjoy the endorsement of the Security Council, while avoiding the process being managed by an external mechanism such as the contact group.

---

12. It was replaced in 1992 by SADC.

The anti-apartheid campaign flexes its muscles

The ANC adopted a strategy to isolate the racist regime through an expanding network of influence. It progressively persuaded thousands that racism, and specifically South African racism, was a moral issue that they could do something about. Sports administrators could influence whether a whites-only team from South Africa should be allowed to compete in an international match. The housewife shopping for her family could act by refusing to purchase those juicy Outspan oranges. It was this strategy that disrupted the Springboks' New Zealand tour in 1981, that galvanised the celebrities who demonstrated outside the South African embassy in Washington, DC, in 1984, and that convinced European parliamentarians to establish their own anti-apartheid network, the Association of European Parliamentarians with Africa, in 1984.

A pact of solidarity concluded with the city of Reggio Emilia, Italy, in 1978 helped to leverage Italian opinion in support of the liberation struggle. An internationally broadcast rock concert at Wembley Stadium in London to mark Mandela's seventieth birthday in 1988 made him the best-known political prisoner in the world and recruited thousands of young people to the campaign demanding his release. The cumulative effect of all these acts persuaded many Western politicians that their constituents demanded action to end apartheid.

The role that the African American church played in the human rights struggle in the United States also had a positive impact on the international ecumenical movement. In 1969, the World Council of Churches initiated its anti-racism programme, with an inevitable focus on South Africa.

A multifaceted relationship with intergovernmental bodies such as the OAU, the UN and the International Labour Organisation, non-governmental organisations, political parties and individual politicians facilitated the ANC's influence spreading well beyond its immediate milieu. The ANC earned the respect of international bodies, politicians and governments because of the conduct of its leadership, whose stature grew over twenty-eight years of relentless campaigning.

By the mid-eighties, international solidarity sustained a host of ANC institutions. In addition to providing food, clothes and other essentials to its personnel in exile, Scandinavian and Dutch funds maintained the Solomon Mahlangu Freedom College, the ANC's school in Tanzania; Dutch NGOs sent canned goods and Dutch Army surplus to MK camps; every two years from 1978 an Italian 'Ship of Solidarity' unloaded cargo at Luanda, Maputo and Dar es Salaam for the ANC; the Soviet Union, Cuba, China and India provided arms and other ordinance in addition to military training; volunteers from many English-speaking countries and the Netherlands actively participated in the ANC underground and assisted MK; Scandinavian countries, especially Sweden, helped fund organisations, including those aligned to Black Consciousness, and engaged in the struggle for democracy within South Africa; funds raised in the US and Europe helped sustain alternative media associated with the democratic movement inside South Africa; and a sustained campaign, spearheaded by African Americans, pushed the Comprehensive Anti-Apartheid Act through both houses of Congress in 1986.

7

The White Laager Wavers

The original 1977 Vorster proposals for constitutional changes that would provide some form of accommodation for Coloureds and Indians generated considerable debate behind closed doors within the NP and the secretive Broederbond. While Vorster's proposals ultimately went nowhere, the internal differences burst into the open and the labels *verligte* and *verkrampte* were given respectively to those who supported this so-called power-sharing and those who were implacably opposed.[1]

After they captured political power in 1948, the NP and the Broederbond became 'the twin central pillars of the entire nationalist edifice'.[2] In the late 1970s, Gerrit Viljoen, chairman of the Broederbond from 1974 to 1980, concluded that the way to meet the crisis evidenced by the Soweto Uprising lay in reforms to the apartheid system. Viljoen's main concern was how to ensure the perpetuation of white privilege and control, without which the Afrikaner *volk* could not survive. His rationale for reform was that there was nothing wrong with the concept of apartheid – it was neither immoral nor evil; the problems arose in the implementation and practice of apartheid. Hence the need for reform. *Verligtheid*, in the thinking of the Broederbond, had clear limits to any claim to enlightenment.

1. *Verligte*, meaning 'enlightened', referred to those who portrayed themselves as the enlightened ones, as opposed to the *verkrampte*, the hardliners or stubborn ones who clung to the past.
2. Dan O'Meara, *Forty Lost Years: The Apartheid State and the Politics of the Nationalist Party, 1948–1994* (Johannesburg: Ravan Press, 1996), p. 43.

When Vorster announced that he was exploring a constitutional alternative to the Westminster model, the executive council of the Broederbond submitted a memorandum. After Vorster announced the proposals for a new constitution, the Broederbond notified its members that 'the contents of our memorandum are in many respects reflected in the new dispensation for Coloureds and Indians'.[3]

There was vigorous opposition in both the NP and the Broederbond. When Botha took over from Vorster and proposed a new set of constitutional amendments in a similar vein, he realised he needed Viljoen's services in government and appointed him to the cabinet as minister of education in 1980. Viljoen relinquished his position in the Broederbond and a battle over the chairmanship began.

Wary of the *verkramptes* who threatened his reforms, Botha took the unusual step of addressing the Broederbond's secret general council before the chairmanship election in 1980. He lost the battle. The Broederbond elected Carel Boshoff, who at the time was the chairman of a think tank promoting the *verkrampte* cause, the South African Bureau of Racial Affairs. Boshoff had been raising the possibility of an Afrikaner retreat to a Whites-only homeland.

Botha was now at odds with the leadership of the Broederbond. Concurrently, the securocrats of the NSMS took control of the government's policymaking and execution.[4] The NP's decline in influence was happening while the expansion of Afrikaner economic power saw the deepening of shared interests between Afrikaner and English business and the rise of monopolies and conglomerates to dominance in the economy.

And the differences could not be contained. In 1982, Andries Treurnicht, the leader of the NP in the Transvaal and a leading *verkrampte*, together with twenty-one members of parliament, left the party and founded the breakaway Conservative Party. Treurnicht had been chair-

---

3. Price and Rosberg, *The Apartheid Regime*, p. 41.
4. The changing relationship between the NP and the Broederbond is dealt with by O'Meara in *Forty Lost Years*.

man of the Broederbond before Viljoen defeated him in 1974 and was a minister in Botha's cabinet in the late 1970s and early 1980s.[5]

In 1983, the pendulum inside the Broederbond swung again. Boshoff resigned and Jan Pieter de Lange, the rector of Rand Afrikaans University, replaced him as chairman. The disarray penetrated the Broederbond to such an extent that it would take De Lange two years to restore order to its ranks.

Botha turned to the white electorate, who were called on to say 'Yes' or 'No' to his tricameral reform proposals in a referendum on 2 November 1983. Seventy-six per cent of the 2.5 million eligible white voters took part in the referendum. Sixty-six per cent of those who voted said 'Yes'. The results showed that Botha had garnered support among English-speaking whites. He exchanged his position of prime minister for the post of executive president of the country and power was centralised in the NSMS. Botha succeeded in limiting his accountability to parliament when the constitutional changes came into effect in 1984.

Differences in the inner councils of the NP and the Broederbond shattered the unity of Afrikaner nationalism. The *verkramptes* saw Botha's reforms as the thin edge of the wedge that would lead inexorably to the end of white rule. The *verligtes* saw the reforms, which were marketed as power-sharing, as necessary to ensure the continuation of white minority power and control. Initially, De Lange explained Treurnicht's and Boshoff's respective departures from the Broederbond as a consequence of them not being able to move with the power-sharing constitution. When recalling the event in 1987, he portrayed the divide as differences 'between those who sought security through exclusion and those who sought it through inclusion'.[6] Whatever the cause, the reality was that Afrikanerdom was a house divided.

---

5. David Harrison, *The White Tribe of Africa: South Africa in Perspective* (Berkeley: University of California Press, 1981), p. 269.
6. Paul D. Williams, 'Intellectuals and the end of apartheid: Critical security studies and the South African transition', PhD thesis, University of Wales, 2001.

Business and the threat of change from below

Law and order ultimately trumped the murmurings of concern among the business community about the Botha government's response to the rise of worker militancy and the Soweto Uprising. Most in business voted 'Yes' to the tricameral system.[7] The shift in position became evident in the different efforts to broaden the constitutional debate initiated by Botha's proposals.

One segment, whose interests were represented by the Progressive Federal Party (PFP), voted 'No'. They were 'among the more far-sighted among the monopolists' and realised that 'new policies were needed'. The 'English-speaking fraction of monopoly capital' had found a home in the PFP.[8]

The PFP had its origins in November 1959, when a breakaway group from the United Party, the official parliamentary opposition, launched the Progressive Party. With Harry Oppenheimer as its chief funder, the Progressive Party advocated for the incorporation of Blacks based on a qualified franchise. The Liberal Party, which had been established in 1953 by Alan Paton and others, had abandoned the qualified franchise in favour of universal suffrage.[9] In 1975, the Reform Party, another break-away from the United Party led by Harry Schwarz, joined forces with the Progressive Party to form the Progressive Reform Party with Colin Eglin as its leader. In September 1977, another small group within the United Party, led by Kowie Marais, joined the Progressive Reform Party, and that led to the formation of the Progressive Federal Party. During the 1970s, the PFP 'became the party of English speaking monopoly

---

7. The Association of Chambers of Commerce and the Federated Chamber of Industries saw the tricameral system as 'a step in the right direction and the start of an evolutionary process of constitutional reform'. Shandler, 'Structural crisis and liberalism', p. 101.
8. Jordan, *Letters to My Comrades*, p. 64.
9. In 1968, the Liberal Party chose to disband rather than obey legislation outlawing multiracial political parties. In 1975, the Liberals believed that the best means of dealing with the threat of African nationalism was through the development and co-option of a black middle class.

capitalism – with its base in AAC [the Anglo American Corporation], but increasingly in other large corporations'.[10]

Jolted by the Soweto Uprising of 1976, the PFP called for reforms that included the convening of a National Convention 'involving all the political interest groups in the country in the process of constructing a constitution', coupled with the enforcement of law and order.[11] Its rationale was that without the reforms they proposed, a revolution from below would overrun South Africa. They saw their role as mediating between the white and black communities. When they talked of the black community, they drew a line in the sand: there was no place for engaging with the ANC. But if not the ANC, then who?

Colin Eglin made it a practice to consult with bantustan leaders, chiefly among them Mangosuthu Gatsha Buthelezi, leader of Inkatha and chief minister of the KwaZulu bantustan. In August 1978, Eglin, Schwarz, Buthelezi and Dr Sibusiso Bhengu, the general secretary of Inkatha, issued a joint statement to the effect that enough common ground existed between Inkatha and the PFP to negotiate and agree on an alternative constitutional framework for the country.

In November 1978, on the recommendation of a commission led by Frederik van Zyl Slabbert, the PFP adopted a platform that stood for the protection of capitalist interests. It abandoned the idea of a unitary state in favour of federalism. It sought to make its proposals attractive to Africans by committing itself to universal adult suffrage. At the same time, it was determined to thwart majority rule, which it equated with 'black domination'. It did this through a combination of provisions for federal decentralisation and minority vetoes. So, while they differed from Botha, their objective remained the same: co-option of sections of the black community to serve the preservation of white control.

Slabbert became the leader of the PFP in 1979, and he was vocal in

10. Jordan, *Letters to My Comrades*, p 63. It would later change its name to the Democratic Party and is presently known as the Democratic Alliance.
11. Dr Frederik van Zyl Slabbert, in an article for the *Citizen*, 1981.

developing and articulating its perspectives. He based his approach to the Botha reforms in the conviction that South Africa needed to embark on a path of 'evolutionary changes in advance of structural pressures and so avoid "revolution, violent or subversive change"'. Slabbert maintained that 'the responsibility and initiative for such change must come from the white parliament, for it alone has the sovereign power to create the conditions for such change'. He explained the rationale behind this stance 'in terms of the immense hold that the state had over the power of coercion which would make the change from below by the black community, i.e. revolution, highly unlikely'.[12]

Underlying the logic of this position was the absence of any fundamental disagreement with apartheid founded on white minority rule. The convergence went further in that Slabbert saw the need for a strong military as a '"shield" behind which evolutionary change could take place'. He was opposed to 'those organisations and groups which seek to bring about revolutionary, violent or subversive change'.[13]

Consequently, during the period from 1979 to 1984/85, the PFP and Slabbert eschewed contact with the democratic movement and the ANC. Instead, they chose to engage with leaders of organisations that were participating in the structures created by apartheid. The collaborators among the Blacks were the moderates in the PFP's view.

Leaders of the Gazankulu, KwaZulu and Lebowa bantustans, the South African Indian Council and the Labour Party agreed to work with the PFP for peaceful change and a National Convention. Slabbert built especially on the relationship cultivated with Inkatha during Eglin's tenure, and it appears that a close personal relationship developed between him and Buthelezi.

Apartheid's programmes to consolidate land allocated to the KwaZulu bantustan gave rise to concerns among some business sectors, espe-

---

12. Shandler, 'Structural crisis and liberalism', p. 57.
13. Ibid., p. 92.

cially the agricultural sector. The Natal Sugar Association, fearing they might lose their land to the bantustan, commissioned Professor Jan Lombard to look into 'Alternatives to the Consolidation of KwaZulu'. His report, published in 1980, argued that separate development could not provide a stable government. He recommended an experiment in 'power-sharing' between races in Natal as a means to 'effective participation of the governed'.[14]

In the meantime, Buthelezi set up a commission in October 1980 to explore a regional constitutional dispensation for Natal, including KwaZulu. It was chaired by Deneys Schreiner of the University of Natal, who had close links with the PFP. Colin Eglin served on the commission as the PFP representative.

The Buthelezi Commission recommended a geographically based federal system. For KwaZulu and Natal, it proposed a consociational agreement which would consist of an executive made up of an equal number of Africans, Whites, Coloureds and Indians. On the basis of one person, one vote, under proportional representation all groups would elect the legislature. A Bill of Rights would protect individual rights, and a minority communal veto would safeguard the rights of minorities.

The Buthelezi Commission published its findings in 1982. In a joint statement, Slabbert and Buthelezi welcomed the report and agreed to work towards a new constitution for South Africa based on negotiations between 'the recognized and accepted leaders from all sections of our population'.[15]

Botha's new dispensation, the PFP proposals, the recommendations of the Lombard report and the Buthelezi Commission all opposed the goals of the national liberation movement, which saw these schemes as representing 'a vital area of ideological convergence amongst the disparate elements, linked to the monopoly capitalist class – either directly

---

14. Merle Lipton, *Capitalism and Apartheid: South Africa 1910–1986* (New Jersey: Rowman and Allanheld, 1985), p 109.
15. Shandler, 'Structural crisis and liberalism', p. 94.

through economic interest, or intellectually – by a commitment to the same objectives'.[16]

The difference between Botha's dispensation and the rest was that the former did not include Africans. In this sense, the other proposals sought to broaden the constitutional debate initiated by Botha while simultaneously ensuring the continuation of the substance of white privilege and control.

Among those who voted 'No' in the 1983 referendum were leading corporate figures such as Tony Bloom, Gordon Waddell, Clive Mennell and Harry Oppenheimer, all of whom had close historical links to the PFP.[17] Their defiance notwithstanding, the tricameral dispensation became law in 1983 and Botha was inaugurated president in 1984. Having urged and voted 'No', the PFP had to decide on their future role. However far-sighted Oppenheimer and those monopolists who promoted the PFP may have been, they could not and would not stray too far from the larger body of monopoly capitalism. Consistent with the views espoused by Slabbert in favour of evolutionary change that could only come through parliament, the PFP decided that, while it would be critical of government, it would work closely with it to influence political reform. Slabbert would radically change his position in late 1985.

While many advanced alternative models to Botha's tricameral system, in essence, they were all the same. Whether described as a division of power (Botha), or as the politics of consultation and joint decision-making (Heunis), or as power-sharing (Slabbert), in the end it amounted to the same thing: maintaining white control.

---

16. Jordan, *Letters to My Comrades*, pp. 70–71.
17. Shandler, 'Structural crisis and liberalism', p. 87.

8

Botha Trips Himself

By the mid-1980s, Botha's plans to destabilise the southern African region had begun to bear fruit. Samora Machel, the president of Mozambique, found his room for manoeuvre increasingly constricted, and the FRELIMO government buckled under the might of apartheid South Africa. The signing of the Nkomati Accord between Botha and Machel in March 1984 was a significant victory for the South African president. Many saw the Accord as a significant step in realising apartheid's game plan of cutting off vital ANC infiltration routes through Mozambique and Swaziland. The regime was in a self-congratulatory mood.

The forces for democracy headed by the ANC, the Frontline States and the worldwide anti-apartheid movement watched the signing of the Nkomati Accord with a mixture of unease, anxiety and even a sense of betrayal. Not one of the leaders of the other Frontline States attended the event. The leaders of the Western powers, led by US president Ronald Reagan, UK prime minister Margaret Thatcher and German chancellor Helmut Kohl, were, however, unreserved in their congratulations to Pretoria.

The Accord could not have come sooner for the Botha regime, as the balance of forces had shifted to its disadvantage. During the period 1980–84, the strategic initiative had passed into the hands of the democratic forces led by the ANC. By 1981, the economy was in recession. It registered negative growth rates for the years 1982 and 1983, and the unemployment rate surged past 20 per cent.

Botha's tricameral parliament was in tatters. The boycott of the elections showed that the Coloured and Indian communities were not on

71

board. Far from dividing the Coloureds, Indians and Africans, the tricameral dispensation brought the three together in ways that confounded the architects of apartheid. The UDF captured the moment in the slogan 'Apartheid divides, the UDF unites'.

Beginning with the uprisings in the Vaal Triangle, townships around the country rose in revolt. No amount of police action was able to contain it. By 1984, SADF troops occupied township after township.

The revolt of the masses, the growing convergence of the community struggle and the workers' struggle on the factory floor, the intensification of MK operations, and the increasing presence of the ANC within South Africa led the people to identify with the ANC as the leader of the democratic forces.

South Africa's military adventures into Angola in support of UNITA suffered setbacks too. On 6 December 1983, the SADF launched Operation Askari. On 3 January 1984, twenty-one members of the SADF lost their lives in engagements with Cuban/Angolan forces at Cuvelai in Angola. Consequently, South Africa, Angola and Cuba signed the Lusaka Accord on 16 February 1984. According to military analysts, 'Operation Askari was the decisive event that led to the signing of the Lusaka Accord'.[1] The agreement defined a no-man's land in southern Angola from which South African, Cuban and SWAPO forces were required to withdraw. From Pretoria's point of view, this would limit SWAPO's direct access from Angola into Ovamboland. SWAPO, however, was not a signatory to the Accord and was therefore not bound by it.[2]

The international anti-apartheid campaign to impose sanctions and

---

1. Papenfus, *Pik Botha and His Times*, p. 553.
2. Ibid., p. 552–3. In Niël Barnard's account of the 1982 agreement with Swaziland, the subsequent Lusaka and Nkomati Accords do not get a mention when considering the factors driving the need for possible negotiations. See Niël Barnard, *Secret Revolution: Memoirs of a Spy Boss* (Cape Town: Tafelberg, 2015), pp. 145–53. Without providing any evidence, Barnard claims there were 'positive sounds behind the scenes from African countries (such as Egypt, Uganda, Kenya and Zambia) towards South Africa, particularly on the basis of our assurances to them that negotiations with the ANC were just around the corner', p. 152.

isolate apartheid South Africa was gaining momentum. The business and financial community in the West began to question the prospects of stability in the country.

The idea that the NP represented the Afrikaner *volk* was shattered. Whereas Botha failed to keep the Broederbond onside in 1980, he felt that with the election of Jan Pieter de Lange as chairman in 1983 there was once more a *verligte* in control. The interests of business now dominated both the NP and the Broederbond. Botha engaged in broadening his reach into the white community as a whole, while seeking to contain the influence of the breakaway parties among the Afrikaner community.[3] Now more than ever he needed to ensure that his Western allies stood by South Africa.

Such were the circumstances when Botha saw an opportunity in the Nkomati Accord. He set out on an extensive tour of eight European countries from 29 May to 8 June 1984. The regime picked the destinations with care. They did not include the Scandinavian countries, which were already committed in their anti-apartheid stance and were rendering humanitarian aid to the anti-apartheid forces, in particular the ANC. The ebullient foreign minister, Pik Botha, who was familiar with the international circuit, accompanied President Botha. They chose to visit Portugal, Great Britain, West Germany, Belgium, France, Austria, Italy and Switzerland.

The *New York Times* of 10 June 1984 reported: 'When Mr Botha's diplomats subsequently put out the word that he would like to invite himself to Western Europe, several leaders found it difficult to ostracise a man who had recently been embracing his black neighbours, notably Mr Machel ... Mrs Thatcher pressed home to Mr Botha a line coordinated with the other governments on his itinerary: South Africa must use

---

3. Botha was primarily concerned by the Conservative Party and the Herstigte Nasionale Party (Reconstituted National Party), a far-right splinter group that had formed in 1969 in response to Vorster allowing the presence of Māori players and spectators during the New Zealand national rugby union tour of South Africa.

its newly won detente with its black neighbours to foster liberalisation at home.' It goes without saying that, in their dictionary, 'liberalisation' excluded the ANC and other liberation movement organisations.[4]

Although Botha's visit provoked anti-apartheid demonstrations, 'his reception by leaders in Lisbon, London and Bonn went a long way toward lessening South Africa's pariah status in the West. "He has been de-isolated," a Bonn diplomat said.'[5]

The regime's success in ramming the Nkomati Accord down the throat of Mozambique and the warm congratulations Botha received from Western leaders led Pretoria to entertain the idea of persuading the Soviet Union to stop 'hostile actions towards South Africa' and 'promote peace and dialogue'. Niël Barnard, the head of the National Intelligence Service (NIS), which replaced the Bureau of State Security in 1980, led the delegation to the talks held in Vienna in August 1984. He used the pitch that 'Pretoria was conducting independent foreign policy and did not want to be closely connected with any superpower'. His team offered the possibility of cooperation between South Africa and the Soviet Union in several fields, including control over a number of strategic mineral resources. However, the Soviet Union rejected 'the idea of exchanging Moscow's support for its friends for a dubious chance of Pretoria's distancing itself from Washington'.[6]

White South Africans saw the Nkomati Accord as a breakthrough signifying the end, or at least the beginning of the end, of South Africa's isolation from the international community. It was a colossal miscalculation. In some ways, it was similar to Vorster's misreading of the success of his outward-looking policy with regard to Africa. But it was of a different order. In many ways, Vorster's actions and reactions were instinctive, whereas those of Botha were based on calculation, albeit that

---

4. 'Europeans give Botha a frosty visit', *New York Times*, 10 June 1984.
5. Ibid.
6. Vladimir Shubin, *The Hot 'Cold War': The USSR in Southern Africa* (Pietermaritzburg: University of Natal Press, 2008), pp. 254–5.

of a streetfighter who chose to interpret the balance of forces from a singular event.

Botha's disinformation campaign backfires

A systematic programme of infiltration and disinformation accompanied Botha's destabilisation of southern Africa. The disinformation campaign took advantage of the problems facing the ANC, including the excesses in the treatment of several apartheid agents held in ANC detention facilities in Angola. Some among them were innocent. The difficult conditions of life in the camps compounded by the eagerness of those trained in the art of war to engage in the struggle within South Africa provided further ammunition for the disinformation campaign.

Apartheid's propagandists used their leverage in the media. During the period 1983 to 1985, the press carried an increasing number of articles by commentators and analysts depicting different kinds of rifts in the ANC in exile. Some forecast a breakdown in the ANC between moderates and hardliners, and between nationalists and communists. Others focused on the clash between the youth and an old guard that was clinging to power. Some reports claimed dissatisfaction with corrupt leadership. The aim was to turn the attention of the membership inwards and cause them to disagree among themselves. The bonus the propagandists sought was disillusionment and disunity among black people.

Throughout history, belligerents have used disinformation to mislead the enemy and sow division in its ranks. During the Cold War, both sides refined the methods and used them extensively. Problems arise when those who engage in disinformation begin to believe their own propaganda, however, and Botha and his cohorts, in their desperation, fell into this trap.

The ANC, for its part, held a consultative conference at Kabwe, Zambia, in June 1985. It was preceded by a preparatory period of more than eighteen months, which involved research, inputs from the membership (both within and outside South Africa), requests for agenda items, and robust discussions at the branch and regional levels that took place before 250 representatives assembled at the conference. The delegates were from the branches as well as the camps. There were vigorous debates and the ANC emerged energised, more united and more determined to intensify the struggle across all four pillars.

Mandela – a problem that won't go away

During his eight-country tour of Europe, the other leaders assured Botha that they would continue resisting sanctions, but said they were finding it increasingly difficult to defend the continued incarceration of Nelson Mandela. Mandela was now into his twenty-second year of imprisonment and in his late sixties. They feared that his death in prison would pour oil on the simmering mass revolt. They urged Botha to show tactical flexibility even while they subscribed to the Cold War mindset. Thatcher was implacably opposed to the ANC, which she labelled a 'terrorist' organisation. She sympathised with Botha when he raised Mandela's commitment to violence as the obstacle to his release. The right-wing leader of Bavaria, Franz Josef Strauss, suggested that Botha offer to release Mandela on the condition that he renounce violence.

The demand for Mandela's release caught the imagination of people both inside South Africa and worldwide. In March 1980, the editor of the Johannesburg-based *Sunday Post*, Percy Qoboza, launched a petition for the release of Mandela and all political prisoners under the banner 'Free Mandela'. It rapidly gained momentum and inspired and reinvigorated the international campaign for the release of all political prisoners in South Africa. Mandela received an avalanche of honours from universities and cities around the world. Over 20 000 mayors from cities on every continent signed the call for the end of his incarceration. The UN Security Council described his release as the only way to achieve 'meaningful discussion of the future of the country'.[7] The Free Mandela

---

7. Sampson, *Mandela,* p. 320.

Campaign encapsulated the need to release all political prisoners and end apartheid.

Was there a way in which to accommodate the concern of apartheid South Africa's European allies without handing a victory to the communists and the 'terrorists'? How could Botha diffuse the campaign for Mandela's release? Apartheid's disinformation campaign had taken advantage of the restlessness in the MK camps in Angola. Botha's success in bringing to heel both Swaziland and Mozambique emboldened him. He remembered the advice given by Franz Josef Strauss.

On his return, Botha told his cabinet that this was a brilliant solution 'because if Mandela refused the whole world would understand why the South African government would not release him'.[8] Some of his colleagues, among them Kobie Coetsee, his minister of justice and prisons, and Louis le Grange, his minister of law and order, warned that Mandela would not play ball.

All the better, thought Botha. His government and the politics of the country were not ready for the possible repercussions should Mandela and his colleagues be released. Botha had no real intention of releasing Mandela. He thought his manoeuvre would wrong-foot Mandela, and because he would extend his offer to all political prisoners, it would split the movement.

The regime remained wedded to the idea that African political rights, including those of Africans in the urban areas, could only find expression in the bantustans. At this stage, the Transkei, Bophuthatswana, Venda and Ciskei bantustans had accepted 'independence', but the programme was meeting resistance even within the bantustans, particularly KwaZulu, which insisted on Mandela's release before any discussion about a constitutional dispensation could take place. Botha's regime felt it could overcome Chief Buthelezi's resistance by manipulating differences between the ANC and Inkatha and employing a carrot-and-stick

---

8. Ibid., p. 335.

policy towards Inkatha. The doors of London, Washington and Bonn were always open to Buthelezi, who had become increasingly vocal in condemning the strategy and tactics of the ANC while insisting on a primary role for himself in any new dispensation. The regime had not come to terms with the fact that any black cooperation would be devoid of credibility unless and until it enjoyed the blessing, if not the participation, of the ANC,[9] and it could not free itself from an approach based on breaking up the alliance between the ANC and the SACP. Its fixation on splitting the ANC rested on a fundamental misconception that there was a pro-violence/non-violence divide within the ANC that could be exploited.[10]

This background enables us to make sense of some of what on the surface seemed to be erratic conduct by the regime, especially during the period from 1984 to 1990. Botha, as already noted, was a calculating man. Often there is method in madness.

Manoeuvrings of a calculating man

In August 1984, Professor Hendrik W. van der Merwe of the University of Cape Town's Centre for Intergroup Studies travelled to Lusaka to meet with ANC leaders to promote the idea of dialogue.[11] At that meeting, Thabo Mbeki and ANC secretary general Alfred Nzo welcomed the idea that he could arrange for them to hold discussions with influential Afrikaners with close links to the NP government. On his return, Van der Merwe approached Wynand Malan and Leon Wessels, both

---

9. It is interesting that one of the issues raised by the PFP delegation led by Slabbert in 1985 was whether the ANC would agree not to oppose a middle way in the form of an anti-apartheid government that did not include the ANC as a participant. They punted this as the best way out of apartheid. Tony Bloom also canvassed this idea at a meeting between business leaders and the ANC held in Mfuwe, Zambia, in September 1985.

10. Buthelezi presented himself as a leader of the ANC of Luthuli, which he claimed was against violence, and alleged that the ANC led by Tambo had deviated from the real ANC when it advocated the armed struggle.

11. Many have confused the Afrikaans pronunciation of the initials H.W. ('Ha-Vee') to mean the professor's first name was Harvey.

National Party parliamentarians, to make the journey to Lusaka, but Botha's disapproval forced them to abandon the trip.

He then approached Willie Esterhuyse and Sampie Terreblanche, two prominent professors at the University of Stellenbosch, both of whom were members of the Broederbond at the time and were close to several ministers, as well as Botha. They expressed cautious interest and put out feelers. 'But no sooner had they begun doing so, the President had them on the carpet,' wrote Van der Merwe years later. '"I hear that Van der Merwe is trying to get you to talk to the ANC," he said. Almost pointing his finger in their faces, he shouted: "I will not let you talk to murderers!" And that was the end of that attempt.'[12] Die Groot Krokodil had spoken.

Next, Van der Merwe applied to visit Mandela in prison. The Security Branch submitted a written report to the Prisons Department advising against it.[13] Nevertheless, in October 1984, Van der Merwe was allowed to visit Mandela at Pollsmoor. That he was able to do so suggests that someone, most likely the NIS, overrode the Security Branch's objection.

In December 1984, the regime turned a blind eye when Van der Merwe took the *verligte* deputy editor of *Beeld*, Dr Piet Muller, to meet with the ANC in Lusaka. Muller had a five-hour interview with Thabo Mbeki and colleagues. Upon his return, *Beeld* published an editorial urging the government to hold talks with the ANC, 'even if it has to be done secretly'. Muller wrote: 'There are people within the ANC who would like to conduct a dialogue with the SA government. It is also just as clear that they must be very careful not to lose their credibility with the ANC's militants.'[14]

12. Hendrik van der Merwe, 'Facilitation and mediation in South Africa: Three case studies', *Emory International Law Review*, 11 (1), Spring 1997.
13. Prison Archive, National Archives and Records Service of South Africa.
14. Quoted in 'Delegations and dialogue between ANC and internal non government groups', South African History Online, available at https://www.sahistory.org.za/article/delegations-and-dialogue-between-anc-and-internal-non-government-groups (last accessed 26 May 2021). *Beeld*'s formulation clearly fed off and into the view that there was a fault line within the ANC that could and should be exploited.

There is no doubt that the regime was aware of Van der Merwe and Muller's trip. Not only was Van der Merwe keeping Maurice van Greunen of the NIS informed of his movements, as we shall see, but he made all arrangements over the phone directly with the ANC's office in Lusaka. Yet when Van der Merwe later tried to facilitate a group of students from the universities of Stellenbosch and Potchefstroom to visit Lusaka to meet the ANC Youth League in 1985, the regime reacted differently. A day after the media carried reports of the proposed trip, officials from the Department for the Interior confiscated each student's passport.[15]

Van der Merwe recalled:

> By the time our plans had taken firm shape, I phoned Maurice van Greunen, a personal contact in the National Intelligence Service (a body that was not part of the police and which reported directly to the President), *and whom I had always kept informed of my movements,* to tell him about this mission. He thanked me for informing him, but told me with a smile that *the Security Police had already done so!*[16]

Neither the NIS nor the Security Branch ever challenged this claim.

Why allow some to go to Lusaka but deny others? Was it a sign of a regime trapped in the chaos of its own making or of bureaucratic bungling? Far from it. The powers that be were interested in reading the alignments inside the ANC to determine whether and how they could deal with it. They allowed people in certain instances to interact with the ANC on the basis that the regime could be a fly on the wall. Such

---

15. Dries van Heerden of *Die Vaderland* was able to visit Lusaka in September 1985. In 1988, Esterhuyse and Terreblanche were allowed to travel freely to meet the ANC.
16. Van der Merwe, 'Facilitation and mediation in South Africa', authors' emphasis. This incident also sheds some light on the cooperation and exchange of information that was taking place between the NIS and the Security Branch, something that those in the top ranks of the NIS have denied in post-apartheid South Africa.

intelligence would be valuable in helping to shape tactics – tactics predicated on the need to divide the ANC and draw Piet Muller's 'moderates' to its side. It required having informants among those meeting the ANC, or at the very least the cooperation of the person organising the visit. Conversely, the authorities refused permission to visitors who were likely to promote within the NP's own constituency the idea that it was all right or even necessary to talk to the ANC.

Let there be no misunderstanding: there is no reason or evidence to suggest that Van der Merwe or Muller were agents of the apartheid intelligence services, the professor's confessed interactions with Maurice van Greunen of the NIS notwithstanding. It is conceivable that he cooperated with the NIS in the belief that this accorded with his desire to serve as a facilitator or mediator. There would be many besides Van der Merwe who, in the coming years, would find their way to the ANC in the hope of being facilitators. The doors of the ANC were never closed.

The regime's political and intelligence analysts would have had a keen interest in an independent reading of the situation inside the ANC by a person of the calibre of Dr Muller. Indeed, he would not have found anything untoward in sharing his understanding with the regime without becoming a paid intelligence agent. No one on the side of the government would question his credentials as a *verligte* Afrikaner. As we shall see, Muller was unrestrained in condemning the delegation of more than fifty Afrikaners that met with the ANC in Dakar, Senegal, a few years later. He supported talking to the ANC, provided it was the 'right ANC' and that such engagements did not permeate and become the practice among Afrikaner intellectuals and opinion-makers.

The ANC, for its part, took into account the links that Van der Merwe may have had with the regime and sought to use him as an intermediary. Minutes of the National Working Committee (NWC) meeting held on 25 March 1987 record a proposal to approach the professor to establish initial contact with the apartheid regime concerning the possibility of a prisoner exchange after Angolan armed forces captured SADF Captain Wynand du Toit, who had led a special task force that attempted to sabotage the oil installations in Cabinda, Angola, in May 1985.[17]

Never underestimate a foe

It was becoming more pressing than ever to find a way around the Mandela conundrum. By 1980, Mandela had become the focal point of the campaign for the release of political prisoners. Since the early seventies, the regime had been considering how to avoid the incarceration becoming a rallying point for the anti-apartheid movement. It had made at least five conditional offers, all of which Mandela brushed aside. On 3 May 1982, P.W. Botha sought strategic advice from the secretariat of the State Security Council as to what to do about Mandela.[18] The SSC had been monitoring Mandela's conversations during visits, his letters to and from family and friends, and even at times bugging cells in Robben Island prison. Different officials had at different times prepared reports evaluating Mandela and his views. For example, on 12 June 1980, Major General Jannie Roux, who during the early 1970s was the commanding officer at Robben Island prison and later became a member of the secretariat of the SSC, interrogated Mandela about his opinions.[19]

There can be no doubt about the bugging of conversations in prison, particularly those between Mandela and his visitors. In his book *Secret Revolution: Memoirs of a Spy Boss*, Niël Barnard admits that they did this behind Mandela's back, but claims that Mandela must have known

---

17. Minutes of the ANC NWC meeting held on 25 March 1987, in the Mark Gevisser Collection at the South African History Archive, AL3284, G.190.
18. Willie Esterhuyse and Gerhard van Niekerk, *Die Tronkgesprekke* (Cape Town: Tafelberg, 2018), p. 65. In the Kobie Coetsee Papers at the University of the Free State, there are several reports dealing with whether to release Mandela and the implications of his continued incarceration and release. The earliest of these appears to be a report by Lieutenant General J.F. Otto, which was considered by a committee of the SSC in June 1982. The SSC decided that Mandela and the Rivonia group should not be released and that the matter be reviewed annually.
19. Esterhuyse and Van Niekerk, *Die Tronkgesprekke*, p. 71–2.

and did not complain. Barnard audaciously asserts that 'the recording of the conversations was a kind of insurance policy for [Mandela]' and that the NIS handled the monitoring 'as ethically as possible'.[20] Yet Barnard exposes the untruthfulness of the claim that the NIS acted 'ethically' when he states that these recordings played a role in determining whether and how the regime should use the information about 'differences between local struggle supporters and the external wing of the ANC'.[21]

Barnard also claims he destroyed the tape recording of the July 1989 meeting between Botha and Mandela, hinting that he may have done this for ethical reasons and to 'protect' Mandela. Because of this claim, scholars have questioned whether there was a secret deal between the regime and Mandela. Barnard, a seasoned spymaster, was no novice when it came to planting disinformation and leading people to make inferences that did not accord with the facts. That is how 'alternative facts' gain currency. Barnard would have done better by justifying his actions using the simple statement that 'all's fair in love and war'.

Barnard seems to have engaged in destroying evidence even in the democratic era. In *Secret Revolution*, he often quotes from discussions that he and his team held with Mandela in prison. He references these quotes as 'Transcript of discussions'. In November 2020, the authors contacted him telephonically and requested access to the transcripts. His responded that he had destroyed them in the late 1990s, after he left national government and took up service in the provincial government of the Western Cape.[22]

It would seem that bugging Mandela's conversations with visitors happened throughout his incarceration and not just from the time of

---

20. Barnard, *Secret Revolution*, pp. 182–4. At least the British kept mum when it was found that they had bugged the liberation movement delegations to the Lancaster House talks that culminated in the agreement regarding the transition in Zimbabwe.
21. Ibid., p. 212.
22. Telephonic conversation with Mac Maharaj in November 2020. Barnard offered no explanation for why the transcripts were destroyed.

the Barnard talks.[23] In any event, the Kobie Coetsee Papers are replete with evidence of in-person monitoring of Mandela's visits and correspondence, as well as covert eavesdropping.[24] Mandela assumed the tracking of his discussions and carefully avoided saying anything that he did not want the regime to hear or know.

By the beginning of 1985, all seemed set for Botha's announcement about the possible release of Mandela. He was due to address parliament on 31 January. But before doing so, he needed to satisfy himself on one aspect: how accurate was the information that Mandela would refuse to renounce violence?

On 30 March 1982, the authorities had moved Mandela, Walter Sisulu, Raymond Mhlaba and Andrew Mlangeni to Pollsmoor Prison in Cape Town. Later, Ahmed Kathrada joined them. Govan Mbeki and Elias Motsoaledi remained on Robben Island. A report prepared in January 1985 by Lieutenant General W.H. Willemse, the commissioner of prisons, for Kobie Coetsee, briefly addressed the motives for their removal from Robben Island.[25] Willemse recorded that 'the purpose of the strategy was to demoralise and detach prisoners like Mandela, Sisulu and Mbeki from the power bases [constituencies]. This was why Mandela and Sisulu were transferred to Pollsmoor and Govan Mbeki left behind on Robben Island. They were separated from each other so

23. See the three-volume study by Karl Edwards of Mac Maharaj for the NIS, which is in the archives of the Mayibuye Centre, Cape Town. In that report, it becomes clear that the cells of certain prisoners in Robben Island prison had been bugged as far back as 1976, if not earlier.

24. Kobie Coetsee, as minister of justice and prisons from 1980 to 1993, presided over the last eight years of Nelson Mandela's imprisonment and started secret talks with him. When he left office, Coetsee took with him a trove of documents. The Kobie Coetsee Papers, as they became known, are archived at the University of the Free State and contain confidential government records, transcripts of clandestine recordings of many meetings between Mandela and his visitors, and monitoring of some other prisoners. These records would normally be the property of the state.

25. Willemse was a regular member of the team headed by Niël Barnard in the discussions that took place in prison from May 1988. He was also aware of the one-on-one meetings that his minister had been holding with Mandela since 1985/86.

that there should not be any possibility of contact and communication between them.'[26]

Jonny Steinberg writes that 'Kobie Coetsee, who pored over every report of his prisoner's conversations ... would write a memo at the time that Mandela was a spent force and that his organisation would soon cast him aside'.[27] Steinberg's conclusion is in accord with the reasons given by Willemse for separating the Rivonia trialists.

From the time he was relocated to Pollsmoor Prison in 1982 to the end of 1984, Mandela was not allowed to receive any international visitors. Suddenly, in January 1985, two prominent international figures were allowed to visit him within a space of three days. Lord Bethell, a member of the European parliament, the House of Lords and the European Working Group on Human Rights, visited on 20 January 1985. Three days later, Coetsee granted permission to Professor Samuel Dash of Georgetown University, who was a member of the International League for Human Rights.

Needless to say, both visits were surreptitiously as well as overtly monitored.[28] Lord Bethell published a report in the London *Mail on Sunday*, dated 27 January 1985, in which he assured the public that Mandela was in good health. While distancing himself from Mandela's position on violence, he called for his release on humanitarian grounds.

Lord Bethell's notes about what happened before he met Mandela are illuminating. Over lunch, Lieutenant General Willemse told Lord Bethell that Mandela and his friends had 'spent 18 years on Robben Island and three in Pollsmoor, all for no worse a crime than conniving at the destruction of property. It is a punishment that far exceeds the offence ...' The problem, said Willemse, 'is that Mandela still supports the armed struggle. For this reason, some human rights bodies such as

---

26. Esterhuyse and Van Niekerk, *Die Tronkgespreke*, pp. 89–90.
27. Jonny Steinberg, 'Poring over Mandela's words, apartheid apparatchiks learnt sweet nothing', *Business Day*, 29 October 2020.
28. Mandela mentioned that a Major Van Sittert sat in during Lord Bethell's interview. See Mandela, *Long Walk to Freedom*, p. 508.

Amnesty International, will not campaign for his release. Also, his case does not appeal to the Parole Board, since he shows no repentance for his past actions – rather the contrary – he makes no secret of his wish to return to the fray. This provides the authorities with the ideal pretext for not putting his name forward to the State President Botha for clemency.'[29] There could have been no more polite and persuasive way of ensuring that Lord Bethell would explore the issue of Mandela's commitment to violence during the visit.

These notes show that Willemse was determined to win Lord Bethell's sympathy for the regime's reluctance to release Mandela and that he wanted to ensure that the issue of Mandela's standpoint on violence featured in Bethell's discussion with him. We can be certain that had the commissioner of prisons publicly stated that Mandela's 'punishment … far exceeds the offence', he would have been summarily dismissed from his post.

After the lunch, Lord Bethell met Mandela. It appears that the latter was, as always, forthright on the question of violence.[30] Bethell's notes indicate that there was no restriction on what they discussed.[31] Mandela later confirmed that 'we discussed the armed struggle and I explained to him it was not up to us to renounce violence, but the government'. In the case of Professor Dash, Mandela stated that 'I told Dash quite candidly that at the moment we could not defeat the government on the battlefield, but could make governing difficult for them.'[32] In an article written for the *New York Times Magazine*, Dash said that 'Mandela left

29. Document 116 in Gail M. Gerhart and Clive L. Glaser, eds, *From Protest to Challenge: A Documentary History of African Politics in South Africa, 1882–1990*, vol. 6: *Challenge and Victory, 1980–1990* (Bloomington: Indiana University Press, 2010), pp. 549–53.
30. At his subsequent meeting with Professor Dash, Mandela informed him of his concern about the carnage taking place and told him, 'I am prepared to play my role in the effort to normalize the situation, and to negotiate over the mechanics of transferring power to all South Africans.' Sampson, *Mandela*, p. 334.
31. Mandela and his ANC colleagues in prison always proceeded in their discussions with the authorities and visitors on the assumption that they were bugged. The eavesdropping yielded nothing new about Mandela's views, but it did show the manipulation and bad faith of the regime.
32. Both quotations are from Mandela, *Long Walk to Freedom*, p. 508.

me with no doubt that, although he intended his statements for my ears, he wanted me to relay them to the white authorities.'[33] Lord Bethell, who gained the same impression, told a journalist that he 'could not detect that Mandela was holding back at all and I think he welcomed the opportunity to get his views on record'.[34]

Both conversations confirmed Mandela's unwillingness to renounce the armed struggle. The visits had served their purpose.[35] Botha was reassured, secure in the knowledge that Mandela would reject his offer.

On 31 January 1985, the state president told parliament that he was sympathetic to the calls for Mandela's release, such as the one made by Lord Bethell. The problem, however, was that Mandela and his associates preferred to stay in prison. 'The government,' Botha said, 'is willing to consider his release in the Republic of South Africa on condition that Mr Mandela gives a commitment that he will not make himself guilty of planning, instigating or committing acts of violence for the further-ance of political objectives, but will conduct himself in such a way that he will not again have to be arrested.' He proceeded to make his challenge explicit: 'It is not the South African government which now stands in the way of Mr Mandela's freedom. It is he himself.'[36]

Botha did not take into account that his challenge gave Mandela an opening that he would not let pass. For twenty-three years, he had been cut off from the public. The country's laws prohibited the publication of any word or statement by a prisoner, or even a photo of one. Mandela the lawyer now came to the fore. He viewed Botha's 'offer' as an attempt 'to drive a wedge between me and my colleagues by tempting me to accept a policy the ANC rejected'.[37] He would not react to the media

---

33. Samuel Dash, 'A rare talk with Nelson Mandela', *New York Times Magazine*, 7 July 1985.
34. Copy of a press report by Joubert/Malherbe in the Kobie Coetsee Papers.
35. The prison records show that Mandela wrote to Dash and Bethell, but the prison authorities never sent the letters. Also, Dash and Bethell wrote to Mandela, but those letters were never given to him.
36. Mandela, *Long Walk to Freedom*, p. 509.
37. Ibid.

reports. Instead, he obtained a copy of the official parliamentary record, commonly referred to as Hansard, and requested an urgent meeting with his wife, Winnie Mandela, and his attorney, Ismail Ayob, to discuss the offer. They were permitted to see him on 8 February.

He delayed formally replying in writing to Botha until 13 February, a response which would be co-signed by his four comrades. He knew that Botha would neither allow his reply to be published nor inform the media of its existence. So, he decided to communicate his message directly to the people of South Africa by dictating his response to Winnie and Ayob. The warders monitoring the visit tried to stop him, but Mandela brushed them aside and continued speaking.[38]

Two days later, on 10 February, Mandela issued a trenchant response through his daughter Zindzi, who read out his statement at Jabulani Stadium, Soweto, at a mass rally to celebrate the awarding of the Nobel Peace Prize to Archbishop Desmond Tutu.

She preceded each substantive point with the words 'My father says'. In his statement, Mandela pledged: 'I cannot sell my birth-right, nor am I prepared to sell the birth-right of the people to be free ... Only free men can negotiate. Prisoners cannot enter into contracts. I cannot and will not give an undertaking at a time when I and you, the people, are not free ...'[39]

When it was over, old and young left the stadium walking taller.

Mandela deftly brushed aside the conditionalities for release in which Botha sought to entangle him. He fixed his attention on negotiations – an issue which, like the legendary genie, was now out of the bottle. What is more, from that moment, the release of political prisoners became inextricably linked as a precondition and precursor to negotiations.

ANC president Oliver Tambo managed to communicate his response to the speech to Mandela in prison:

---

38. Ibid., p. 510.
39. The full text of Mandela's statement is available at http://www.mandela.gov.za/
   mandela_speeches/before/850210_udf.htm (last accessed 26 May 2021).

Tambo was delighted with the speech's reception, and wrote via Adelaide [Tambo's wife] to Mandela in his code which called the ANC 'the Church' and Mandela 'Bishop Madibane'. He praised the Bishop's 'brilliant' and stirring message which spread from congregation to congregation ... it struck a powerful unifying note, and revealed a remarkable degree of identity of approach to the ever-changing terrain of the church-going world.[40]

Botha was outfoxed. He had underestimated his adversary. Shortly after the Jabulani rally, he turned to Coetsee and said: 'You know, we have painted ourselves in a corner. Can you get us out?'[41] His nose bloodied, Botha needed someone else to redeem his tarnished reputation and find a way forward. That became Coetsee's licence to engage with Mandela. But he would play safe. He was not one to readily expose his back, particularly to his president. Coetsee chose to play a lone game. He held a strong hand as Mandela's keeper, but plausible deniability shielded Botha.

Mandela's public response to Botha's offer was consistent with the written response dated 13 February 1985 that all five of the prisoners jointly sent to the president. Botha did not disclose it to parliament or the public. At the same time, political prisoners on Robben Island and in other prisons considered the offer since it also included them. Not one of the black prisoners who supported the ANC accepted the offer. There was no fault line for Botha to exploit.

Trapped in a no-win situation

What the regime may have conceived of as a period for rolling out constitutional initiatives combined with ruthless enforcement of law and order, side by side with a diplomatic push consolidating the gains of the Nkomati Accord, had run out of steam. While Botha toyed with some

---

40. Sampson, *Mandela*, p. 336.
41. Ibid.

minor changes to his new dispensation that never saw the light of day, he locked himself into relying on more and more repression in a bid to retain control over the future of South Africa.

The wave of uprisings that began in the Vaal Triangle on 3 September 1984 had spread across the country. Stimulated by the birth of the UDF, consumer boycotts became popular. Progressive trade unionism changed the terrain with the formation of COSATU on 1 December 1985. At the height of the township uprisings, radical churchmen came to the fore in support of the struggle. The activities of the Detainees' Parents Support Committee and, even more ominously for the regime, the emergence of the End Conscription Campaign (ECC), which superseded the Conscientious Objectors Campaign, reinforced the work of organisations like the Black Sash. With troops fighting a war in Angola for reasons they could not understand and occupying townships charged with tasks for which they were not trained, conscripts and their families began to waver in their support for conscription. Soon the regime stopped publishing data relating to the number of conscripts evading the call-up.

MK operations were on the rise. In June 1985, the Security Branch arrested Klaas de Jonge, a Dutch citizen, for smuggling arms and ammunition for MK into South Africa. He escaped from custody and took refuge in the Dutch embassy. On 18 October, in defiance of international calls for clemency, the regime executed Malesela Benjamin Moloise for allegedly killing a police officer. In June 1986, two car bombs exploded in Johannesburg. In the same month, a car bomb outside the Magoo's and Why Not bars killed three and injured sixty-nine people.

The ANC argued that the regime was setting the rules of war. At its Kabwe Conference in June 1985, the ANC authorised its leadership to drop certain self-imposed restraints and demanded that MK strike at enemy personnel and take the war into white areas. At a post-conference press briefing, Tambo explained that the distinction between 'soft' and 'hard' targets would disappear in an 'intensified confrontation ... an escalating conflict'. He went on to explain: 'I think the distinction between

hard and soft targets is being erased by the development of the conflict
… It is happening every day. It happened two days before we started
our conference – a massacre in Gaborone.'[42] Tambo was referring to a
military raid by apartheid security forces into Botswana on 14 June 1985,
in which they killed twelve people and injured six. Among the dead were
seven ANC members, including prominent artist and MK member
Thami Mnyele.

The war was becoming dirtier. On 26 June 1985, eight activists lost
their lives and seven were wounded in explosions involving booby-trapped
hand grenades in Duduza, KwaThema and Tsakane in the Transvaal.
It transpired that they had been provided with the hand grenades by
Vlakplaas operative Joe Mamasela, masquerading as an MK operative.
The minister of law and order, Adriaan Vlok, had authorised the
operation.

On 20 July 1985, the first instance of 'necklacing' took place at a
funeral for one of the slain Duduza activists on the East Rand.[43] The
victim of this gruesome practice was a young woman named Maki
Skosana. The crowd believed a rumour that she was the informer who
had led to the activist's death. Later, at the TRC, it was revealed that
this rumour was spread by Joe Mamasela to deflect attention from the
real perpetrators, including himself. It thus emerged at the TRC that
necklacing was incited by agents of the regime. Activists had no way of
knowing this at the time. Many began to support the necklacing of suspected informers and the ANC had to work hard to persuade activists
and combatants to end this practice.

On 15 October 1985, the South African Railways Police worked with
the security police to crush a gathering of youths protesting against
the apartheid government in Cape Town. They loaded a South African

---

42. Hugh Macmillan, *The Lusaka Years: The ANC in exile in Zambia, 1963 to 1994*
    (Johannesburg: Jacana, 2013), p. 195.
43. Necklacing was the term given to extrajudicial summary execution and torture
    carried out by forcing a rubber tyre filled with petrol around the victim's arms and
    chest and setting it alight.

Railways truck in a way that created a hidden space in the middle, in which armed police officers hid. They drove the vehicle down Thornton Road and, once in the middle of the protest, the officers sprang up and opened fire, killing three young people – Jonathan Claasen, aged twenty-one, Shaun Magmoed, aged fifteen, and Michael Miranda, aged eleven – and injuring several others. The incident became known as the Trojan Horse Massacre.

On 3 March 1986, members of the South African Police lured the 'Gugulethu Seven' into a trap and killed them. It was publicised as a successful ambush of MK activists.

The regime's dirty tricks included cross-border raids and other illegal activities. In 1984, during one such raid into Botswana, the security forces murdered three people execution-style. The June 1985 raid into Botswana was followed by another, this time into Lesotho, on 20 December 1985. That raid resulted in nine deaths. On 19 May 1986, simultaneous ground and air attacks against Botswana, Zambia and Zimbabwe killed three. All these so-called pre-emptive strikes, themselves a unilateral extension of hot-pursuit strikes, were questionable in terms of international law.[44]

Besides the Treurnicht–Boshoff breakaway, other developments in the white community raised the NP's concern. The launch of the End Conscription Campaign took place at the Claremont Civic Centre, Cape Town, in October 1984. By September 1985, its 'Troops out of the Townships' campaign was attracting thousands at rallies. According to a government report to parliament, 7 589 conscripts failed to respond to the January 1985 national call-up. The number was worrying, having risen from 1 596 for the whole of the previous year. It would be the last

---

44. On 19 October 1986, President Samora Machel of Mozambique and members of his entourage were killed in a plane crash in the Lebombo Mountains near Mbuzini, South Africa. Jacinto Veloso deals with the concerns that led to the view that South African authorities had a hand in causing the plane crash. See Veloso, *Memories at Low Altitude: The Autobiography of a Mozambican Security Chief* (Cape Town: Zebra Press, 2012), pp. 158–64.

time the government revealed the number of draft dodgers. In August 1988, the authorities banned the ECC under the state of emergency regulations.[45]

Pretoria was feeling the heat. It was under pressure to assure the international community that it was in control of the situation. On 21 July 1985, it imposed a partial state of emergency covering thirty-six magisterial districts to quell the uprisings and resistance.

International pressure continued to mount. On 31 July 1985, Chase Manhattan Bank announced that it would not roll over credits and grant new loans to South Africa. This action precipitated the calling in of short-term South African debts by several international banks. The resulting pressure on the country's foreign exchange reserves caused the government to impose a four-month freeze on the repayment of debts on 2 September 1985. To discourage large capital outflows, it reintroduced the dual currency system comprising a commercial and a financial rand.[46]

How seriously did the regime view the actions of Chase Manhattan and other banks? Pik Botha recounts that shortly before Chase Manhattan Bank announced its decision, rumours reached Barend du Plessis, the minister of finance:

> I will never forget the night of 31 July when Barend du Plessis phoned me. I still perspire when I think of it. [Du Plessis said]: 'Pik I must tell you that the country is facing inevitable bankruptcy ... The process has started. An American bank has decided to demand the immediate repayment of all its loans to South Africa. Can you help? Is there not someone in the United States who could talk to the bank?'[47]

45. 'End Conscription Campaign', South African History Online, available at https://www.sahistory.org.za/article/end-conscription-campaign-ecc (last accessed 26 May 2021).
46. Carole Cooper, Jennifer Shindler, Colleen McCaul, Frances Potter, Melanie Cullum, Monty Narsoo and Pierre Brouard, *Survey of Race Relations in South Africa: 1985* (Johannesburg: South African Institute of Race Relations, 1986).
47. Pik Botha, 'Die land was op pad na ekonomiese verwoesting', *Rapport*, 6 June 2010, quoted in Giliomee, *The Last Afrikaner Leaders*, p. 191.

According to Carl von Hirschberg, the deputy director general in the Department of Foreign Affairs, Botha 'implored retired secretary of state Henry Kissinger to intervene, but Kissinger called back to say nothing could be done and that other banks would soon follow suit'.[48]

The Department of Foreign Affairs under Pik Botha set out on a massive public relations exercise to counter the rising tide of international condemnation. The foreign minister and his team put out the word that President Botha would announce a radical shift in policy at the opening of the National Party's congress in Durban on 15 August 1985. Pik Botha personally briefed leading Western governments. Expectations in the media, especially in the Western countries, soared. Pik Botha marketed the forthcoming address as a crossing of the Rubicon. He ensured there would be a media frenzy. *Time* magazine speculated that it would be the 'most important announcement since the Dutch settlers arrived in South Africa 300 years ago'.[49] P.W. Botha's address was screened live to a world audience of about 200 million people. Tambo made special arrangements with the Zambian broadcasting authority so that he and some other members of the ANC could view it live.

The hard-line stance Botha took when he eventually delivered his address crushed all expectations. There would be no substantial shift in policy. Instead, Botha insisted that he and his government would not yield to pressure and agitation from abroad. The world witnessed a finger-wagging president stridently warning: 'Don't push us too far.'

The foreign exchange value of the rand plunged to thirty-four American cents – the lowest point ever reached, leading to a summary suspension of trading on the Johannesburg Stock Exchange for three days from 28 August. In October 1986, the United States Congress passed the Comprehensive Anti-Apartheid Act, which banned new investment and loans, withdrew landing rights, and severely curbed imports of coal,

---

48. Giliomee, *The Last Afrikaner Leaders*, p. 191.
49. Quoted by Hermann Giliomee in 'The day apartheid started dying', *Mail & Guardian*, 26 October 2012.

uranium, iron and steel. The European Community and the Common-wealth imposed a variety of milder sanctions.

In his 2012 book *The Last Afrikaner Leaders*, historian Hermann Giliomee wrote: 'Even a well-packaged, eloquent speech would not have dispelled all the serious doubts about the country's growth prospects, but Botha's speech had made the situation far worse.'[50]

This disastrous public relations exercise compounded the problems facing the regime, pointed to differing situation appraisals inside the ruling NP and caused business to look for other possibilities for a way forward for the country.

50. Ibid.

9

Shaping Setbacks
into Opportunities

The signing of the Nkomati Accord in 1984 posed a new kind of challenge to the ANC. President Machel of Mozambique urged Tambo to consider the need to find a negotiated settlement with the Pretoria regime. Though they did everything to maintain the unity of the Frontline States, some other leaders began to raise the possibility as well.

Tambo was bitterly disappointed by Machel's actions. But it was not the time for kneejerk reactions. After the signing, Tambo appointed a subcommittee made up of Pallo Jordan (convenor), Thabo Mbeki, Simon Makana (aka Nkokheli) and Hermanus Loots (aka James Stuart) to look into the question of negotiations.[1] The committee was of the view that negotiations were not feasible, because the regime was not serious about negotiating change. It recommended that it would be prudent for the ANC to set up a 'constitutional think tank under the supervision of a sub-committee' that would enable the ANC 'to develop

1. Some writers incorrectly claim that an extended meeting of the NWC appointed this committee in 1983 'in anticipation of the Nkomati Accord' of 1984. Another incorrect claim is that the NWC 'in anticipation of negotiations' set up a President's Committee consisting of Alfred Nzo, Thomas Nkobi, Joe Slovo, Dan Tloome and John Nkadimeng 'to manage the interface of any talks and negotiations'. This President's Committee was tasked with the organisational restructuring of the ANC in the light of the 1985 Kabwe Conference decisions. There was no President's Committee to manage the talks and negotiations.

its own set of concrete proposals (not merely the Freedom Charter), otherwise, we will be forced to react to the other side's proposals'.[2]

After the Kabwe Conference and in response to a request from Tambo, Pallo Jordan prepared a paper titled 'The new face of counter-revolution: A briefing paper', dated July 1985. Tambo circulated the document among members of the NEC for discussion. Jordan argued that the 'offers that the ruling class has put on the table amount to a number of soft options for the Black elite ... We must at all costs work towards detaching the elite from the ruling class, not merely rendering it neutral but committing it to our objectives ... [T]he best means of doing this at this juncture would be the adoption of a Bill of Rights.' He added that the constitutional rights and liberties embodied in the Bill of Rights could have a tremendous impact on the political scene at home and abroad. It should not replace the Freedom Charter. Instead, it should 'be an extensive and comprehensive exposition of the rights and liberties South Africans would enjoy under an ANC government'.[3]

It was an interesting strategic proposal – one which was in keeping with the best traditions of the ANC going at least as far back as the African Claims of 1941.[4] Jordan said it would 'put the ball in the courts of our opponents amongst the ruling class' and that 'if we adopt and

---

2. Document 129: 'A submission on the question of negotiations', in Gerhart and Glaser, *From Protest to Challenge*, vol. 6, p. 589. The report notes that, due to other duties, Mbeki did not attend any of the meetings of the subcommittee. The summary in the form of Document 129 is dated 27 November 1985, that being the date when it was formally tabled at an NWC meeting. The unabbreviated version had been developed much earlier (interview with Pallo Jordan).

3. Z. Pallo Jordan, 'The new face of counter-revolution: A briefing paper', Lusaka, July 1985. The paper is reproduced in Jordan, *Letters to My Comrades*, pp. 51–75.

4. 'African Claims in South Africa' was the product of a twenty-eight-person committee, chaired by Professor Z.K. Matthews, set up at the ANC's annual conference in 1942. It was inspired by the Atlantic Charter adopted by British prime minister Winston Churchill and US president Franklin Roosevelt in August 1941 and included a Bill of Rights that the ANC adopted as its objectives in December 1943. The document anticipates the leitmotif of the Pan African Freedom Movement's 1945 conference where the right of the oppressed peoples of Africa, Asia and the Caribbean to use whatever means were necessary to attain their freedom was endorsed. See Karis and Carter, *From Protest to Challenge*, vol. 2, p. 209.

publicise the document at the appropriate moment, it will become the focal point of political discourse inside the country. No one, not even our worst enemies will be able to ignore it, and as such it will be an intervention that puts all other options in the shade.'[5]

Jordan also proposed that the ANC 'explicitly pronounce ourselves on the question of political pluralism (i.e. a multiplicity of political parties and political space for the loyal opposition)'. He explained that there is 'no reason in principle, why we should oppose a multi-party system ... [A]s long as the ANC and its allies are capable of demonstrating, through political argument, debate and open contestation, that we have both the correct policies and the practical ability to address the burning social and political problems facing the people, we have nothing to fear from such a system.'[6]

In due course, these two ideas – a Bill of Rights and a multiparty democracy – developed into ANC policy positions and found their way into the January 8 statement of the NEC in 1987.

The importance of ideas in a political formation such as the ANC is that they undergo processing within its structures, where they are scrutinised and modified until they become policies of the movement. In this way, they morph into the action plans of the organisation.

Tambo was alive to the importance of the work of the subcommittee and the proposals and briefing papers it produced. During the latter half of 1985, he sent the document prepared by Jordan to members of the NEC with a covering note. 'We are poorly briefed and are lagging behind the enemy's "think tanks",' he noted, adding: 'The whole issue needs a thorough and comprehensive study by a collective which is being set up.'[7]

As a follow-up, Tambo inaugurated the Constitutional Commission

---

5. Jordan, *Letters to My Comrades*, pp. 51–75.
6. Ibid.
7. The note, signed 'OR', is attached to the Jordan briefing paper, 'The new face of counter-revolution' (in the private collection of Z. Pallo Jordan).

chaired by Jack Simons, which met on 8 January 1986.[8] He carefully outlined the challenge facing the commission. Apartheid South Africa, the US and the United Kingdom were looking at the idea of a constitution for South Africa that would avoid a future envisaged in the Freedom Charter. The ANC should not be caught unprepared by the recommendations of the research groups and think-tanks set up by the regime. The commission was, therefore, required to investigate various constitutional proposals 'and look beyond the Freedom Charter'. They 'would be expected to draw up a constitutional frame work which shall not be a blueprint prescription of the future constitution of SA'.[9]

Contrary to notions of the authoritarian nature of the ANC in exile, Tambo explained that the commission's task was to assist the NEC in tackling some of the significant constitutional problems it might be occasionally required to solve. Its work would be confidential. He added that 'democratic lawyers at home will have to be consulted from time to time as their input will be necessary and important'.[10] In fact, not only were legal minds from within South Africa drawn into the consultations, but so too were legal experts from abroad, including many from the Western countries.

The commission held its first session on 8–11 and 14 January 1986. The meeting appointed Albie Sachs as rapporteur and Pallo Jordan to liaise with the NWC. Among other things, the commission discussed the Freedom Charter clause by clause.

Once launched, there began a process of exchange of views between the commission, the NWC and the NEC. Upon receipt of the first report of the Constitutional Commission on 14 January 1986, Tambo

---

8. The commission was at times referred to as the Constitutional Committee. Zola Skweyiya was appointed as vice chair and Z.N. Jobodwana as secretary.
9. Minutes of the Constitution Commission proceedings, 8 January 1986 (in the Simons Papers, UCT).
10. Ibid.

appointed a subcommittee to study it and guide discussion in the NWC.[11] This mechanism – consisting of the Constitutional Commission headed by Simons, the NWC subcommittee convened by Jordan, the NWC and the NEC – was at the centre of developing the ANC's strategic policy positions on negotiations. It ensured that the organisation consolidated and widened its support base within South Africa and beyond its borders. Tambo took an active interest in the process and steered it with an acute appreciation of the need to make the ANC the strategic centre of the negotiations when that moment arrived.

The ANC reaches out to white South Africa

Strategically positioning the ANC in the event of negotiations converged with the overall strategy of mobilisation. In terms of the latter, the ANC was steadily engaging with members of the white community inside South Africa. Walter Sisulu succinctly captured the tactical and strategic approach of the ANC towards the white community in an essay he wrote in prison in 1976:

> For the revolution to succeed, it is essential to pare away the strength
> of the enemy and to pin it down to the narrowest limits ... Every
> reduction of the enemy's strength has a much greater effect than
> absolute numbers. At this level there are two aspects to weakening
> the enemy – that of winning sections onto the side of the revolution
> and that of neutralising sections of the enemy camp. To achieve both
> we have to take account of the fact that white supremacy benefits all
> sections of the white community. This means we have to look more

---

11. 'Report of the NWC Sub Committee on the Report of the Legal and Constitutional Commission' (in the Simons Papers, UCT). The report bears a handwritten note '23/2/86', 'Rec. 16/9/86'. The subcommittee was composed of Pallo Jordan (convenor), Simon Makana and Joe Slovo. It appears that at a later stage this subcommittee came to be composed of Pallo Jordan (convenor), Simon Makana, James Stuart and Thabo Mbeki, but the latter does not seem to have attended any of its meetings.

closely at the structure of their societies and the different forces and currents of thought among them and devise appropriate tactics.

This means that we must be alive to the contradictions among the white population group.[12]

As far back as 1976, Sisulu maintained that, while the NP was perceived to be the 'authentic voice of a united Afrikanerdom', changes had been taking place among Afrikaners and the National Party was experiencing difficulties in projecting a convincing image that it represented all Afrikaners.[13]

The ANC's 1984 January 8 statement looked at the immediate challenges this posed and urged:

We must go further to say that our white compatriots, with even a modicum of anti-apartheid feeling, have to abandon the delusion that they can use Botha's constitutional institutions to bring about any change. The forces struggling for a new order in our country are outside these structures.[14]

In his political report to the 1985 Kabwe Conference, Tambo alerted delegates to the new opportunities and challenges:

The growing crisis of the apartheid system is, in any case, causing some sections of the white population to consider ways in which they can defuse the situation. *Among these are elements from the big capitalists of our country, representatives of the mass media, intellectuals,*

---

12. Walter Sisulu, 'We shall overcome', published in Mac Maharaj, ed., *Reflections in Prison: Voices from the South African Liberation Struggle* (Cape Town: Zebra Press, 2001), p. 78.
13. Ibid.
14. 'Statement of the National Executive Committee on the occasion of the 72nd Anniversary of the ANC – 8 January 1984', South African History Online, available at https://www.sahistory.org.za/archive/january-8th-statements-statement-national -executive-committee-occasion-72th-anniversary-anc (last accessed 26 May 2021).

politicians and even some individuals from the ruling fascist party. Increasingly these seek contact with the ANC and publicly put forward various proposals which they regard as steps that would, if implemented, signify that the racist regime is, as they say, moving away from apartheid.

This poses the possibility that our movement will therefore be in contact with levels of the ruling circles of our country that it has never dealt with before. Our organisation and the democratic movement as a whole must be of one mind about this development to ensure that any contact that may be established does not have any negative effects on the development of our struggle.[15]

Earlier we noted that the first of these overtures in the post-Nkomati era began in 1984 with Professor H.W. van der Merwe. He introduced himself as someone with access to leading personalities within the Afrikaner establishment who wanted to engage with the ANC, and he offered his services as a facilitator. The offer opened a new dimension in the ANC's access to the white community.

As previously recounted, in August 1984 Van der Merwe met with Alfred Nzo and Thabo Mbeki in Lusaka. From the perspective which Tambo placed before the Kabwe Conference, Van der Merwe offered the ANC an opportunity to come into contact with the upper reaches of the Afrikaner community, to understand it and the changes and thinking taking place within it. Such interaction would better equip the ANC to pursue its goals. The proposal included the possibility of coming face to face with those at the heart of the establishment.

In April 1985, the editor of *Leadership*, Hugh Murray, proposed to Mbeki a meeting between business leaders and the ANC. The idea was

---

15. 'Political report by Oliver Tambo on the National Executive Committee to the National Consultative Conference of the African National Congress, 17 June 1985', South African History Online, available at https://www.sahistory.org.za/archive/political-report-oliver-tambo-national-executive-committee-national-consultative-conference (last accessed 26 May 2021), authors' emphasis.

for Gavin Relly, who had recently taken over the chairmanship of Anglo American, to lead a delegation of business leaders, but many business-people, including Relly's predecessor Harry Oppenheimer, baulked at the suggestion.[16] When the meeting did eventually take place in September 1985, hosted at Mfuwe by Zambian president Kenneth Kaunda, the only other business leaders present were Zach de Beer, also from Anglo American, and Tony Bloom of the Premier Group.[17] Also in attendance were Peter Sorour of the South African Foundation; Harald Pakendorf, editor of *Die Vaderland*; Tertius Myburgh, editor of the *Sunday Times*; and Hugh Murray.[18]

Tambo's notes show how seriously he took the meeting organised by Murray and how carefully he prepared himself and his delegation. He addressed the questions: 'What do we require from the monopolists?' and 'What do the big capitalists want?' The ANC's task was to get South African business to increase pressure on the regime, which 'should be consonant with creating an atmosphere in which the issue of talks about talks can be broached'.[19]

'Our role,' he wrote, 'must be to try and bring about a split between the regime and the monopolists/exacerbate what tensions exist between the two.' He cautioned: 'Nothing we do or say during the discussion must indicate that we are willing to bargain away their claims in return for some vague promises from the monopolists. We must ensure that they leave here determined to demonstrate to us that they are distant from Botha. Place before them a number of conditions to prove their bona fides.'[20]

---

16. At the meeting, Relly confided that at least two leading Afrikaner business leaders submitted to pressure from Botha and withdrew at the last minute.
17. The ANC delegation was led by its president, O.R. Tambo, and consisted of Thabo Mbeki, Chris Hani, James Stuart, Pallo Jordan and Mac Maharaj.
18. For years there were suspicions that an 'editor-in-chief' was working with the regime. It subsequently became clear that Tertius Myburgh was the mole while he was editor of the *Sunday Times*, a position he rose to in 1975. See John Matisonn, *God, Spies and Lies: Finding South Africa's Future Through its Past* (Vlaeberg: Missing Ink, 2015), pp. 214–15.
19. Notes contained in the private collection of Z. Pallo Jordan.
20. Ibid.

Nelson Mandela and F.W. de Klerk address the media following the Groote Schuur talks on 2–4 May 1990.

Walter Sisulu addresses the media after Raymond Mhlaba, Oscar Mpetha, Andrew Mlangeni, Walter Sisulu, Ahmed Kathrada, Elias Motsoaledi and Wilton Mkwayi were released from prison on 15 October 1989. Although the ANC was a banned organisation at the time, Sisulu opened the briefing with the words: 'This is a press conference of the African National Congress.'

Enuga Sreenivasulu (E.S.) Reddy demonstrating at the United Nations in 1946. This photo was taken when Mrs Vijaya Lakshmi Pandit first raised the issue of South Africa at the UN. From then on, 'apartheid' became a regular feature on the agenda of the UN General Assembly. Reddy devoted his life to the anti-apartheid struggle and led the UN Special Committee Against Apartheid until the mid-1980s.

Looksmart Khulile Solwandle Ngudle was the first person to lose his life in detention without trial, on 5 September 1963 at Pretoria Central Prison. The Security Branch claimed that Ngudle committed suicide.

On 16 June 1976, students marched through Soweto in protest against the imposition of Afrikaans as a language of instruction. The police opened fire and a number of youths were killed. Soweto became a battleground and the revolt spread across the country.

Nelson Mandela, Andimba Toivo ya Toivo, leader of SWAPO, and Reuben Ntlabathi (aka Gizenga Mpanza) in Robben Island prison. This picture was taken during a press visit in 1977 to showcase the treatment of political prisoners.

On 15 May 1977, Winnie Madikizela-Mandela was banished to this house at 902 Mothupi Street in Majwemasweu township, Brandfort, Orange Free State.

Percy Qoboza, editor of the *World*, before his arrest and the banning of the newspaper in 1977. In 1980, Qoboza launched the Release Mandela Campaign in the *Post*.

Steve Bantu Biko, the charismatic leader of the Black Consciousness Movement, addressing a students' conference. Biko was arrested, brutally tortured and died in detention on 12 September 1977.

Oliver Tambo addressing cadres of the ANC at Lilanda, Lusaka, on 16 December 1977. To his left is John Nkadimeng. Mac Maharaj is at the other end of the table.

ANC president Oliver Tambo and Samora Machel, president of the People's Republic of Mozambique, at a public gathering in Maputo in 1981.

A group of ANC women, with Swedish guests, celebrate International Women's Day at Kabwata, Lusaka, Zambia, on 8 March 1982. To the left in black is Dulcie September, who was assassinated in Paris on 29 March 1988.

Ruth First in her office at Eduardo Mondlane University, Maputo, where she was assassinated by a parcel bomb on 17 August 1982. Pallo Jordan, who was with her at the time, sustained severe injuries.

Oliver Tambo mourns the massacre of forty-two comrades and Basotho civilians in Maseru, Lesotho, after a military attack by the SADF on 10 December 1982.

SIPHIWO MTIMKULU STUDENT LEADER

DETAINED. POISONED.

MISSING.

ANC/IDAF

Source unknown

Above left: Tambo addressing a Maseru massacre funeral attended by King Moshoeshoe II.
Above right: Poster issued in 1982. At the TRC in September 1997, the then retired General Nic van Rensburg admitted that he, Colonel Gideon Nieuwoudt and Colonel Herman du Plessis had arrested Siphiwo Mthimkhulu and Topsy Madaka, then tortured and killed them. They burned their bodies and disposed of the remaining fragments in the Fish River. After that they drove the activists' car to the Lesotho border to create the impression that the two had fled the country.

Source unknown

Prime Minister P.W. Botha and President Samora Machel during the signing of the Nkomati Accord near Komatipoort, South Africa, on 16 March 1984. The Accord was a major setback for the South African liberation struggle and the ANC.

Source unknown

The National Executive Committee of the United Democratic Front, 1984. *Back row*: Hans Hlaletwa, Sabelo Ndzuta, Popo Molefe, Mosiuoa Lekota, Christmas Tinto. *Middle row*: Mohammed Valli Moosa, Virgil Bonhomme, Derrick Swartz, Ram Saloojee, Makhenkesi Stofile, Hintsa Siwisa, Andrew Boraine, Cheryl Carolus, Moss Chikane, Joe Phaahla, Cas Saloojee, George du Plessis, Yunus Mahomed and Trevor Manuel. *Front row*: Prince Msuthu, Mewa Ramgobin, Mildred Lesia, Archie Gumede, (empty chair for Albertina Sisulu), Oscar Mpetha, Edgar Ngoyi and Aubrey Mokoena.

Rashid Lombard

Reverend Allan Boesak speaking at the funeral of the Cradock Four – Matthew Goniwe, Fort Calata, Sparrow Mkonto and Sicelo Mhlauli – who were kidnapped on 27 June 1985 and murdered by the Civil Cooperation Bureau, apartheid's top-secret hit squad.

Olof Palme, the prime minister of Sweden, and ANC president Oliver Tambo enjoyed a close friendship. Palme was assassinated in Stockholm on 28 February 1986. Tambo was the keynote speaker at a New York commemoration held at the Riverside Church, a historic venue during the civil rights struggle, attended by the Swedish and other UN delegations.

A finger-wagging P.W. Botha, nicknamed *Die Groot Krokodil* (The Big Crocodile), in full flight.

Poster by the End Conscription Campaign.

Funeral for those massacred outside a church in Queenstown on 17 November 1985. The youth are carrying wooden replicas of the AK-47 rifle – a symbol of resistance and the armed struggle.

Jay Naidoo (left) and Elijah Barayi (right) were elected general secretary and president respectively at the launch of COSATU in December 1985.

Jack Simons was the chair of the Constitutional Commission established by the ANC in January 1986.

Rashid Lombard

In July 1987, Frederik van Zyl Slabbert led a group of 61 mainly Afrikaans-speaking South Africans to a meeting with a 17-person delegation of the ANC in Dakar, Senegal. This photo was taken when the two delegations were hosted by General Thomas Sankara, the president of Burkina Faso.

Dale Cherry/Daily Mirror/Mirrorpix/Getty Images

To celebrate Mandela's 70th birthday, a concert was held on 11 June 1988 at Wembley Stadium, London. It was broadcast live to an audience of 600 million viewers in 67 countries.

The last of the Mells Park meetings was held in June 1990 in London. The talks involved teams led by Thabo Mbeki and Willie Esterhuyse. They met eight times between 1987 and 1990.

P.W. Botha secretly met Nelson Mandela at Tuynhuys on 5 July 1989. Shortly after, he seemingly 'let slip' this information to his colleagues at a bosberaad. Was it a genuine slip of the tongue, or was it deliberately made to look like one?

The police killed 23 demonstrators during the stayaway campaign of 3–4 September 1989. Outrage at the killings spurred defiant marches in the main centres of South Africa. F.W. de Klerk, who became the president of the country in mid-August 1989, was left with no option but to allow marches like the one below to take place.

In September 1989, religious leaders, academics and trade unionists came forward to head a mass march in Cape Town. *From left to right*: Jay Naidoo, general secretary of COSATU, Jakes Gerwel, vice-chancellor of the University of the Western Cape, Sheikh Nazeem Mohamed, head of the Muslim Judicial Council, Desmond Tutu, archbishop of Cape Town, and Reverend Allan Boesak, president of the World Alliance of Reformed Churches.

General Willie Willemse, Nelson Mandela, Dr Niël Barnard, Minister Kobie Coetsee and Fanie van der Merwe. Mandela met Coetsee at least 15 times between 1986 and 1990, and he met the team led by Barnard at least 48 times between 1987 and 1990.

On 11 February 1990, the day of his release from Victor Verster Prison, Mandela addressed the crowd from the balcony of City Hall, overlooking the Grand Parade in Cape Town.

Mandela and others meet Oliver Tambo in Sweden where he was recuperating, March 1990.

Oliver Tambo, the man who guided and led the ANC during its thirty years in exile, was welcomed home by rapturous crowds wherever he went. This photo was taken at Kingsmead Stadium, Durban.

After the meeting, Relly told the media that 'we felt, they [the ANC] and us, that this has been a very important contribution to the process of seeking ways and means of ending the violence of apartheid'.[21] While still on Zambian soil, Relly went so far as to say that more talks might follow. That he never returned tells us something of the pressure exerted by the regime on any person, including influential people in business, who sought detente. And that business still saw the need for the shield that the apartheid state provided. Nevertheless, the meeting played a significant role in countering the demonisation of the ANC and beginning the 'safaris' to meet with them.

When a delegation from the Progressive Federal Party, led by Frederik van Zyl Slabbert, met the ANC in Lusaka a month later, in October 1985, they pursued a matter that had been raised at the Relly meeting. Slabbert and Chief Buthelezi were promoting the idea of a National Convention Alliance. Slabbert believed in finding 'the middle ground' between repression and revolution, rooted in opposition to violence and committed to the rule of law. As the ANC would not renounce violence, he thought it was necessary to exclude them if South Africa was to move forward. It was his view that the priority had to be the ending of the Botha regime, but he realised that any middle path would need, at the very least, a nod from the ANC. Without this, whether implicit or otherwise, such an initiative would not gain mileage. The ANC brushed aside this proposal.

When Slabbert was elected head of the PFP in 1979, the party was searching for ways to expand its membership. He had an academic background, came from the Afrikaner community and played rugby. The PFP felt that with Slabbert at the helm, the party would reach into the Afrikaner community. That did not happen, and they had to come to terms with the fact that no one saw them as an alternative to the NP government. Consequently, the PFP entertained the idea that it might gain a

---

21. Blaine Harden, 'S. African businessmen meet with exiled guerrilla leaders', *Washington Post*, 14 September 1985.

majority in the House of Representatives and the House of Delegates and thereby acquire leverage in the tricameral parliament. That idea died when Dr Jerry Coovadia, speaking on behalf of the UDF, warned

> that the PFP had no moral right to try to corrupt and erode our sense of unity. The PFP must come and ask the coloured and Indian communities whether they want to participate in the tricameral parliament. Yet 82% did not participate in the sham elections last year. If the PFP have not learnt that yet, they must learn that now, otherwise we will find ourselves on different sides of the fence. And we don't want that.[22]

In September 1985, Slabbert and Buthelezi jointly sought to launch the National Convention Alliance. They drew into its steering committee Reverend Stanley Mogoba, who had served time on Robben Island as a PAC member. The launch attracted the presence of several business leaders, including Raymond Ackerman of Pick n Pay, Zach de Beer of Anglo American, Chris Ball of First National Bank, Mike Rosholt of Barlow Rand, Tony Bloom of the Premier Group, Chris Saunders of Tongaat Hulett, and Sam Motsuenyane, president of the National African Federated Chamber of Commerce. Archbishop Tutu and the general secretary of the South African Council of Churches, Reverend Beyers Naudé, sent messages of support.

Despite this support, the initiative died away. The UDF and the Mass Democratic Movement refused to participate. The ANC brushed aside Slabbert's call at the Lusaka meeting, explaining that the dismantling of apartheid was a precondition for calling a National Convention. While the participation of business was a sign of their increasing concern regarding the failure of Botha's reforms, many in industry had shied away from meeting with the ANC when Botha condemned Murray's preparations.

---

22. Shandler, 'Structural crisis and liberalism', p. 118.

Not unexpectedly, the PFP delegation also questioned the ANC's commitment to the armed struggle. Once again, the ANC was able to show how it was always for a peaceful resolution, but that it was apartheid violence that forced it to resort to arms. The pressing question, therefore, was whether the PFP would shoulder responsibility for helping create the conditions for a peaceful resolution. In a joint communiqué, both parties supported the demand for the release of Nelson Mandela and all political prisoners, the lifting of the state of emergency and the unbanning of prohibited organisations. The parties claimed that this could open a pathway to a peaceful resolution of the conflict in South Africa. Tambo's notes in preparation for the meeting with the delegation led by Relly a month before remained the guideline for the ANC delegation that met with the PFP, and the joint communiqué demonstrated that it could gain traction in interactions with leaders and intellectuals within the white community.

On his return to South Africa, Slabbert, as leader of the opposition in parliament, considered it appropriate to brief the state president. Botha felt the PFP was undermining the unity necessary to confront the menace of communism and terrorism, which the ANC represented. Slabbert defended his position. Using the image of a tiger, he urged that if you wanted to defang the tiger, you had to get close to it. Unbeknown to Slabbert, Botha recorded this conversation. In early 1986, when Slabbert gave up his seat in parliament, Botha released a transcript of the recording in an attempt to rubbish his image. More than anything, this incident provided insight into how Botha operated.

Of greater significance was the fact that the meeting in Lusaka with the ANC certainly contributed to Slabbert and another PFP MP, Alex Boraine, re-examining their views. Slabbert later explained that he 'knew very little about the ANC and extra-parliamentary politics. I did not know people in the ANC. I had never met them. I never really understood, practically, "the struggle of the people".'[23]

---

23. Ibid., p. 92.

By the time Slabbert returned from Lusaka, he had exhausted his efforts based on parliament being the font from which incremental change would come. Tambo's message to white South Africans in his January 8 statement of 1984 had entered Slabbert's consciousness: the locus of change was outside parliament, which was irrelevant and illegitimate. And on 8 February 1986, Slabbert said so to all South Africans, primarily white South Africans, from the rostrum of parliament when he announced his resignation as leader of the opposition and a member of parliament, explaining that he no longer viewed the apartheid-era parliament as the locus from which to bring about change in South Africa.

Slabbert's colleagues condemned his action. Those sections of business that were becoming insecure under the existing order felt that he had let them down. The NP played down its significance. For the democratic forces, it was confirmation from within the white community that parliament and apartheid had lost all legitimacy. Above all, there was no future for the country without the ANC. It was time to force a different narrative from the one with which the ideologues of apartheid had conditioned white South Africa. When Slabbert announced that he was quitting parliament, Thabo Mbeki released a statement on behalf of the ANC welcoming Slabbert as a 'new voortrekker'.

Tambo on violence and negotiations
The myth that the ANC and its allies were a bunch of terrorists who worshipped violence was the centrepiece of the narrative which the regime and its Western allies could not abandon. Tambo found an opportunity to address this matter when the editor of the *Cape Times*, Tony Heard, sought an interview and undertook to publish it in full. Tambo was head of a banned organisation, the ANC. Here was an editor of a leading English-language daily willing to breach a twenty-five-year prohibition and risk running foul of the law. Mandela had forced his voice into the public domain in February 1985. Now the president of

the ANC had the opportunity to speak to South Africans through the cooperation of an editor willing to defy the powers that be.

Tambo confronted the issue of violence in a way that could not have been more explicit about his personal standpoint. In the interview published on 4 November 1985, he explained:

> As individuals and certainly as an individual, I don't like violence. But I was in full support of the policy of non-violence because we thought it would bring us the fulfilment of our objectives. When that failed, then we had to look for an alternative. We found the alternative in combining political and armed actions and it is one of those things that you have to do as there is no alternative. I think that many people in the ANC would be glad if there was no need for violence, but the need is there and we have got to go ahead with it, bitter as it is ...[24]

'Is there a possibility of a truce?' asked Heard.

Tambo responded that those who made it a precondition that the ANC abandon the armed struggle were not seeking negotiation but capitulation. He couched his response concretely and carefully: 'There is always the possibility of a truce. We see the possibility of a truce. It would be very, very easy, if for example, we started negotiations ... with the government when they are ready because at the moment they are not ready.' He went on to describe the right climate for such talks – they were the conditions identified by the NWC subcommittee that would be tabled later: 'Lift the State of Emergency; pull the troops from the townships; and the police. And release the political prisoners. We have even said unban the ANC. Do these things to create a climate.'[25]

---

24. Quoted in Luli Callinicos, *Oliver Tambo: Beyond the Engeli Mountains* (Cape Town: David Philip, 2004), p. 585.
25. Ibid. The report of the NWC subcommittee referred to is Document 129, dated 27 November 1985, in Gerhart and Glaser, *From Protest to Challenge*, vol. 6, pp. 589–92, which included the cessation of all political trials and the repeal of all politically repressive laws.

While he addressed the white community, Tambo knew that his words would be eagerly absorbed by the oppressed, including Mandela and his comrades in prison. Mandela, who was at the time in Volks Hospital in Cape Town, found confirmation of a meeting of minds between Tambo and himself. The interview equipped him with his guard rails. Mandela made it his priority to disabuse government of the notion that negotiation required an abandonment of the armed struggle.[26]

At a meeting with British businesspeople, Tambo returned to the question of negotiations and armed struggle. 'Governments often negotiate while there is a war being fought,' he said.[27]

Alongside these tactical responses and positioning, the ANC's 1986 January 8 statement emphasised that the strategic initiative had passed from the hands of the Botha regime. It was now the central task of the democratic movement to retain the initiative by going on the offensive on all fronts, in particular across all four pillars of struggle, freely and with the immediate objective of continuing to make South Africa ungovernable and apartheid unworkable.

Botha shoots down the Eminent Persons Group

It was under these circumstances that the Commonwealth Heads of Government met in Nassau, Bahamas, in October 1985 and the potentials and pitfalls of negotiations came to the fore. British prime minister Margaret Thatcher had come to the meeting determined to stave off the imposition of sanctions against apartheid South Africa. She did not conceal her intense antipathy towards the ANC. Other member states were supportive of the ANC's calls to isolate the country through sanctions.

A confidential letter from Thatcher to P.W. Botha gives insight into the extent to which Britain was batting for the apartheid regime while at the same time vigorously attempting to encourage Botha to pursue

---

26. In his memo to President F.W. de Klerk dated around the latter half of November 1989, Mandela specifically mentions this interview given by Tambo.
27. Callinicos, *Oliver Tambo*, p. 586.

his agenda of reform and repression. Thatcher's letter, dated 31 October 1985, gives her version of what happened at the Bahamas meeting:

> In short, as your message acknowledged, the debate was a highly unpleasant and bitter one; and there is no doubt that the issue of sanctions will not go away, despite my success in preventing the Commonwealth from adopting them at this meeting.
>
> My other main purpose was to secure Commonwealth backing for dialogue between the South African Government and representatives of the black community in the context of a suspension of violence by all sides.
>
> The concept of course comes from your earlier letter to me: and I hope you will agree that it is no small achievement to have persuaded the Commonwealth to put its name to a suspension of violence ...[28]

The Commonwealth meeting searched for a compromise. It eventually agreed on an accord that sought to hold together the divergent standpoints while at the same time striving for ways to align itself on the side of ending apartheid without removing the issue of sanctions, as Thatcher wished. The heads of state called on South Africa to dismantle apartheid, lift the state of emergency, release Mandela and unban the ANC. The meeting appointed a group of seven 'eminent persons' (known as the Eminent Persons Group or EPG) charged with the task of 'establish[ing] a basis for negotiations between the Nationalist government and its opponents, principally the African National Congress' and reporting back within six months.[29]

---

28. 'Letter from British Prime Minister Margaret Thatcher to South African President PW Botha, October 31 1985', full text available at https://www.politicsweb.co.za/documents/free-nelson-mandela--margaret-thatcher (last accessed 26 May 2021).
29. Ralph Lawrence's review of *Mission to South Africa: The Commonwealth Report – The Findings of the Eminent Persons Group on South Africa* (Harmondsworth: Penguin Books for the Commonwealth Secretariat, 1986), available at http://www.sahistory.org.za/sites/default/files/DC/resep86.4/resep86.4.pdf (last accessed 26 May 2021).

The ANC met the establishment of the EPG with caution: Margaret Thatcher was of one mind with the Reagan administration in seeking to use incentives as a means of encouraging South Africa to move away gradually and incrementally from apartheid. The US advanced 'constructive engagement' as an alternative to economic sanctions and divestment from South Africa. Chester Crocker, the assistant secretary of state for African affairs, had sought through 'constructive engagement' to link the independence of Namibia to an easing of the arms embargo against South Africa and the withdrawal of Cuban troops from Angola.

The ANC was alert to the possibilities that the EPG exercise could lock it into premature negotiations or develop into a manoeuvre to place the fate of South Africa in the hands of outside forces. It was necessary to keep in mind the support the Western powers were giving to the apartheid regime and their determination to prevent the ANC from coming to power. At the Lancaster House talks in 1980, ZANU and its military formation ZANLA had been forced to the table by some of the Frontline States that were its principal backers. The ANC wanted to avoid a similar situation. Tambo said that 'what came out at Nassau was very disturbing. Not only did Thatcher abort the efforts of the Commonwealth, but she also bought Botha a way out of the tight corner he was in.'[30]

The ANC's response to the EPG had to take into consideration all these concerns.

On 26 April 1986, Thabo Mbeki and Johnny Makatini reported to a special meeting of the NWC and provided an outline of the key elements of a proposal that Olusegun Obasanjo, the co-chair of the EPG, was putting together:

1. Negotiations can only take place in the absence of violence.
2. Botha should take steps to begin dismantling apartheid.
3. Botha should move away from group concept and adopt a non-racial vision.

---

30. Minutes of the NWC special meeting on 26 April 1986 (in the Simons Papers, UCT).

4. Practical measures, including abolishing pass laws, lifting bans on illegal organisations, ending repression, removing troops from the townships, and suspending detention without trial.

In the discussions that followed, some saw the Obasanjo proposal as a starting point, while others were deeply concerned about the bona fides of the regime. Tambo carefully crafted the way forward, warning that 'the chief danger we have to guard against is the EPG getting us entangled in negotiations just when we are getting on top of the situation'. He reminded the meeting that it was 'in deference to our friends' that the ANC did not shoot down the EPG. Rather, it was necessary to 'pin the EPG down to the original understanding of Nassau – all the conditions must be met – only then can we move towards the reduction of violence by both sides'.[31]

Tambo was especially concerned about the EPG's proposal that the 'absence of violence' be a precondition for negotiations. He maintained that 'we must at all costs avoid a *quid pro quo* situation in which we are expected to make reciprocal moves in response to the enemy moves. On negotiations – we stick to our position that negotiations are not dependent on cessation of hostilities. We stress too that it is the other side who are not ready.'[32] The wording of this proposal was also ambiguous. 'Absence of violence' clearly implied much more than a suspension of armed activity by MK, but the language papered over the issue that the source of the violence was the apartheid system. Accordingly, the proposal gave the regime the space to force the ANC to take responsibility for and prevent any form of 'violent' activity in the black communities and to police the actions of all the democratic forces.

Obasanjo drafted a negotiating concept document which the EPG then took on the road. The group visited South Africa, where they met

---

31. Ibid.
32. Ibid.

with government ministers, black leaders and even Nelson Mandela in Pollsmoor Prison. Mandela accepted Obasanjo's draft document 'as a starting point' and hoped it would enjoy the support of his colleagues.[33] He couched his response carefully, as he met with the EPG in the presence of Minister Coetsee, who secretly recorded the conversation. Mandela told the EPG: 'The problem is that what you are actually interested in is not my view. But my view to express the view of the organisation to which I belong [sic] … My problem is that that I have no contact with my colleagues inside prison and outside prison in South Africa.'[34]

On 16 May, during another visit from the EPG in Pollsmoor, Mandela asked whether Botha was taking the 'negotiating concept' seriously. The EPG had not received a clear answer from Botha by the time they reached Lusaka the following day to present the concept to the ANC. Tambo, like Mandela, suspected Botha of employing delaying tactics and was suspicious of his good faith. He avoided dismissing the proposals out of hand and suggested that the concept was likely to enjoy the support of his ANC colleagues. He was not committing the ANC, but he was keeping the door open. The preconditions of the Nassau Commonwealth meeting were the responsibility of the government.[35]

The EPG returned to Cape Town on 19 May to put their proposals to a committee of cabinet ministers. Botha's hardliners insisted that the ANC renounce violence and not just suspend it, as the EPG now recommended. They wanted the ANC dehorned, or, as Slabbert put it to Botha, rendered toothless, before they would meet at the negotiating table.

At this critical moment, while the regime and the EPG were still talking, military airstrikes and raids were launched, with Botha's approval, against alleged ANC facilities in Lusaka, Harare and Gaborone. The EPG

33. Sampson, *Mandela*, p. 348.
34. Esterhuyse and Van Niekerk, *Die Tronkgespreke*, pp. 128–9.
35. Document 134: 'Report by Commonwealth Eminent Persons Group on meeting with ANC representatives in Lusaka, May 17, 1985', in Gerhart and Glaser, *From Protest to Challenge*, vol. 6, pp. 599–601.

returned to London, knowing that their mission was over. In their final report, the EPG concluded:

> It is our considered view that, despite appearances and statements to the contrary, the South African Government is not yet ready to negotiate ... (for the establishment of a non-racial and representative government) except on its own terms. Those terms, both in regard to objectives and modalities, fall far short of reasonable black expectations and well-accepted democratic norms and principles.[36]

Botha claimed that the raids in late May were 'the first installment' and that they showed that 'South Africa has the capacity and the will to break the ANC'.[37]

What led Botha to shoot down the EPG?

The records of a special meeting convened by the Coordinating Intelligence Committee in October 1985 provide a clue.[38] On the agenda was whether it was possible to avoid a settlement with the ANC. Attended by the most senior generals and intelligence personnel in the country, the meeting took into account the 'massive national and international support for the ANC and ... the widespread perception that the government was losing ground ... [T]he consensus was that any negotiation should take place from a position of strength, not weakness[,] and a settlement should be avoided until the balance of power could be shifted. In the words of General [Tienie] Groenewald: "This is the stage when

36. *Preparing for Power: Oliver Tambo Speaks*, compiled by Adelaide Tambo (London: Heinemann, 1987), p. 260.
37. Alan Cowell, 'South African president warns of further raids', *New York Times*, 22 May 1986. Swedish prime minister Olof Palme was assassinated in Stockholm in the same month, February 1986, that the EPG first visited South Africa. Although South African involvement was suspected, the Swedish authorities closed the case in 2020 without establishing who committed the crime.
38. The Coordinating Intelligence Committee (Koordineer Inligting Komitee) was established in 1981 and was a substructure of the National Statutory Council. It was chaired by Dr Niël Barnard, the head of NIS. Note that the committee met during the same month that the Commonwealth established the EPG.

one can negotiate from a position of strength and can afford to accommodate the other party, given that it has largely been eliminated as a threat."'[39] The regime was in no such position at the time of the EPG mission. Pretoria was feeling the heat.

While the EPG was seized with the matter, Botha and Coetsee searched for other ways around the impasse. On 14 March 1986, Coetsee wrote a letter to Botha confirming the latter's consent to informal confidential discussions with Mandela and that the Mandela issue was being looked at by a committee consisting of departmental heads. The letter recorded that Coetsee's overture to Mandela was not a matter for this committee and that he would proceed to hold discussions with Mandela on that basis.[40]

Coetsee wrote this letter before the first of the Mells Park talks between a South African delegation led by Willie Esterhuyse and an ANC delegation headed by Thabo Mbeki in October 1987, and well before a team led by Barnard met Mandela in May 1988.

There was disagreement inside Botha's cabinet around the EPG proposal that the ANC should commit itself to a moratorium on violence for a limited period. Some ministers insisted that the ANC commit to the cessation of violence rather than a moratorium. To this day, it remains unclear as to what, if any, intelligence assessment informed this debate. F.W. de Klerk, Pik Botha and Niël Barnard, who was head of the NIS and chair of the Coordinating Intelligence Committee, all failed to shed light on this episode. In his book, Barnard simply dismisses the EPG, citing it as an instance where 'other countries throughout the world [wanted] to hijack the South African peace process'.[41]

In his review of the EPG report, Professor Ralph Lawrence observed:

The exchange of letters between the Commonwealth co-chairmen, [former Australian prime minister Malcolm] Fraser and Obasanjo, and

---

39. Report of the Truth and Reconciliation Commission, vol. 2, p. 37.
40. Esterhuyse and Van Niekerk, *Die Tronkgespreke*, p. 201.
41. Barnard, *Secret Revolution*, p. 188.

the two Bothas, P.W. and Pik, gives us a rare insight into how the leading lights in Pretoria think and conduct themselves away from the glare of publicity. These letters make sombre reading. Now, with the benefit of hindsight, one can see quite plainly that P.W. Botha resented what he saw as the Commonwealth's intrusion in South African domestic affairs. Nor was there any chance of his government agreeing to bargain with the ANC on equal terms for that would be seen as granting the organisation a legitimacy his Cabinet was not prepared to concede. Furthermore, the EPG believed that for negotiations to get underway both sides would have to suspend violence. The South African government did not accept the premise that it perpetrates violence. Moreover, it demanded that the ANC renounce violence, not merely suspend hostilities temporarily. The State President refused to budge and preferred instead to pander to his domestic constituency by authorising military raids against Zimbabwe, Zambia and Botswana.[42]

The principal tactical victory the ANC won as a result of Botha's intransigence was that it radically shifted opinion in the US Congress. Within days of the release of the EPG's report, the Comprehensive Anti-Apartheid Act sailed through both houses with a sufficient majority to thwart a presidential veto by Ronald Reagan.

The latest raids confirmed that the ANC was right to be wary. The conflict had reached a stage where the path to negotiations demanded clinical analysis, deft tactical manoeuvring and a strategy that allowed for the long haul without constricting the space for the ANC to act timeously and decisively as the situation developed. It required a constant sensitivity to avoid pitfalls and grasp any opportunities that may arise. All this while keeping in mind the overarching necessity for the ANC to consolidate and keep the democratic forces marching in step while

---

42. Lawrence's review of *Mission to South Africa*.

winning the support of new friends and neutralising old enemies. The ANC had to avoid the promise of negotiations demobilising one or more of its pillars of struggle, otherwise it could find itself mired in the quid pro quo about which Tambo had warned. The struggle was entering the stage of 'talks about talks', which would open another front where the ANC had to stamp its authority, demonstrate tactical flexibility and exercise strategic initiative.

10

Seizing the Initiative

Who blinks first?

One of the hurdles in any attempt to end conflict through negotiation is who among the protagonists will make the first move. Usually, this is seen as a sign of weakness and is framed around the question: who blinks first? Mandela believed that his isolation afforded him the freedom to take the first steps. It 'furnished my organisation with an excuse in case matters went awry: the old man was alone and completely cut off, and he took his actions as an individual, not as a representative of the ANC'.[1]

By the end of 1985, South Africa was in the grip of a partial state of emergency. The country was burning. The news of Mandela's hospitalisation from 3 to 23 November at Volks Hospital caused alarm among cabinet ministers, who feared that in the event anything went wrong, they would shoulder the blame. The commanding officer of Pollsmoor Prison warned that civil war would break out if Mandela died. Kobie Coetsee paid him an unannounced 'courtesy' visit. Mandela had not received a reply to an earlier request to see Coetsee and he now suspected the minister 'might want to make some kind of deal, but he did not let on'.[2]

Upon his discharge from hospital, Mandela was separated from his comrades in Pollsmoor and housed on the ground floor with three large cells all to himself – one for sleeping, one for exercise and one for studying. They were damp, dark and bleak, with hardly a view. When he saw his comrades a few days later, they told him the regime was trying to divide them and that they wanted to object to his isolation. Mandela

---

1. Mandela, *Long Walk to Freedom*, pp. 514–15.
2. Sampson, *Mandela*, p. 343.

thought differently. His focus was not on himself and his plight. He did not complain about being segregated from his comrades. 'Something good may come of this,' he told them.[3]

Mandela read his isolation as signalling the arrival of the moment to engage the regime and persuade them it was time to talk to the ANC. He did not consult his four comrades, because he feared they would veto his decision. Mandela knew that such a step did not contradict the long-standing strategy of the liberation struggle, but he took the precaution of sending a message via George Bizos to Tambo, reassuring him that he would not commit to anything without the approval of the ANC. With the green light from Tambo, he was ready to make his move.

It was while Mandela sought to reassure Tambo that the EPG made its first visit to South Africa in February 1986. As we have seen, their shuttle diplomacy ended when South African military forces raided Lusaka, Harare and Gaborone in May. The idea of talks was over. In June 1986, Botha embarked on a total crackdown when he imposed a nationwide state of emergency.

Mandela wrote two further letters to Kobie Coetsee, to which there was no response. Although Coetsee had a mandate from Botha to find a way out of the impasse, he was hesitant to engage with Mandela. In April 1986, Coetsee requested the South African Law Commission 'to investigate and make recommendations regarding the definition and protection of group rights ... and the possible extension of the existing protection of individual rights'.[4] The Broederbond, under the chairmanship of Pieter de Lange, was in the throes of discussions that culmin-

---

3. Walter Sisulu's interview with George Houser and Herbert Shore, September/October 1995, quoted in Sampson, *Mandela*, p. 346.
4. Heinz Klug, *Constituting Democracy: Law, Globalism and South Africa's Political Reconstruction* (Cambridge: Cambridge University Press, 2000), p. 84. In June 1986, the Broederbond Constitutional Policy Committee distributed to all its branches a document for confidential discussion by its members titled 'Basiese staatkundige voorwaardes vir die voortbestaan van die Afrikaner' (Basic political policy conditions for the survival of the Afrikaner), which is in the Erfenisstigting Archive, ref. AB 10/32/2/1, at the Voortrekker Monument.

ated in a position paper in June 1986. The intelligence services were also monitoring developments closely and keeping as fully informed as possible of the meetings held by the stream of delegations visiting Lusaka and elsewhere to engage with the ANC.[5] And Coetsee was aware of Mandela's willingness to use the EPG 'negotiating concept' as a starting point for negotiations to begin.

Mandela persisted. In June 1986, he asked to see the commissioner of prisons, Lieutenant General Willemse, whose headquarters were in Pretoria. Within four days, Willemse was in Cape Town. Mandela asked him to forward a request for a meeting with the state president. Willemse phoned Coetsee, who ordered that Mandela be brought immediately to his residence, Savernake, in the Groote Schuur ministerial estate. The two talked for three hours and over two successive days.[6] Then the contact ceased. Mandela wrote to Coetsee once more, but there was no response.

Then, just before Christmas, the deputy commander of Pollsmoor casually suggested that he and Mandela take a drive through the city of Cape Town. Over the next few months, there were more such sight-seeing trips. Mandela speculated: 'I sensed they wanted to acclimatise me to life in South Africa and perhaps at the same time, get me used to the pleasures of small freedoms that I might be willing to compromise to have complete freedom.'[7] Mandela was now allowed more visits from family and friends too.

Contact between Coetsee and Mandela resumed in early 1987 just as abruptly as it had stopped in 1986. They met three times during the year at Savernake, followed by a meeting on 6 October at Kommaweer, a guesthouse meant for visiting generals in the Pollsmoor prison complex.[8] These talks played a part in the regime's decision to free Govan

---

5. Kobie Coetsee was previously deputy minister of defence and intelligence.
6. Mandela, *Long Walk to Freedom*, pp. 518–19. See also the handwritten prison records which indicate that Mandela and Coetsee met at least fifteen times between 1985 and 1990.
7. Mandela, *Long Walk to Freedom*, pp. 520–21.
8. This is according to handwritten notes in Afrikaans kept by the prison authorities.

Mbeki and Harry Gwala on 5 November 1987. The administration was feeling its way around how to manage and manipulate the inevitable release of Mandela himself. For Mandela, his release from prison could not be a standalone event. It had to be part of a broader process leading to the ending of the conflict that had brought them to prison in the first place.

Before his release, Mbeki was taken from Robben Island prison to meet Mandela, who briefed him about his talks with the regime. Mbeki was unhappy that Mandela had not fully confided in him, and he made it known to many leading activists after his release.[9]

The dilemmas facing the regime, and Coetsee in particular, are perhaps best captured in an appraisal of the political climate during 1987 by an unnamed NIS source:

> South Africa finds itself, internationally and nationally, in a dead-end street. The sole question is how it can get out of the dead-end street with a modicum of political self-respect. The key is to talk with Nelson Mandela and to release political prisoners. He has become the international and national face of freedom and of the wickedness of apartheid. Talking with Mandela is the only way out. Mandela is now South Africa's most influential and powerful leader. The only question is who should speak with him, when and about what. Is this possible? What kind of process and by whom should it be set in motion by us [sic] in order to bring about a negotiating table?[10]

Until this moment, the idea had been to trade Mandela's release for his co-option. Now a shift was taking place in their thinking. What were the prospects for negotiations with Mandela among those at the table? Who else in the ANC could be part of the process? Coetsee knew it was

---

9. Sampson, *Mandela*, p. 384.
10. Quoted in Esterhuyse and Van Niekerk, *Die Tronkgespreke*, p. 104.

time to get down to talking seriously with Mandela by adding an additional strand in the form of talks between Mandela and a committee led by Dr Niël Barnard, the head of the NIS. Coetsee's advice was that this committee's talks should 'demystify' Mandela.[11]

According to Willie Esterhuyse and Gerhard van Niekerk in their book *Die Tronkgespreke*, President Botha met with Coetsee, Barnard and director general of justice S.S. 'Fanie' van der Merwe in his office and informed them that he was setting up a working group. Its task would be to think of a strategy and tactics for the release of Mandela and the other Rivonia Trial prisoners. The team would consist of Barnard, who would head it, Van der Merwe, Lieutenant General Willemse, and Mike Louw, the deputy director of the NIS.[12] The first formal meeting between Mandela and this committee took place on 25 May 1988.

Mandela later wrote that he was 'disturbed' when he learned that Barnard would be part of the team. 'His presence made the talks more problematic and suggested a larger agenda. I told Coetsee that I would like to think about the proposal overnight.' But Mandela ultimately concluded that 'my refusing Barnard would alienate Botha ... If the state president was not brought on board, nothing would happen ... I sent word to Coetsee that I accepted his offer.'[13]

There is some confusion about how, why and to what extent Niël Barnard replaced Coetsee. The letter Coetsee wrote to Botha on 14 March 1986 makes it clear that he and Botha had agreed that he would engage with Mandela on the understanding that this was kept separate from other initiatives. Documents in the Kobie Coetsee Papers indicate that Mandela and Coetsee engaged in substantive discussions material to the regime and the ANC reaching the negotiating table. Yet Coetsee did not attend any of the meetings held by Barnard's team with Mandela. Barnard acknowledges that there were 'sporadic meetings ... over the

---

11. Ibid., p. 197.
12. Ibid.
13. Mandela, *Long Walk to Freedom*, p. 522.

next three years' between Mandela and Coetsee.[14] Of the document that Mandela wrote in preparation for a possible meeting with Botha, Barnard writes that 'Mandela only gave us the document at the end of July 1989 but it had been sent several months earlier, without my knowledge, via Minister Kobie Coetsee to the president.'[15]

Prison records show that between 1985 and 12 December 1989 Coetsee and Mandela met at least fifteen times.[16] During April 1989 – the month Mandela sent his document to Tambo – they met at least three times, on 19, 20 and 26 April, while Barnard and the prison commissioner met Mandela only once, on 12 April.[17] It is possible that it was during this period that Mandela first sent his preparatory notes to P.W. Botha. Mandela may have sensed that Barnard wanted to control the process and claim principal credit for the negotiated transition, and therefore chose to use Coetsee as his intermediary instead.

By December 1989, the committee had met Mandela forty-eight times and, according to Barnard, 'the first seeds of the peaceful revolution that was destined to change the history of South Africa forever had been planted in secret'.[18]

The 'Mandela document', as his 1989 memo to Botha became known, is the most unambiguous indication of what Mandela set out to achieve when he began to engage with the regime.[19] It adheres to the explanation he gave to a concerned Tambo when the latter smuggled

14. Barnard, *Secret Revolution*, p. 154.
15. Ibid. Both P.W. Botha (via Coetsee) and Tambo (via Vula) had received the document by April 1989. This indirectly confirms that Tambo and Mandela were in communication with each other without the NIS's knowledge.
16. Mandela always sought to talk directly with Botha, but Barnard seemed resistant to the idea. Why? Giliomee says that an ex-NIS official described Barnard as follows: 'Barnard believed in stealth, diplomacy, outwitting and outthinking the enemy.' (Giliomee, *The Last Afrikaner Leaders*, p. 144)
17. See faxed communication from the director of specialist services of the Prisons Department to 'Komvang', dated 24 January 1990, accessible at the Centre for Memory, Nelson Mandela Foundation.
18. Barnard, *Secret Revolution*, pp. 246–7. The first time Professor Willie Esterhuyse and two others met the ANC in the UK was in October 1987.
19. See Annexure A for the unabridged text of Mandela's memo to P.W. Botha.

a message into jail asking him what he was up to behind those prison walls. ('A meeting between the ANC and the government,' was Mandela's curt response.[20]) The memo keeps to the parameters of talks about talks, focusing on the government's reasons for refusing to meet the ANC. Mandela robustly challenges the government's precondition that the ANC renounce violence, and defends the alliance of the ANC and the SACP. He disabuses the government of its claim that socialism was the ANC's goal and insists that the Freedom Charter envisaged a mixed economy. Mandela also rejects the government's condemnation of the principle of majority rule, which he insists is a necessary condition for stability and peace to prevail in South Africa.

'[M]ajority rule and internal peace,' Mandela argued, 'are like the two sides of a single coin, and white South Africa simply has to accept that there will never be peace and stability in this country until the principle is fully applied.' His discussions with Coetsee and the Barnard team had led him to hone his argument, and Mandela urged that 'the key to the whole situation is a negotiated settlement, and a meeting between the government and the ANC will be the first major step towards lasting peace in the country'.[21]

He crisply set out the challenge that negotiations would have to confront:

Two political issues will have to be addressed at such a meeting: firstly, the demand for majority rule in a unitary state, secondly, the concern of white SA over this demand, as well as the insistence of whites on structural guarantees that majority rule will not mean domination of the white minority by blacks. The most crucial task which will face government and the ANC will be to reconcile these

---

20. Sampson, *Mandela*, p. 366.
21. O'Malley Archive, 'Notes prepared by Nelson Mandela for his meeting with P.W. Botha, 5 July 1989', available at https://omalley.nelsonmandela.org/omalley/index.php/site/q/03lv01538/04lv01600/05lv01640/06lv01642.htm (last accessed 27 May 2021).

two positions. Such reconciliation will be achieved only if both parties are willing to compromise.[22]

The talks with Coetsee and the team led by Barnard had reached the point where both sides understood the core issues that negotiations should address. By this time, Tambo had secretly briefed Mandela about what later came to be known as the Harare Declaration. The Harare Declaration, adopted on 21 August 1989 by the OAU subcommittee on southern Africa at its summit in Harare, Zimbabwe, urged the apartheid regime 'to take measures to create a climate for negotiations, to put an end to apartheid and define a new constitutional order based on a set of democratic principles (also listed in the declaration). It also elaborated on the conditions for the negotiations to start.'[23] Any hopes that the regime may have entertained of detaching Mandela from the ANC were dashed. The country continued to hurtle towards what many began to see as its Armageddon.

Tambo made sure he had fully canvassed the heads of the Frontline States by the time the ANC NEC met on 8 August 1989 to finalise the draft of the Harare Declaration. That evening, he suffered a debilitating stroke which rendered him out of action. He had devoted all his energy to ensuring that the draft would be adopted by the Frontline States, who in turn would sponsor it at the OAU, who in turn would take it to the UN for its imprimatur.

Parallel to these developments, another initiative was unfolding. The Mells Park talks had their origins in a meeting between Tambo and a group of British businesspeople in London in June 1986.[24] Michael Young, the political advisor to Rudolph Agnew, chairman and group chief executive of Consolidated Gold Fields, had approached Tambo to ask

---

22. Ibid.
23. Harare Declaration summary on United Nations Peacemaker, available at https://peacemaker.un.org/node/2074 (last accessed 27 May 2021).
24. The list of attendees at this meeting is in the Michael Young Papers, Borthwick Institute for Archives, University of York, ref. UOY.

what a company such as theirs could do. Tambo asked him to '"help build a bridge between the ANC and those Afrikaners close to government" as progress was impossible without some form of communication'.[25]

After securing Agnew's approval, Young approached senior figures in the Afrikaner establishment. They included academics such as Willie Esterhuyse and Sampie Terreblanche. Both appear to have been members of the Broederbond at the time and would therefore have been privy to the June 1986 Broederbond document titled 'Basic political policy conditions for the survival of the Afrikaner'.[26] There is a correlation between the views advanced in this paper and the line of questions posed by Esterhuyse and Terreblanche at the Mells Park talks.

Esterhuyse was approached by Fleur de Villiers, a consultant for Consolidated Gold Fields, who called him from London to brief him on Young's proposal. A few weeks later, he received a phone call from Pretoria requesting a meeting. This led to a discussion with Koos Kruger and Möller Dippenaar of the NIS at Esterhuyse's home in Stellenbosch. Esterhuyse felt that, in light of the Consolidated Gold Fields project, cooperating with the NIS would give him the opportunity to advance a process of peace and democratisation. After that, he received regular, intensive briefings from the NIS in various safe houses, even meeting NIS head Niël Barnard at some stage.[27]

In his record of the second bilateral Mells Park meeting held from 22 to 24 February 1988, Young states that Esterhuyse 'briefed the State President following the October session. Both the State President and Dr Niel Barnard, Director General of the National Intelligence Agency

---

25. Michael Young Papers, p. 1.
26. According to notes by Tony Trew of the ANC, this was the view of Willie Breytenbach. See section 'V. The Positions and Outlooks of the Participants', in the record titled 'Meeting with people from home – 22–24 February 1988', a copy of which is in the possession of Mac Maharaj. The Broederbond document titled 'Basiese staatkundige voorwaardes vir die voortbestaan van die Afrikaner' is in the Erfenisstigting Archive, ref. AB 10/32/2/1, at the Voortrekker Monument.
27. Willie Esterhuyse, *Endgame: Secret Talks and the End of Apartheid* (Cape Town: Tafelberg, 2012), p. 18 and pp. 28–32.

[sic], had asked Esterhuyse to ensure the continuance of the dialogue.'[28] In a memo dated 31 May 1988, Young adds that 'since the last round of discussions held at Eastwell Manor from 13–15 February 1988 the State President has been fully briefed and is now positively in favour of further discussions. He appears to trust the forum as one in which dialogue can take place in secrecy, and he and the National Intelligence Agency accept and welcome the contribution [of] CGF [Consolidated Gold Fields] as facilitators of the dialogue.'[29] In his book *Endgame*, Esterhuyse does not indicate whether he consulted P.W. Botha, as he did in 1984 when he was approached by Professor H.W. van der Merwe.

Niël Barnard has chosen to be silent on this aspect in his two books, save for a giveaway remark that 'years later, when the unrest was over and the struggle won, some of them related tales of their heroic deeds with progressive-minded friends under the oaks at Stellenbosch, but when they had to stand up and be counted in the SSC and elsewhere, they were quiet as mice'.[30] However, according to the notes of Michael Young, 'Esterhuyse tells me, in precise detail, what Thabo M'Beke [sic] reported back to his National Executive and this confirms my view that the ANC is anxious to participate in the next round at the most senior level. Such precise intelligence suggests the presence of a security informer on the ANC Executive.'[31]

Three things stand out. First, President Botha was privy to the dis-

28. Memorandum dated 1 March 1988, addressed to Agnew, in the Michael Young Papers.
29. Memorandum dated 31 May 1988, addressed to Agnew, in the Michael Young Papers. Since none of this information featured in the notes made by Tony Trew and Michael Young, it can be inferred that Young and Esterhuyse privately engaged in separate discussions outside the formal meetings.
30. Barnard, *Secret Revolution*, p. 150. The records show that Barnard was determined that the process of talks about talks and negotiations take place strictly under his control.
31. The question arises: from whom did Esterhuyse get his information, if not from the NIS? According to Terry Bell and Dumisa Buhle Ntsebeza, Gordon Brookbanks, a Rhodes University graduate who also held a British passport, was the handler of the ANC chief representative in London, Solly Smith. He is also credited with having recruited the NEC member, SACP Central Committee member and historian Francis Meli as an informer. Bell and Ntsebeza, *Unfinished Business: South Africa, Apartheid and Truth* (London: Verso, 2003), p. 226.

cussions at Mells Park. Second, the NIS was involved at least through Esterhuyse, if not others as well. Third, Thabo Mbeki knew of the NIS connection, but Esterhuyse did not inform him that Botha was aware of the talks. While Esterhuyse conceived of his role as a facilitator, the NIS and the ANC had their own plans. Both were using the talks to gather information about the other and to understand their respective bottom lines if and when talks between the regime and the ANC were to take place. Indeed, at least in the early stages of the meetings, the NIS was still probing to discern fault lines within the ANC. It was during 1988 that the regime realised that negotiations concerning the way out of the crisis could not exclude the ANC.

We dwell on the regime's direct links with the talks through Esterhuyse because he privately informed Mbeki of his contact with the NIS when the two met for the first time in February 1988. This information changed the scenario from previous ANC interactions with groups from South Africa.[32] Later, Esterhuyse became the conduit through which the first face-to-face meeting between the ANC and the NIS took place in Lucerne, Switzerland, in September 1989. It is necessary to note that while Esterhuyse claimed in 2016 that the Mells Park engagement in February 1988 when he met Mbeki was the start of 'talks about talks', he did not make this claim in his book published in 2012. And Mbeki did not make any such characterisation in his report to the NWC in September 1988.

In *The Thabo Mbeki I Know*, published in 2016, Esterhuyse writes that on 21 February 1988, '[u]nderneath a tree in the icy grounds of Eastwell Manor, I told him [Mbeki] – in a serious tone – that our dialogue group actually amounted to "talks within talks", one form of dialogue involved the whole group; the second was private and personal

32. To some extent, because the NIS link could legitimately be interpreted as an information-gathering exercise. Knowledge of Botha's involvement would have changed the scenario. Tony Trew's notes of the Mells Park meeting of 21–24 August 1988 suggest that the exchanges had moved beyond information gathering into the terrain of 'talks about talks'.

between him and me and related to my National Intelligence connection'. He adds, 'I stressed the fact that I had no mandate and that I had no knowledge of the NIS's game plan.'[33]

While Esterhuyse was privately briefing both P.W. Botha and Young, Young was secretly briefing the UK government. Much as Tambo was determined to keep Thatcher out of any negotiations, she was nevertheless brought into the loop by Young. In the Michael Young Papers, there is a copy of a letter written by Young and headed 'Note for Mr R.I.J Agnew'. It states: 'I attach herewith the minutes of the last Bilateral Meeting held in December. I much look forward to discuss how we progress the matter with No. 10 Downing Street.' There is evidence that he was liaising with other ministers in the Thatcher government, too. According to Tony Trew, who was the note-taker for the ANC team during the Mells Park talks, Young raised the possibility of Thatcher's involvement on several occasions. On each occasion, Mbeki outlined reasons why she was unsuitable as an intermediary/mediator and urged that she change her stance and attitude.[34]

It does not appear that Esterhuyse informed the NIS that Young was sharing information with the British government. Just as the ANC was wary of outside involvement, the regime, and Barnard in particular, was also determined to keep all outsiders away from any moves to find a solution to South Africa's problems.

---

33. Sifiso Mxolisi Ndlovu and Miranda Strydom, eds, *The Thabo Mbeki I Know* (Johannesburg: Picador Africa, 2016), pp. 490–93. Esterhuyse is obsessed with pitting the talks with Mbeki against the Barnard–Mandela talks with a bent to write into history that the Mbeki talks were the real talks and that these preceded talks with Mandela. This is not borne out by Mbeki's report to the NWC on 9 September 1988 (Minutes of NWC, dated 08/09/1988), Tony Trew's notes and Barnard's account in his book *Peaceful Revolution: Inside the War Room at the Negotiations* (Cape Town: Tafelberg, 2017).

34. The discrepancies between Trew's and Young's notes as to what transpired at the meetings when the issue of Thatcher arose puts the spotlight on Young's agenda. The ANC and Tambo in particular were dead set against any involvement by Thatcher, as becomes clear from the minutes of the NWC and Tambo's communications to Operation Vula. When news of the Mells Park talks was leaked to the media, the UK government issued a statement to the effect that it was aware of the meeting without having knowledge of its content.

The Mells Park talks enabled the regime and the ANC to gain a better understanding of their respective concerns and positions and graduated, like the Mandela meetings, into talks about talks by the time the NIS and the ANC met in Lucerne in September 1989. Initially, Esterhuyse described his delegations as 'message bearers' and 'facilitators ... developing and expanding the political dynamic of exposing key figures within the establishment to ANC thinking and vice versa'.[35] However, the notes taken by Tony Trew indicate that by the meeting of 21–24 April 1989, and more clearly the meeting held on 29 September 1989, an element of 'talks about talks' had become a feature. Trew records explicitly that 'it was noted that our meetings, with the character of informal discussion, were distinct from any official contacts between government and the ANC which might take place – (quite possibly in the near future, it was said by one of the people from home).'[36] It is important to note that F.W. de Klerk became leader of the NP in February 1989 and was inaugurated president of South Africa on 14 September. The first direct meeting between the ANC and the NIS took place on 12 September, at a time when De Klerk was acting president. The ANC NEC had already approved of talks between Mandela and the government.[37]

These observations should be set alongside Niël Barnard's reasoning for the talks taking place in the shadows. He records that: 'The aim of the secret discussions was not to reach conclusive agreement on governmental issues, but rather to learn about each other's opinions on important matters first-hand, to identify common ground and to create a climate of mutual trust and understanding.'[38]

---

35. Notes by Tony Trew of the meeting held on 21–24 August 1988.
36. Notes by Tony Trew, 'Meetings with people from home, September 1989', p. 109. A copy of the full set of notes, including the meeting that began on 29 September 1989, made by Tony Trew of all the Mells Park talks are in the possession of Mac Maharaj.
37. See message from Slovo to Mandela in maharaj/vula comms/1989/.
38. Barnard, Secret Revolution, p. 211.

The ANC prepares itself

In the interim, the ANC was steadily delimiting the parameters for possible negotiations. It was changing the terms of the public debate, much in line with the approach suggested by Pallo Jordan in his 1985 discussion document, 'The New Face of Counter-Revolution'. In its feedback on the first report of the Constitutional Commission, the NWC advised that, contrary to the proposal of the commission, it 'would be unwise to draw up a constitution [for a future South Africa] at that point in time'.[39] Underlying this advice was a vital process issue. In September 1986, the Constitutional Commission reported back to the NEC, saying:

> Our proposal is that at this stage the NEC consider the adoption and publication of the guidelines in the form of a document that will be entitled 'Proposed Foundations of Government in a democratic South Africa'. The document could then be presented to our people as a whole inviting their active participation and contribution towards preparing a final document.[40]

This approach, which sought to bring on board not only ANC members and supporters, but all South Africans, was aimed at ensuring maximum buy-in and limiting the space within which the apologists could operate.

An exchange of views on the proposed guidelines between the commission and the NWC led to the adoption and publication of a policy paper titled 'Constitutional Guidelines for a Democratic South Africa' ('The Guidelines') in August 1988. The Afrikaner group at Mells Park engaged with these guidelines during the sixth Mells Park meeting held at the end of September 1989. The document drew considerable attention. The UDF and COSATU discussed it, as did some media outlets,

---

39. 'Report of the NWC sub committee on the Report of the Constitutional Commission', in the Simons Collection, UCT, BC1081, file P25.
40. 'Memorandum to the NEC by the Constitution Committee, September 20, 1986', in the ANC Collection, Lusaka/London, Box 042, Folder 1, University of Fort Hare Archives. The commission attached a draft of this proposal to the memo.

such as the *Mail & Guardian*. The first engagement on constitutional matters with lawyers from the National Association of Democratic Lawyers from within South Africa took place in 1988.[41]

The Guidelines were preceded by a public commitment in the ANC's 1987 January 8 statement to a list of fundamental individual rights and an explicit rejection of group rights. 'The revolution,' said the NEC, 'will guarantee individual and equal rights of all South Africans without regard to any of these categories (which define our people by race, colour or ethnic group) and include such freedoms as those of speech, assembly, association, language, religion, the press, the inviolability of family life and freedom from arbitrary arrest and detention without trial.'[42]

The statement made the achievement of democracy the primary focus of any negotiations. It asserted that 'we shall translate that fundamental democratic principle into practice whereby each person shall have the right both to vote and to be voted to any elective organ in the new united and non-racial South Africa'. The statement expressly invoked the experience of the people of South Africa and linked it to an internationally recognised experience when it came out in support of a multiparty system with clear boundaries. It proclaimed that:

all should be free to form and join any party of their choice, without let or hindrance. But as a people, we must state clearly that democracy in our country cannot succeed if it permits the organised propagation of ideas of fascism, racism and ethnicity. Apart from our own experience, we cannot, in the name of democracy, tolerate the organised sustenance of conceptions which led to the Second

---

41. A meeting with a group of predominantly Afrikaner lawyers and jurists took place in Harare in early 1989.
42. 'January 8th Statements – Statement of the National Executive Committee on the occasion of the 75th anniversary of the ANC – 8 January 1987', South African History Online, available at https://www.sahistory.org.za/archive/january-8th -statements-statement-national-executive-committee-occasion-75th-anniversary-anc (last accessed 27 May 2021).

World War and which have since been categorised and dealt with as a crime against humanity.

The message to friends and foes, and those yet to be won over, was loud and clear. The ANC was taking occupation of specific strategic sites in the terrain: the battle for positions had begun on a battlefield named 'negotiations'. The statement posed a crucial question: 'Is it possible today and in the future to enter into negotiations with self-confessed enemies of democracy with the aim of creating a democratic South Africa?' And it provided an unequivocal answer:

> We reiterate our commitment to seize any opportunity that may arise, to participate in a negotiated resolution of the conflict in our country. This we would do in the interests of the masses of our people and those of Southern Africa as a whole, with the specific aim of creating a democratic, non-racial and united South Africa ... Let those in our country who, in the face of our mounting offensive, have started talking about negotiations, commit themselves publicly to this perspective. In addition, and of decisive importance, they must demonstrate by practical deeds their commitment to this objective as well as their acceptance of a rapid and irreversible process leading to the emergence of such a South African society.

Were the positions taken in this January 8 statement philosophically or ideologically driven? The answer lies in an appreciation of the multi-class, anti-colonial national character of the ANC. The glue that bound the diverse classes and communities within the ANC was a commit-ment to destroy apartheid and build a South African nation based on the Freedom Charter. Among its members and in its deliberations, all schools of thought housed within these parameters were given the space to address the challenges the movement faced. The overriding condition was not the label on your sleeve, but the solutions you brought. In its deliberations, the weight your views enjoyed on a particular matter included the track record of the usefulness of your positions in the past rather than that of the philosophy or ideology you espoused.

Scrutiny of the documents from this period reveals how the ANC arrived at its positions concerning negotiations and the constitution for a future South Africa. The NWC and its subcommittee debated the kind of democracy envisaged by the ANC. The subcommittee examined the nature and experiences of democracies around the world and sought to adapt these to our specific circumstances. To this end, the 1987 January 8 statement noted that 'in many parts of the country you [the people in united action] have given concrete form to that emerging alternative power by destroying the enemy's structures of government and setting up organs of people's power'.

The interaction between the Constitutional Commission, the NWC subcommittee and the NWC demonstrates a thriving democratic practice. However, this internal process was constrained by the illegal conditions under which the struggle was waged. It is also at odds with the received wisdom that portrays the ANC in exile as autocratic, paranoid and conspiratorial, seeks to create an exile/'inzile' divergence in its political culture, and attributes the problems that currently bedevil our country to an authoritarian top-down culture imported from exile.

Those who cast the debates within the ANC in terms of personalities, individual roles and labels do not take into account that people who hold differing views may change their opinions over time. While it is important to consider personalities and individual roles, and analyse positions taken in terms of categories and labels, those who treat these as the engine fail to understand the dynamics within the ANC.

In a public lecture on 28 May 1987, Tambo took note of the position of the Western powers that had recently entered into official contact with the ANC. They did this, he said, because the argument that they were seeking change in South Africa by talking exclusively to the Botha regime had become unsustainable. The EPG had found that the majority of people within South Africa 'recognised the ANC as their political representative'. This finding meant that, 'if the Western Powers were still interested to project themselves as brokers, honest or otherwise, these Governments would have to be seen to be talking to the ANC,' Tambo stated. It did not mean that they had changed their attitude towards the ANC. 'On all major questions … the coincidence of views between the Pretoria regime and the Powers that be in most of the West persists.'[43]

Tambo acknowledged that 'repeated calls have been made on the Botha regime to enter into negotiations with its opponents', but that 'nothing is said about how this regime will ultimately be brought to the negotiating table'. The EPG, he said, had noted that the apartheid government 'is not yet prepared to negotiate fundamental change, nor to countenance the creation of genuine democratic structures, nor to face the prospect of the end to white domination'.

Furthermore, said Tambo, the EPG's report had stated that the 'test of the genuineness of the call for negotiations must necessarily turn on the willingness of those who make this call to change the attitude of the Pretoria regime towards these negotiations'. Instead of appeasing the Botha regime, he said, the international community should direct its efforts towards ending the apartheid system. 'Any new international initiative seeking to bring about negotiations would be grossly misplaced … because the Botha regime is not prepared to address this fundamental question.'

The NEC devoted considerable time to assessing the situation as events unfolded during 1987, taking into account the question of negotiations raised by both the Pretoria regime and the various Western powers. It shared its views with the public in a statement titled 'The Question of Negotiations' on 9 October 1987, in which it reaffirmed the ANC's willingness 'to enter into genuine negotiations provided they are aimed at the

---

43. '"South Africa at the Crossroads", Canon Collins Memorial Lecture by Oliver Tambo, London, 28 May 1987', South African History Online, available at https://www.sahistory.org.za/archive/south-africa-crossroads-canon-collins -memorial-lecture-oliver-tambo-london-28-may-1987 (last accessed 27 May 2021). Also published in *Review of African Political Economy*, 14 (40), 1987.

transformation of our country into a united non-racial democracy'. It emphasised that 'this, and only this, should be the objective of any negotiating process'. The NEC ruled out the unilateral abandonment or even suspension of the armed struggle, because 'cessation of hostilities would have to be negotiated and entail agreed acts by both sides'.[44]

It drew attention to the regime's co-option manoeuvres and rejected 'without qualification the proposed National Statutory Council (NSC) which the Botha regime seeks to establish through legislation to be enacted by the apartheid parliament. This can never be a genuine and acceptable mechanism to negotiate a democratic constitution for our country ... The National Statutory Council is ... nothing but a device intended to enmesh all who sit on it in a bogus process of meaningless talk which has nothing to do with any genuine attempt to design a democratic constitution for our country.'[45]

The NEC's deliberations took into account, among other things, a message from Winnie Mandela. She reported that she had engaged with Minister Kobie Coetsee, who indicated that there was a need for a 'face-saver' that would enable the government to release Mandela and his Rivonia comrades.

The potentials and pitfalls that surfaced during the EPG exercise continued to bedevil the talks about talks. The 1987 January 8 statement, the October 1987 statement on negotiations and the August 1988 'Constitutional Guidelines for a Democratic South Africa' constituted critical beacons guiding the democratic forces as they navigated their way through uncharted waters. They also formed the platform for the Mells Park talks, the numerous engagements with delegations from South Africa

---

44. O'Malley Archive, 'Statement of the National Executive Committee of the African National Congress on the Question of Negotiations, October 9th, 1987', available at https://omalley.nelsonmandela.org/omalley/index.php/site/q/03lv03445/04lv040 15/05lv04051/06lv04054/07lv04055.htm (last accessed 27 May 2021).

45. In an attempt to address criticism that the tricameral system did not accommodate the African population, P.W. Botha punted the idea of a National Statutory Council on which individuals from all populations would serve in an advisory capacity to the president of the republic. It never reached the stage of being legislated.

organised by the Institute for Democratic Alternatives in South Africa (IDASA), as well as ANC engagements in international forums and with foreign governments.

While these beacons helped set the course, they were not sufficient to ensure that the initiative remained in the ANC's hands, especially given the number of moving parts that were at play.

Fine-tuning strategy and countering disarray

How would the ANC manage the balance between the four pillars of struggle and the pursuit of negotiations? Success brought to the fore new challenges for the ANC, which at times threatened the unity of the democratic forces.

Developments in the fields of culture and sports within South Africa provide a useful backdrop to appreciate the complex nature of the challenges that arose. What had begun as a straightforward boycott of South African goods in the UK in 1959/60 had grown into a powerful worldwide movement to isolate South Africa. Non-racial sports bodies were developing in the womb of an imprisoned society, and an alternate culture, one related to the struggle for emancipation, was being fashioned. The boycott campaign had to consider these developments. It did so by spelling out that its objectives were to isolate apartheid South Africa and act in solidarity with the democratic and anti-racist forces in the country.

Given the relatively undefined topography of this new front of struggle, there was much room for debate, misunderstanding and even disagreement. The necessity for secrecy – sometimes self-imposed, sometimes the result of unavoidable circumstance, at other times keeping secret what should be public, or making public what should be confidential – compounded the appraisals.

Misunderstanding and disagreement within the ANC and among the democratic forces was like oxygen for the regime, which was determined to define the terrain, promote disunity within the ANC and its allies, and control the process. Sometimes what appeared to be a positive development for the struggle had counterproductive seeds buried within it. As an example, *Beeld* carried an editorial in 1985 suggesting that it was time to meet the ANC. However, when a large contingent of Afrikaner intellectuals met the ANC in Dakar in 1987, Piet Muller, the *Beeld* journalist who had visited Lusaka in 1985, wrote an opinion piece in *Rapport* that the Dakarites were 'stupid' and had no understanding of the rules of the 'new game', claiming that they had handed the ANC a propaganda coup.[46] When he had called for secret talks with the ANC in 1985, he had not meant that white South Africans, in general, should do so. On this score, his thinking at the time was perfectly aligned with P.W. Botha, Barnard and the Broederbond.

Other challenges included the manufacturing of alternative facts. *Beeld*, for example, was the first to suggest there were ANC leaders who wanted to talk with the regime, however, the paper claimed, they lived in fear of the militants within the organisation.

Whether the work of the enemy or mischievous propaganda by well-meaning individuals, externally produced misinformation was just part of the problem the ANC faced. Sometimes inadequate internal communications, lack of information and the matter of tactics in a rapidly changing situation would contribute to heated debates even in authorised meetings with parties from within South Africa.

To overcome such problems, in 1981 the Revolutionary Council of the ANC set up Area Political Committees (APCs) inside South Africa. Their principal task was to ensure that mass mobilisation undergirded and ran parallel to the development of the armed struggle. But the devil was in its implementation. The need to create internally based regional leaderships that would lay the basis for a national political-military leadership within South Africa had two aspects: the integration of the

---

46. Piet Muller, 'Dom doktore van Dakar' (Stupid doctors of Dakar), *Rapport*, 1987. Muller wrote that they 'do not know the rules of the new game. It has already given the ANC a propaganda coup by way of a call on the Government not to handle the people in too rough a manner' (translated from Afrikaans).

political and military structures and the integration of leaders previously based externally with those who had developed as leaders inside the country.

These were among the concerns that led the NEC to authorise Tambo, assisted by Slovo, to launch Operation Vulindlela, also known as Operation Vula, in 1986. According to Padraig O'Malley:

> Vula was an ambitious project aiming to locate senior leaders, including members of the NEC and PMC, within South Africa to take overall charge of the struggle ... It was to provide local all-round leadership, working with the internal leadership, in Natal and the Witwatersrand, in order to bring about effective coordination of underground political work, mass mobilisation and military activity. It was to set up the infrastructure for a people's war, including on-the-spot military recruitment and training, and the importation and caching of arms. It had to establish political structures to ensure that all areas of activity, including military activity, were conducted under the overall political guidance of the ANC.[47]

At other times, misunderstanding and disagreement within the ANC and among the democratic forces may even have been due to a lack of internalising the meaning and responsibilities that go with leadership. The NWC, therefore, had to look at its style of work and find ways to improve it.

Tambo was not present at an NWC meeting held on 22 February 1988 where it emerged that Thabo Mbeki was away in London for a meeting with 'Afrikaner intellectuals'. Chris Hani sharply questioned on whose authority Mbeki had entered into discussions with them. In

---

47. Padraig O'Malley, *Shades of Difference: Mac Maharaj and the Struggle for South Africa* (New York: Viking Penguin, 2007), p. 244. It should also be noted that the claim that Operation Vula was undertaken as an 'insurance policy' in the event that negotiations failed is incorrect. It does not square with the facts, because Vula was initiated in 1986, before the possibility of negotiations arose.

the absence of a satisfactory explanation, the NWC postponed the matter. It agreed that in future all delegations should be appointed by the appropriate structures.[48]

The matter arose again at the NWC meeting of 9 March 1988, when Mbeki was once more absent. Tambo treated allaying the concerns raised as an opportunity to articulate internal ground rules for the ANC. Firstly, he affirmed the principle of the NWC choosing its delegations and that interlocutors should not be allowed 'to specify whom they would like to meet in the NEC'.[49] As there was a lack of clarity at the meeting as to whether there had been a decision authorising Mbeki's discussions with the Afrikaner intellectuals, Tambo urged that in such a situation 'we must assume Cde Thabo acted in good faith'.[50] Unless one based oneself on this assumption, it would be meaningless to speak about collective leadership and unity of purpose.

While this restricted the room for disagreement and for concerns to turn into threats to the unity of the organisation, it never entirely closed the space. From time to time, debates would turn into disagreements. Their management became a continuing challenge. Tambo used the skills he had acquired in dealing with such situations. History thrust upon him the task of ensuring that the ANC and the broad range of democratic forces succeeded in rising to the challenge.

The difficult circumstances under which the talks about talks were taking place surfaced in a meeting between the ANC and the all-white South African Rugby Board (SARB) in late 1988. SARB president Danie Craven, Louis Luyt of the Transvaal Rugby Union, former Springbok rugby player Tommy Bedford, and Ebrahim Patel of the SACOS- and

---

48. Minutes of NWC meeting, 22 February 1988, in the Simons Papers, UCT.
49. At the meeting between the NIS and the ANC in Switzerland in September 1989, Barnard insisted that Slovo, a prominent communist, should not be in the ANC delegation to meet the South African government. Mbeki refused to budge. Slovo, with his trademark red socks, was present at the Groote Schuur meeting.
50. Minutes of NWC meeting, 9 March 1988, in the Simons Papers, UCT.

UDF-affiliated South African Rugby Union (SARU) met with representatives of the ANC in Harare in October 1988.[51]

A study of the meeting provides insight into the conditions under which the ANC was operating at the time. Members of the leadership were continually on the road. They attended to the military camps in Angola and the needs of MK. They saw to the needs of the internal struggle through meetings in neighbouring countries and elsewhere. They were responsible for promoting the international campaign, mobilising resources and training for prosecuting the struggle within South Africa, as well as managing the Solomon Mahlangu Freedom College and transit facilities in Tanzania and other SADC countries. Members were often unable to keep informed about decisions taken at different levels and in different places.

At the IDASA-sponsored Dakar Conference held in July 1987, Slabbert and Tommy Bedford suggested that 'nothing would aid the wooing of white SA as much as a move from the ANC to facilitate the re-entry of SA rugby into international competition'.[52] They contacted Danie Craven and Louis Luyt. Craven sent Luyt to meet the Pahad brothers, Essop and Aziz, in London in February 1988 and Mbeki in Frankfurt three months later. These became the building blocks for the meeting held in Harare between the SARB, SARU and a contingent from the ANC headed by Alfred Nzo on 15 and 16 October 1988. The ANC, however, ensured that they first held a separate meeting with the non-racial SARU.

As it turned out, Craven, a veteran Broederbonder, had his own game plan, and so too did Luyt, whose true colours became evident in the

51. Minutes of NWC meeting, 20 October 1988, in the Mark Gevisser Collection at the South African History Archive, AL3284, G1.97. The ANC was represented by secretary general Alfred Nzo, treasurer general Thomas Nkobi, assistant secretary general Henry Makgothi, Thabo Mbeki, Steve Tshwete, R. Mpongo, and Barbara Masekela.
52. Mark Gevisser, *Thabo Mbeki: The Dream Deferred* (Johannesburg: Jonathan Ball, 2007) p. 515.

nineties. For both men, the Harare meeting was just another attempt to circumvent the isolation of white South African rugby from the international arena. In the months leading up to the meeting, Craven had made a public attack on apartheid, creating the impression that he had undergone his Damascene conversion.

Luyt claimed that, in Harare, the two rugby unions agreed that 'South Africa come under one non-racial controlling body', and that 'the ANC undertook to speed the code's passage back into the international arena'.[53] The joint communiqué that came out of the meeting, however, did not support this view. In the aftermath, there was a public spat between the SARB and SARU. The general council of SARU explained the matter in a press statement:

> The meeting [attended by representatives of the SARB, SARU and the ANC in Harare in October 1988] came about because of a common desire on the part of all the participating organisations to ensure that rugby in South Africa is organised according to non-racial principles. The meeting confirmed this position and agreed that South African rugby should come under one non-racial controlling body.
>
> They agreed to work together to achieve these goals and called on all people of goodwill inside and outside South Africa to support this process. They also agreed that the accomplishment of the goals stated here is a necessity for South African rugby to take its rightful place in world rugby.[54]

There is no ambiguity in the last sentence of this statement. Bringing rugby under 'one controlling body' was a necessary precondition for South African rugby's return to the international stage. But even that

53. Louis Luyt, *Walking Proud* (Cape Town: Don Nelson, 2003), p. 173, cited in Gevisser, *Thabo Mbeki*, p. 516.
54. SARU press statement, available at http://www.historicalpapers.wits.ac.za/inventories/inv_pdfo/AG3403/AG3403-A1-2-6-004-jpeg.pdf, p. 107 (last accessed 27 May 2021).

would not have achieved the end of apartheid in rugby and therefore could not constitute a sufficient condition.

The minutes of a subsequent NWC meeting do not support Luyt's claim that the ANC promised to facilitate the return of rugby to the international arena if the administration came under one controlling body. The report to the NWC, presented by Steve Tshwete and supported by Nzo, stated that ANC policy on boycotts recognised that an alternative culture was developing within South Africa, that it was the responsibility of the movement 'to widen fissures appearing on hitherto monolithic Afrikanerdom', and that there was full agreement between the ANC and SARU on all positions adopted at the Harare meeting.[55]

NWC members expressed concern about the wording in the joint communiqué, which was open to different and worrisome interpretations. The main concern aired at this meeting was that the policy of boycotting apartheid South Africa was being adapted in recognition of the need to support democratic South Africa. This was a policy departure. Several critical issues would follow if the ANC adopted such a policy. Did 'Boycott Apartheid South Africa' imply that apartheid could be reformed? What were the implications for the slogan in light of SACOS's 'There can be no normal sports in an abnormal society'?

In his lecture delivered in London on 28 May 1987, Tambo had observed:

In the recent period intense debates have arisen about the academic and cultural boycotts ... The boycott campaigns, from their inception in the late fifties, were aimed at the total isolation of apartheid South Africa. This objective is inviolate and needs to be pursued with even greater vigour ... At the same time, we must take into account the changes that have taken place over time ... In almost every field of human endeavour in South Africa there has emerged a definable,

---

55. Minutes of NWC meeting, 20 October 1988.

alternative, democratic culture – the People's Culture … [W]ithout doubt, the developing and vibrant culture of our people in struggle and its structures need to be supported, strengthened and enhanced. In the same way as apartheid South Africa is increasingly isolated internationally, within South Africa this People's Culture is steadily isolating the intellectual and cultural apologists of apartheid. The moment is upon us when we shall have to deal with the alternative structures that our people have created and are creating through struggle … Not only should these not be boycotted, but more, they should be supported, encouraged and treated as democratic counterparts within South Africa of similar institutions and organisations internationally.[56]

No one in the NWC discussion referred to Tambo's statement. One member indicated that the International Solidarity Conference held in Arusha, Tanzania, in December 1987 had agreed on a policy of 'boycott apartheid and support democratic South Africa'. Those present seemed to be unaware that hard on the heels of this conference, Amsterdam had hosted the arts festival 'Culture in Another South Africa' that same month. At the festival, the ANC, the international solidarity movements and representatives from within South Africa that included leading artists and writers endorsed this carefully nuanced policy position.[57]

The shift in policy necessitated by changes within South Africa had repercussions that went beyond the issue of the white SARB and the non-racial SARU. It sharpened the differences inside the country about the stance of SACOS, whose membership had become almost exclusively Indian and Coloured. SACOS was opposed to having any dealings with

56. '"South Africa at the Crossroads", Canon Collins Memorial Lecture by Oliver Tambo, London, 28 May 1987'.
57. The 'Culture in Another South Africa' festival was preceded by a festival in Botswana under the theme 'culture and resistance' and attended by artists, or 'cultural workers' as they called themselves at the time, from South Africa. The festival was organised by the Medu Art Ensemble (*medu* meaning 'roots' in SePedi) in 1982.

white sports bodies such as the SARB. It had elevated its tactical slogan – 'There can be no normal sports in an abnormal society' – into a principle. It also caused the South African Non-Racial Olympic Committee (SANROC) and the ANC to repudiate Dennis Brutus's negative interpretation of the Harare communiqué.[58]

There was another complication. SARU, which was part of the UDF, was affiliated to SACOS, but the latter had not joined the UDF. The differences influenced another joint communiqué issued after a meeting between the ANC, the International Campaign Against Apartheid Sport and SANROC held in Lusaka on 23–24 February 1989. The three organisations affirmed that:

> The main focus of the meeting was the international isolation of Apartheid Sport and how to assist the non-racial sports movements inside South Africa.
>
> The meeting paid tribute to the various organisations inside South Africa for their commendable efforts to establish non-racial sport in the country. However, the meeting re-affirmed the policy agreed upon with the non-racial sports bodies inside South Africa that the creation of non-racial sports organisations does, in no way, imply their immediate entry into International Sports competitions.[59]

Discontent with SACOS's stance eventually led to the formation of the National Sports Congress in the late eighties and a break with SANROC led by Sam Ramsamy and Dennis Brutus, a founder member of SANROC.

---

58. Dennis Brutus was an educator, journalist and poet who had played a leading role, together with Sam Ramsamy, in the campaign to have South Africa banned from the Olympic Games.
59. Joint communiqué, available at http://www.historicalpapers.wits.ac.za/inventories/inv_pdfo/AG3403/AG3403-A1-2-6-004-jpeg.pdf, p. 109 (last accessed 27 May 2021). The International Campaign Against Apartheid Sport's chairman, Fekrou Kidane, and Sam Ramsamy, executive chairman of SANROC, attended the meeting.

11

Botha in a Bind

By 1988, Botha found himself in a difficult position. What led him to authorise Coetsee to set up the Barnard team to engage more systematically with Mandela? What led him to also allow Coetsee to continue with his separate engagements with Mandela? What was he seeking to achieve when he allowed Barnard to engage with the ANC in exile?

Despite the setbacks the regime suffered in the mid-1980s, Botha insisted on pushing ahead with his twin strategy of repression and reform, with the latter premised on the condition of white control. Coloureds and Indians had rejected his tricameral reform, which had drawn Coloureds, Indians and, most importantly, the African community into a common, mass-based struggle that brought into sharp relief apartheid's reliance on the local municipal structures intended to co-opt urban Africans. Despite the Nkomati Accord and the challenges it presented to the prosecution of the armed struggle, MK remained active and a potent threat. Botha's finger-wagging 'Rubicon' speech at the National Party Congress in August 1985 neutralised all the goodwill he had mustered during his eight-nation European tour. The brutal manner in which the regime shot down the EPG mission in May 1986 raised serious concerns among its allies. Without the release of Mandela, there was no chance that promises of change would enjoy any credibility.

Botha realised that he would need to release Mandela, but he believed that he should not appear to be acting from a position of weakness. He needed to create the right moment through some carefully designed manoeuvres directed at Mandela as well as the ANC.

In his mind, the rejection of the tricameral parliament had exposed a lacuna. He planned to address this through a forum composed of co-opted Africans. He attached what he thought was a sufficiently attractive bait to the hook. It would be a structure at the national level. He would call it the National Statutory Council and it would have a direct line to him, the president of the country. The hook? He would appoint it and it would be advisory.

But where would he find and how would he cultivate the credible African leaders for the NSC? Even if he succeeded in drawing in some individuals from within the ANC, it is doubtful that Botha entertained living with an NSC dominated by such individuals. That would have exposed his flank, as was the case in the House of Representatives, to which he had welcomed the Labour Party though he found its conduct irritating if not problematic.[1]

Botha believed that in the absence of 'intimidation' and boycotts, the local government councils for urban Africans would produce a critical number of collaborators. The Urban Bantu Councils were an essential component of the bantustan strategy. Botha now fixed his attention on ensuring that the local municipal government elections in October 1988 took place in the appropriate circumstances.

To achieve this, he had to crush the opposition gathered under the umbrella of the UDF and silence all the voices of sympathy and support it and its affiliates enjoyed. The instruments he needed were already operational: the NSMS machinery, state-sponsored vigilantes, and the dirty-war techniques in the form of murders, kidnappings, assassinations and poisonings with which his security forces had been experimenting. The nationwide state of emergency was in place; he just needed to unleash its full power.

The crackdown came in February 1988 in the form of regulations

---

1. In 1987, P.W. Botha derided Reverend Allan Hendrickse, the leader of the Labour Party which was a member of the House of Delegates, on prime-time television for swimming at a whites-only Port Elizabeth beach.

promulgated in terms of the state of emergency. The UDF and seventeen other organisations were the first to suffer restrictions. They could not conduct any activities that promoted 'a revolutionary climate or endangered public safety'.[2] A little while later, thirteen more organisations, including the End Conscription Campaign, were added to the list. The restrictions included measures to prevent the listed organisations from receiving foreign funding. As much of this funding reached them via the SACC, the SACC, too, found itself in the gunsights of the regime.

It was necessary to whip the media into line as well. The *New Nation*, with a circulation of 60 000, was suspended for three months while its editor, Zwelakhe Sisulu, languished in detention. The regime suspended other print media for shorter periods. Some received warnings that they faced suspension. The intention was obvious: *Crisis News* and *Al-Qalam*, both of which openly supported the call for a boycott of the October municipal elections, had their print runs confiscated before distribution. It became an offence for the media to quote any official of a restricted organisation.

The universities came under pressure to suppress protests. The regime threatened to withdraw their subsidies if they failed to cooperate. The minister of education, F.W. de Klerk, threatened five universities.

During the second state of emergency, thousands were detained without trial. They remained in detention, while many more joined them. At one time in 1988/89, about 30 000 people were in detention without trial. Youth activists were detained, released after a stint in custody and then detained again. Detention was used to paralyse organisations and break individuals. The regime also used it to plant suspicion about who among the detainees remained loyal to the struggle. Some leaders of the UDF were rendered inactive by being placed under restriction. Others spent their time evading arrest.

---

2. Gerhart and Glaser, *From Protest to Challenge*, vol. 6, p. 165.

Botha avoided the outright banning of organisations as the NP had done with the ANC and the PAC in 1960 for fear that such action would be counterproductive. He chose instead to impose restrictions and detentions under the state of emergency. He succeeded in disrupting the UDF but failed to stifle opposition.

The churches and trade unionists rose to the challenge. The clergy used the pulpit to preach defiance and called for the boycott of the upcoming municipal elections. Clerics marched at the head of demonstrations. In May 1988, the SACC and the Southern African Catholic Bishops' Conference jointly agreed to plan for a civil disobedience campaign. In resistance circles, Archbishop Desmond Tutu, Reverend Allan Boesak, Reverend Frank Chikane, Reverend Beyers Naudé and Father Smangaliso Mkhatshwa became household names. Twenty-six churchmen defiantly signed a statement in June 1988 calling for the boycott of the municipal elections.

The voice of the clergy resounded in the capitals of the Western powers and resonated with the growing anti-apartheid movements around the world. The regime no longer had the free hand it had enjoyed during the sixties. There was turmoil in the townships. Emboldened, in June, COSATU and the National Council of Trade Unions jointly called a three-day stay-at-home strike. The regime ranted and raved against the defiant clergy but did not pursue them in the courts. Instead, the security forces targeted them with dirty tricks.

While the UDF and its affiliates searched for new ways to function and new forms of resistance, such as rent boycotts, the SACC and the trade unionists stood up to lead the outraged masses. Under the banner of the Mass Democratic Movement, a broader anti-apartheid coalition emerged. Academics Gail Gerhart and Clive Glaser describe the MDM as 'a political formation with no headquarters, office-holders, or letterhead stationery – in short, an entity which could not be legally banned or restricted. Being in the MDM meant sharing a commitment to a future of a unitary, non-racial and democratic South Africa; beyond that, it was not necessary to support any particular political views, strategies or economic policies for a post-apartheid future.'[3]

The results of the October 1988 municipal elections were telling. African turnout nationwide was just above 20 per cent. In the Pretoria–Witwatersrand–Vaal region, the average turnout was just 12 per cent. There was not the slightest chance that this election would provide the core of credible collaborators that Botha sought. The bantustan leaderships were compromised.

Buthelezi, who had some claim to credibility, was proving to be a handful. Though he had broken ties with the ANC, he was consorting with the PFP. Furthermore, he refused to participate fully in the regime's plans unless and until Mandela was released. The ANC summarily rejected the NSC – it did not even make it to the starting block. Not only was the idea stillborn, but Botha's time was also running out.

Talks about talks continue

What was Botha's game plan with regard to Mandela and the ANC? It is clear that he authorised the interactions between Mandela and Kobie Coetsee, as well as the Mells Park talks, but in a way that covered him should leaks cause adverse reactions. Plausible deniability was part of the process. In October 1987, Coetsee had informed Mandela that, in the coming year, discussions would take place with a team that included Niël Barnard. That same month, the first Mells Park talks went ahead, but only once the regime had ensured the NIS would have an inside track and thus be able to steer the conversation. The notes kept by Michael Young and Tony Trew are fascinating when read from this perspective.

At the first meeting, which took place at Eastwell Manor on 7 October 1987, the Afrikaner delegation talked about creating a climate for negotiations and sought to create a quid pro quo framework with the

---

3. Ibid., p. 173.

ANC. The government, they said, had painted itself into a corner concerning the renunciation of violence. The government needed a face-saver, and the ANC could provide this by responding positively to the release of political prisoners, in particular Govan Mbeki, whose release was imminent. They claimed that 'the security establishment distinguished the release of prisoners and the unbanning of the ANC as two distinct matters – the second might follow if the first occurred successfully, i.e. if the ANC accepted it as a genuine step towards negotiation'.[4] Esterhuyse and Terreblanche did not hesitate to dangle the carrot while wielding the stick. They went on to say that 'the ANC should not turn it [the release of Govan Mbeki] into a damp squib or "move the goalposts" by asking new demands'.[5] It appears the NIS was attempting to tie the ANC's hands, and the way Esterhuyse raised the matter suggests that the NIS had made contact with him before the first meeting took place.

The pursuit of a step-for-step trade-off became more evident at the second meeting in February 1988. Esterhuyse reported that Govan Mbeki's release had meant to be a prelude to the freeing of Mandela, but that 'Kobie Coetzee and others believe it is necessary to have ANC involvement to achieve a controlled release' and that, crucially, '[t]here had been a drastic change in the climate since the release of Mbeki, and that it would take a long time to recreate in the white establishment a climate that favoured more releases'.[6] Thabo Mbeki deflected Esterhuyse's attempts and refused to commit to a trade-off. In short, while Mbeki envisaged a scene of dominoes falling, he would not entertain a quid pro quo in any shape or form.

Botha clearly had a well-thought-out strategy with regard to the Mandela and Mells Park discussions. By March/April 1989, Mandela had held at least five meetings with Coetsee and at least nine with the team led by Barnard. The meetings had disabused the regime of any

---

4. Notes by Tony Trew, 'Report of meeting of 31/10/87 to 1/11/87', pp. 5–6.
5. Ibid.
6. Notes by Tony Trew, 'Meeting with people from home – 22–24 February 1988', pp. 15–18.

possibility of cajoling Mandela to serve on the NSC or detaching him from the ANC led by Oliver Tambo. It is also reasonable to assume that the regime was not ready to consider any action that would raise public expectations that talks between the government and the ANC were likely. Mandela kept pressing for this, however.

Gerhart and Glaser sum up the Botha–Mandela skirmish as follows: During the NIS talks

> Barnard, Botha's point man in the secret committee, pressed Mandela relentlessly regarding the armed struggle, the ANC-SACP alliance, and the impossibility of majority rule given white fears of black domination. Mandela gave no ground on fundamental ANC positions, instead patiently explaining over and over, the rationale for ANC policies, how they had evolved historically, and also why the ANC was committed to racial reconciliation. Little by little, as Barnard and the committee came to realise that detaching Mandela from the core ANC policies was going to be impossible, they also began privately to let go of some of their own preconceived assumptions about the African struggle for democracy and to recognise that a viable negotiated settlement was possible.[7]

The realisation that the regime would have to meet the ANC, and that Mandela's release could not be postponed indefinitely, explains why the NIS had found it necessary to have the SSC adopt a new resolution on 5 July 1988. According to Barnard, on that date, 'with the help and full knowledge of PW Botha, NIS had piloted a decision through the State Security Council (SSC) to take out a bureaucratic insurance policy on the secret talks, of which the SSC was unaware. It read as follows: "The Security Services and Prison Service should study the Mandela question

7. Gerhart and Glaser, *From Protest to Challenge*, vol. 6, p. 181. See also Steinberg, 'Poring over Mandela's words, apartheid apparatchiks learnt sweet nothing'.

continuously and remain in touch with the situation on the ANC leadership."[8] The resolution protected the NIS against possible future accusations that it had engaged with the ANC without the SSC's authorisation. The formulation 'study the Mandela question continuously and remain in touch' was deliberately vague and allowed for an interpretation that the resolution authorised the NIS to talk with the ANC. It was an insurance policy intended to cover both the actions of the NIS and Botha's back. In light of the rivalry between the NIS and Minister Coetsee, it is also noteworthy that the resolution specifically mentioned both the security services and the prison service.

Partly driven by an internal fight in the NP, Botha decided to meet Mandela to ensure that when he was eventually released and/or talks with the ANC commenced, Botha would be the one to get the credit. This was the basis for his meeting with Mandela on 5 July 1989, which the government made known to the public shortly thereafter. By making it public knowledge, Botha was forcing the hand of his party, over which he had begun to lose control. But, like Slabbert, Botha did not know Mandela and the ANC.

Botha stakes a claim to the future

By the time Botha agreed to meet the man who was causing him so much trouble, events within the NP were developing in such a way that Botha could do nothing in the little time left to him as president of the country. By now he was locked in a bitter power struggle with F.W. de Klerk.

After suffering a stroke on 18 January 1989, Botha had resigned as leader of the NP while remaining president of the republic.[9] The NP parliamentary caucus had elected De Klerk as the party's new leader on the same day Botha stepped down, 2 February 1989. This separation of state president and party leadership proved fertile ground for tension

---

8. Barnard, *Secret Revolution*, p. 217.
9. During the period of Botha's convalescence, Chris Heunis was acting president.

and conflict, which manifested even before Botha resumed office on 15 March. The power struggle centred on the question as to who had the necessary authority to interpret and implement NP policy. On 10 March 1989, while Botha was still recuperating, the NP federal council decided in favour of the principle that the leader of the NP as the majority party should hold the office of state president. And, on 3 May 1989, it scheduled the next general election for 6 September that year.

Another flashpoint between Botha and De Klerk arose when the latter began to develop contacts with political leaders in Europe and Africa. In June 1989, De Klerk visited Margaret Thatcher in the UK, Helmut Kohl in Germany, Aníbal Cavaco Silva in Portugal and Giulio Andreotti in Italy. In July, he visited Joaquim Chissano, the president of Mozambique, and was scheduled to meet Kenneth Kaunda of Zambia in late August.

This was the context in which Botha finally decided to meet with Mandela. Throughout his tenure, he had avoided direct contact with the ANC. Interactions over a prisoner exchange between Angola and South Africa during the last years of his presidency highlight his determination not to be at the same table as the ANC.

Pretoria was keen to get back SADF captain Wynand du Toit, who had been captured by Angolan forces in a botched raid on oil installations in Cabinda in May 1985. The oilfields in question were jointly run by the Angolan government and Gulf Oil of the US. Around 1987, a plan was hatched to free Angolan soldiers who had been captured by South African forces operating in Angola in support of UNITA in exchange for Du Toit. In discussions between Angola and the ANC, the possibility arose of including prisoners awaiting execution in South Africa, as well as Klaas de Jonge, who was holed up in the Dutch embassy in Pretoria. The ANC approached the Dutch government to include De Jonge in the exchange.[10]

At that stage, Botha was not prepared to release black prisoners or

---

10. Minutes of an NWC meeting held on 25 March 1987, in the Simons Papers.

engage with the ANC. He maintained his stance even when the ANC NWC sought to intervene through Professor Hendrik van der Merwe, and despite that fact that Coetsee was already in talks with Mandela and plans for Esterhuyse and others to meet the ANC abroad were in the pipeline.[11] It took the intervention of the Netherlands to eventually get Botha to agree to De Jonge's inclusion.[12]

The prisoner exchange took place on 7 September 1987 and involved 133 Angolan soldiers, two Frenchmen serving relatively short sentences in prisons in the Ciskei bantustan, and Klaas de Jonge, in exchange for Captain du Toit and the remains of two South African Special Forces commandos who had been killed in the Cabinda raid. The deal involved five governments – Angola, South Africa, the Netherlands, France and Mozambique – and representatives of UNITA, as well as the Ciskei in a belated attempt to force de facto recognition of the bantustan.[13]

Faced with developments within his party and De Klerk's growing contact with Western leaders, Botha sensed that his power to shape events was rapidly diminishing. So, he agreed to meet with Mandela, to poke a finger in De Klerk's eye and to stake a claim that it was he who pioneered a pathway to negotiations with Mandela and the ANC. For Botha, the meeting on 5 July 1989 was merely a pawn in the NP's internal power struggles.

As mentioned previously, news of the meeting went public. Botha deliberately leaked the story, but in a way that appeared accidental. The event was supposed to be kept secret, but during a hunting trip shortly afterwards, Botha showed some cabinet members a photo of himself,

---

11. Ibid.
12. The NWC minutes reflect contact between the government of the Netherlands and the ANC on this matter. The inclusion of the two Frenchmen did not feature in the ANC list. In the 2014 film *Plot for Peace*, the focus is on the role of a Frenchman, Jean-Yves Ollivier, described as a cereal, oil and coal trader who appears to have made a living in sanctions-busting. The film does not mention anything about how De Jonge and the two Frenchmen came to feature in the exchange.
13. William Claiborne, 'Prisoners returned in 4-way swap', *Washington Post*, 8 September 1987.

Willemse and Barnard with Mandela and told the story of the prison talks. The secret was out.[14]

On 10 August 1989, Reuters reported from Lusaka that De Klerk and Kaunda had agreed to meet on the 28th. The power struggle reached its denouement. Four days later, P.W. Botha resigned as state president and F.W. de Klerk assumed the mantle. De Klerk fought the election of 6 September on a mandate for 'negotiated' reform. Although the NP was returned to office, its majority was significantly reduced by Treurnicht's Conservative Party and the Democratic Party, which had formed from the merger of the PFP and two smaller parties.

Parallel to these developments, mass action by the democratic forces was intensifying despite the state of emergency. The ANC, COSATU and the MDM met in Lusaka in June 1989 and agreed to mount a mass civil disobedience campaign. Black patients began seeking treatment at 'white' hospitals, groups of black bathers invaded 'white' beaches and students demonstrated against segregated schools. On 20 August, MDM leaders declared at a rally at St George's Cathedral in Cape Town that the UDF was unbanning itself. The police, in their efforts to suppress a national stayaway called for 5 and 6 September, killed twenty-three people. This led to the intensification of the defiance campaign with mass marches in Cape Town, Johannesburg, Durban, East London and other urban areas during the month of September.

On the international front, De Klerk had to contend with the threat of new sanctions from the Commonwealth Heads of Government meeting due to be held in October 1989, as well as manage delicate negotiations to reschedule South Africa's debts.

The democratic forces close ranks

By 1987/88 it was clear that a new front of struggle was taking shape. Mandela had held several discussions with Kobie Coetsee, the first

---

14. Barnard, *Secret Revolution*, pp. 24–41.

of which took place in June 1986. The release of Govan Mbeki on 5 November 1987 came about partly as a result of these discussions.[15] These interactions culminated in the talks between Mandela and the government team headed by Barnard, while Mandela continued to meet with Coetsee separately. The discussions between the Afrikaner group and the ANC team led by Mbeki at Mells Park were also in progress. The regime had declared group rights and the protection of minority rights as its core position. It had insisted that abandonment of the armed struggle be a precondition. It had offered the unilaterally proposed National Statutory Council as the forum to advise the government and parliament on a constitution for a future South Africa, but there had been no credible takers.

The state of play in the international arena was changing too. Since 1985, more than seventy American companies had left or announced their intention to exit South Africa. They included Kodak, General Motors, IBM and Coca-Cola. In October 1986, after the House of Representatives, the US Senate voted overwhelmingly in favour of a comprehensive sanctions bill imposing bans on new investments, airport landing rights and exports of oil. From its headquarters in London, Barclays Bank, the first major European investor, announced that it was exiting South Africa. The UK's foreign secretary, Geoffrey Howe, found it prudent to meet Oliver Tambo in September 1986, and the US followed suit when US secretary of state George Shultz met the ANC president in Washington in January 1987.

The contours of the negotiation's terrain were slowly taking shape. Without a clear topographical map, it would be hazardous to deploy

---

15. Vula communications (in maharaj/vula comms/1989): Tambo (Alphons) and Slovo (Janet) sent a report to Govan Mbeki (Rachel), which states in paragraph 6 that Mandela 'had discussions on three different occasions before the latter was released from prison' and in paragraph 8 that Mandela 'is definitely negotiating with the government on this issue and the release of GM [Mbeki] is the result of such negotiations'.

one's forces and determine the requisite armaments required. In such a relatively undefined terrain, one could easily be blindsided. Losing a skirmish could snowball into a rout.

The primary effect of the *Beeld* editorial of December 1985 was its unintended contribution to demolishing the decades of demonisation of the ANC. The editorial sought to explore chinks in the armour of the ANC as well as appease the *verkramptes*. Based on a five-hour interview with Mbeki, the editorial alleged that the moderates within the ANC who were in favour of talks were fearful of militants.[16]

Until he relinquished power in 1989, P.W. Botha pursued a divide and co-opt strategy combined with the iron fist of law and order. Whatever one makes of the assurances of Barnard on the matter, the ANC would have been foolhardy if it did not factor in such a strategy on the part of the regime.

Through channels opened by Operation Vula in late 1988, Tambo and Mandela were able to communicate secretly, bypassing the reach of bugging devices. Tambo used the first opportunity to give Mandela an assessment of the state of play, the positions of the different players and would-be players, and cautioned about becoming entangled in a quid pro quo. Mandela was thus able to see more clearly how he could align the efforts he was making to the overall strategy and tactics of the ANC. He, in turn, smuggled the text of his memorandum to Tambo in early April 1989. In the meantime, Tambo consulted Mandela on the draft of

---

16. There is no evidence that this was an approach inserted by the regime. Our observation does not assume Piet Muller or the editor of *Beeld* were in cahoots with the regime. They were, however, part of the *verligte* camp. We do not know whether Muller was a member of the Broederbond. At the same time, one should not ignore the claim that in 1976 an agent of the Bureau of State Security, the journalist Gordon Winter, alleged that he was told by the head that the bureau had thirty-seven South African journalists on its payroll and that these included parliamentary correspondents. One was an editor-in-chief and eight worked on news desks. See Matisonn, *God, Spies and Lies*, p. 199.

the Harare Declaration.[17] By the time Tambo was incapacitated by a stroke in August 1989, the positions taken by the ANC, Mandela and the MDM were substantially in alignment.

The Vula communications channels also enabled Tambo to provide comprehensive briefings to Govan Mbeki, who was under restrictions in Port Elizabeth, and Harry Gwala in Pietermaritzburg. Both had expressed concerns about the talks that Mandela was having with the regime. The communications provide valuable insight into Tambo's thinking. They also show how he sought to close the gaps that were opening in the ranks of the ANC.

Pretoria is boxed in

In mid-May 1989, Tambo advised Mac Maharaj, who was heading Operation Vula inside South Africa:

We're under intense pressure from friends & allies, & also because of Margaret Thatcher-led drive by the west to evolve a strategy that belongs to [a] period following the independence of Namibia. The race for who'll control developments in our country has started in earnest, & we should be in the lead. Our friends, no less than we, don't [want us to] leave the running to MT [Margaret Thatcher] & other allies of the regime. The question being pressed on us from every corner is 'what is to be done? What is the new strategy, or new approach? We need to evolve a kind of '435' for South Africa, formu-

---

17. Interview with Mac Maharaj. Confirmed by Ivan Pillay, who was based in Lusaka and was the administrator of Operation Vula, which was under the direct command of Oliver Tambo, assisted by Joe Slovo. The bulk of the Vula communications in their possession in Lusaka was destroyed when the Vula arrests took place in July 1990. A part of the communications, mainly those that were found unenciphered in a safe house in Durban and which were in the possession of the lawyer representing the security police, was retrieved by O'Malley. A substantial part is available on the O'Malley Archive and the hard copy is in the possession of Mac Maharaj. The Security Branch were only able to access what was captured in an unencrypted form in Durban. The security police did not manage to crack the code used.

lated by us [the ANC and MDM], sold to the FLS etc. & used to control & channel pressures, including MT & Co that we can take charge of what needs to be done in our country.[18]

'435' is a reference to UN Security Council Resolution 435, adopted in 1978, which unequivocally called for an end to South African occupation of Namibia. The Namibian independence movement had necessarily involved the international community, being a UN trust territory. But, in the process, the Namibians themselves were regularly excluded from discussions and decisions affecting their country. The ANC leadership was determined to avoid finding itself in a similar situation.

At a meeting of the OAU, one of the West African states suggested that it was time for the liberation movements to hold considered negotiations with Pretoria. Tambo parried this with the need for him to consult. The OAU set up a special committee to look into the matter and report back at its meeting scheduled for mid-July 1989. It was the trigger that set Tambo on a high-pressure process that culminated in the adoption of the Harare Declaration by the OAU Ad-hoc Committee on Southern Africa on 21 August 1989.

In the same communication, Tambo briefed Maharaj and Siphiwe Nyanda about a meeting with Allan Boesak. The latter had gone to Lusaka to consult on his and Archbishop Tutu's behalf, after which they were due to visit the US. At the Lusaka meeting, it emerged that 'according to *Radio Deutsche Welle*, the US administration had upgraded the status of the ANC, that President Bush intends to meet OR' and that 'Hank Cohen of the US administration agrees entirely with the ANC's objection to Margaret Thatcher as honest broker'. Furthermore, Tambo's message stated that 'the imperialists are moving carefully towards mediation at the present time. That is why we need the commitment of the FLS & OAU.'[19]

---

18. Vula communications (in maharaj/vula comms/1989/17 May 1989).
19. Ibid.

From as far back as 1985, Tambo had consistently argued that the suspension of violence could not be a precondition for meaningful negotiations to take place. By the end of May 1989, the Reagan administration had come to acknowledge this too. In a detailed appraisal of the situation to Govan Mbeki, Harry Gwala and Mac Maharaj dated 3 June 1989, Tambo and Joe Slovo wrote that 'the US administration through Schultz accepted the logic of our argument, as Johan Hayes [*sic*; Heyns] now has. But the call for negotiations persisted unabated, with Schultz demanding of the regime to "start negotiations so that violence can stop".'[20]

Tambo advised that the '435' idea for South Africa was under intense discussion in the NWC and that a committee was reworking the draft.[21] On 6 June 1989, the ANC informed a UDF/COSATU delegation that it was in the process of working out its position on negotiations and asked for their inputs. On 16 June, Tambo tasked Vula to get comments within ten days from several individuals, including Mandela, in different parts of South Africa. A joint meeting of the NECs of COSATU and the UDF held on 26 June discussed the matter and agreed on a programme of action that included convening the Conference Towards a Democratic South Africa. The conference aimed to ensure that the ANC and the MDM spoke with one voice.[22]

Tambo and his drafting team consulted the leaders of the Frontline States and carefully took on board their observations and advice. Tambo wanted to ensure that the final product enjoyed not only the approval of the NEC, but also ownership by the Frontline States. Tambo, in particular, worked with a sense of urgency. President Kaunda of Zambia

---

20. Vula communications (in maharaj/vula comms/June). Johan Adam Heyns, moderator of the General Synod of the Nederduitse Gereformeerde Kerk, had come to the view that it was unethical to demand that Mandela renounce violence before he was released. Heyns was assassinated on 5 November 1994. No one has been arrested for his killing. It was widely believed that it was the work of white right-wing extremists.
21. Vula communications (in maharaj/vula comms/1989/5 June 1989).
22. The report is in maharaj/vula comms/1989/26 June 1989.

obtained the services of an eight-seater aircraft to enable Tambo and his team to hurry from one Frontline State to another.

The draft took final shape and was approved by the ANC leadership on 8 August 1989. That evening, while the drafting team cleaned and polished the text, Tambo suffered a debilitating stroke. But the task he had set for himself had been finalised and now just awaited the OAU's endorsement.

Mandela's memo to Botha on April 1989 had provided a compass. Under Tambo's stewardship, the 1987 January 8 statement, the October 1987 statement on negotiations and the Constitutional Guidelines for a Democratic South Africa of August 1988 had set the parameters for talks. The Harare Declaration of August 1989 became the road map to enable South Africa to reach the goal of a united, democratic and non-racial country. Tambo had given every ounce of himself to ensure that whatever path events took, democracy would be the outcome. He had steered a course in stormy and uncharted seas.

In doing so, he not only kept the ANC intact, but also succeeded in ensuring that the democratic forces stayed united. According to Padraig O'Malley:

> giving his benediction to both Thabo Mbeki [the Mells Park talks] and Mac Maharaj [Vula operation] in their endeavours reflected Tambo's holistic approach to the struggle ... Prudence required him to plan for different outcomes. Thus he had to plan for a seizure of power as well as for a protracted armed struggle, ways of balancing the four pillars of struggle, strangling the regime through economic isolation, and a negotiated settlement. Each course of action had to be pursued. The various pursuits were interrelated: Mac's Vula and Mbeki's Mells House Park talks complemented each other. Tambo orchestrated both, and he knew too ... that Mandela was in contact with the SA government.[23]

---

23. O'Malley, *Shades of Difference*, p. 261.

Around this same period, Mandela too, from the limited space of prison, set about requesting meetings with groups of individuals who were playing an influential role in various formations of the Mass Democratic Movement. In each case, he sought to brief them about his talks, allay the rumours and concerns, and ensure they appreciated the possibilities of the times. There was an amusing incident which showed how lines of communication in the underground could get tangled. Billy Nair was in a delegation visiting Mandela. He returned from the visit to confront Mac Maharaj, because he had noticed that Mandela had briefed them about the contents of the draft Harare Declaration from a thin strip of paper about two and a half centimetres wide with tiny print. It was similar to the strip of paper that Maharaj had used when he consulted Nair before the latter went to see Mandela. Nair accused Maharaj of secretly being in touch with Mandela without sharing that information with him.

At its meeting on 21 August 1989, the OAU subcommittee on southern Africa gave the 'Declaration of the OAU Ad-hoc Committee on Southern Africa on the question of South Africa' (more commonly known as the Harare Declaration) its stamp of approval.[24] This was followed by endorsement from the OAU, the Non-Aligned Movement and the United Nations. Though it became public knowledge that the driving force behind the declaration was the ANC, the proposal was put together in such a way that none of these powerful agencies found cause to make any substantive changes to it. Pretoria was boxed in.

The declaration succinctly spelt out the goal of negotiations as a united, democratic and non-racial state based on a multiparty system with universal human rights protected in an entrenched Bill of Rights. It envisaged a South Africa with an independent judiciary, founded on an economic order that would promote and advance the well-being

---

24. The document is better known as the Harare Declaration because the OAU AD-hoc Committee that adopted it met in Harare, Zimbabwe.

of all South Africans. The declaration demanded that Pretoria create the necessary climate for negotiations to take place. The preconditions included the unconditional release of all political prisoners and detainees; the lifting of all bans and restrictions on all prohibited and restricted organisations and persons; the removal of troops from the townships; an end to the state of emergency; the repeal of all legislation designed to circumscribe political activity, such as and including the Internal Security Act; and the cessation of all political trials and political executions. Furthermore, the declaration included a section on guidelines for the process of negotiations as well as a programme of action. The Harare Declaration became South Africa's road map to democracy.

De Klerk had ascended to the presidency of the country at a time when the regime's space to manoeuvre was severely constrained.

12

New Terrain, New Challenges

De Klerk had to demonstrate that he was in control of the situation. Thatcher was urging him to release Mandela, but he feared this might heighten black expectations. To diffuse the tension caused by police brutality during the stayaway of 5–6 September and to deal with the growing mass defiance, De Klerk allowed the post-election demonstrations and marches to proceed without police interference. On 15 October 1989, he freed five of the Rivonia trialists – Walter Sisulu, Ahmed Kathrada, Andrew Mlangeni, Elias Motsoaledi and Raymond Mhlaba – and three other prisoners: Wilton Mkwayi and Oscar Mpetha, both of the ANC, and Jafta Masemola of the PAC.

Mandela's release was now a foregone conclusion and negotiations likely. In rejecting Botha's offer in January 1985 to release him if he renounced violence, Mandela had fashioned a link between his freedom and negotiations to resolve the South African conflict and had ensured the removal of the renunciation of violence as a precondition.

The question now was when and how these negotiations would commence. The Harare Declaration enjoyed world support and placed the onus on Pretoria to demonstrate its willingness to negotiate, whether De Klerk was ready or not.

During the latter half of 1989, Mandela met with justice minister Kobie Coetsee; Gerrit Viljoen, the former chair of the Broederbond whom De Klerk had appointed minister of constitutional development in his new cabinet; and the team led by Barnard.[1] Mandela also met

---

1. Vula communications (in maharaj/vula comms/1989/2 October 1989).

with leaders from the MDM, and with Walter Sisulu on 20 October, shortly after the latter's release.[2]

It was clear to both sides that the release of the Rivonia trialists had unleashed events that made negotiations inevitable. The focus was now on ensuring that the regime created the right climate for negotiation. In this regard, the release of Mandela and all other political prisoners, particularly those serving life sentences, was top of the agenda. So, too, was the removal of all restrictions on political activity. The nub of the discussions shifted to ensuring a meeting between the government and the ANC. The principle was a foregone conclusion. What stood in the way now was how to get there.

The logistics of the release of political prisoners had been the subject of many meetings, including those between the ANC and the NIS. The latter had sought to draw the ANC into an undertaking that, after their release, the Rivonia trialists would not fan unrest and the people's defiance.

On 10 October 1989, just five days before the release of Sisulu and the others, Coetsee and Viljoen met with Mandela. They indicated that they expected 'a commitment from your colleagues [i.e. Sisulu and the others] that they will strive towards a peaceful and orderly integration into society without upheaval ... and won't make it difficult'. Mandela countered that unconditional releases 'will look dignified'.[3]

Armed with the Harare Declaration, in late November/early December 1989 Mandela wrote to De Klerk on the issue of 'creating a climate of understanding'. He pressed for a meeting between the government and the ANC. He was determined not to allow his impending release to be a standalone event, detached from moving to negotiations about the future of the country. He proposed a two-phased approach. During phase one, government and the ANC would settle the five preconditions for

---

2. Vula communications (in maharaj/vula comms/1989/20 October 1989).
3. Esterhuyse and Van Niekerk, *Die Tronkgesprekе*, pp. 226 and 228.

negotiations. Phase two would involve the actual negotiations regarding the future, including restoring peace.[4]

De Klerk, Coetsee and the team led by Barnard were seemingly not prepared to reveal their hand just yet, but the Kobie Coetsee Papers open a window into their thinking.

On 8 December 1989, Mike Louw, a member of the Barnard team, penned a memo to Coetsee headed '913: Besinning [Reflection]',[5] which begins with the question: From a subjective perspective, where do we stand on Mandela? Louw briefs Coetsee on the team's reading of the situation. He states that Mandela insists on convincing De Klerk of the need for peaceful negotiations. The white community now accepts that Mandela will be released – the only question is when. There has also been dramatic progress concerning the issue of violence as a precondition for release. Louw writes that a more nuanced formula has been found about commitment to decision-making in connection with peace, though this formulation is a headache for the ANC. Louw ends by stating that what was unthinkable and considered dangerous when the SSC met in December 1984 – namely, the release of Mandela – has now become, in all likelihood, the best starting point.[6]

It seems Barnard's team had come round to Mandela's proposition that the way ahead revolved around a meeting between the government and the ANC. It was the same conclusion that Coetsee himself had reached, as well as the NIS from their reading of the interactions at the Mells Park talks and their meeting with the ANC in Switzerland. It was the message carried by the Mass Democratic Movement[7] and by the Conference for a Democratic Future held in Johannesburg on 8–9 December 1989 and attended by 4 600 delegates.

---

4. The twelve-page letter is available at the Nelson Mandela Centre of Memory.
5. '913' is the prison number used for Mandela in the Kobie Coetsee Papers.
6. Esterhuyse and Van Niekerk, *Die Tronkgespreke*, p. 233.
7. At an IDASA-organised meeting between delegations from South Africa and the ANC in Paris in late November 1989, as part of the bicentennial of the French Revolution, one of the Afrikaner delegates announced that De Klerk had decided to take the ANC on politically, rather than through repression.

'Today's politics is tomorrow's history'

Would De Klerk remain trapped in his conservative past the way Botha had imprisoned himself with a strategy of co-option? The opening of parliament on 2 February 1990 became the focus of attention.

In pursuit of a comprehensive negotiation strategy, De Klerk organised a bosberaad between 3 and 5 December 1989, where – as he recalls in his autobiography – the cabinet agreed 'on the importance of government seizing the initiative and of occupying the moral high ground ... We also considered the enormous risks involved in reform and discussed fall-back positions should things go wrong.'[8] The cabinet accepted the full logical consequences of power-sharing – provided there would be reasonable protection for minority rights – and agreed that the ANC would have to be part of the process. 'This would require a strategy to bring the ANC to the negotiating table,' De Klerk later wrote. 'We reached consensus on the need for an approach that would surprise our opponents and give us the early initiative. We would have to ensure that we would, throughout, stay in control of the process, and maintain good government and law and order.'[9]

Concerning his speech to the opening of parliament, De Klerk wrote that 'the key decision I had to take for myself was to make a paradigm shift'. He had to move in a way that would 'convince important players that we were not negotiating under pressure, but from the strength of our convictions'. What he envisaged was 'an orderly step-by-step process of meaningful negotiation'.[10]

He presented the package to 'the cabinet in its entirety on 31 January 1990'. The contents of the speech were broken to the media at a special briefing under lockdown conditions at 6 a.m. on 2 February. De Klerk believed that with the delivery of the speech in parliament, 'We had

---

8. F.W. de Klerk, *The Last Trek – A New Beginning: The Autobiography* (London: Macmillan, 1999), pp. 161–2.
9. Ibid.
10. Ibid., pp. 162–3.

succeeded in catching the media, the political opposition and the world completely by surprise.'[11]

Whatever the facts, with that speech De Klerk had opted to take a decisive step designed to disarm his detractors and opponents and take occupation of the moral high ground.

Did De Klerk have a strategy as he claims, or was he flying by the seat of his pants? An adequate response to this question would require an examination of his actions right up to the April 1994 elections. At this stage of our narrative, we can only hazard a limited answer based on developments that brought the country to the Groote Schuur meeting of 2 May 1990.

According to De Klerk, at the bosberaad held in early December 1989, it was agreed that the release of Mandela, the unbanning of the ANC and talks with the ANC were to be part of the process of moving forward. The discussions between Mandela and Coetsee between 1986 and 1990, the exchanges between Mandela and the Barnard team between May 1988 and 1990, and the Mells Park talks that first took place in October 1987 made this possible. But had the outcomes of these talks been sufficient to move De Klerk from his hard-line position of perpetuating white control?

When he was elected leader of the NP by the party parliamentary caucus on 2 February 1989, De Klerk still believed that reform would come through the tricameral parliament. De Klerk had considered resigning from the cabinet in 1988, but his stated reasons were Botha's 'surliness, aggression and poor human relations'.[12] He said not a word about substantive policy differences. De Klerk had been a member of

---

11. Ibid. Pallo Jordan was in Harare on 2 February 1990. He recalls receiving the text of De Klerk's speech two hours before delivery from Comrade Ike Maphoto, who had been a commander during the Sipolilo Campaign. Jordan faxed a copy to Lusaka with the request that it be sent to Sweden where Walter Sisulu, Alfred Nzo and others were visiting Tambo. By the time Jordan reached Lusaka that same afternoon, the ANC had released a statement from Stockholm in response to De Klerk's address.

12. Ibid., p. 130.

Botha's SSC from the time of its inception. He had a track record as a hardliner in the NP.

His elder brother, Wimpie de Klerk, could not join the second Mells Park talks held from 22 to 24 February 1988. He sent an apology stating that 'he was ready to take part in such a meeting at any time', and he kept his word.[13] Many of the key personalities at the Groote Schuur talks in May 1990, and in the negotiations that followed, had links to the Broederbond, of which F.W. and Wimpie de Klerk were both members. It is therefore reasonable to assume that De Klerk was aware of the Mells Park talks.

The Broederbond had even established a subcommittee, the Constitutional Policy Committee (*Komitee vir Staatkundige Aangeleenthede*), whose task was to address the question of constitutional change for South Africa. The debates in this forum were confidential and conducted in secret. Relations between the NP and the Broederbond had changed over time, and the latter's influence over government policy had weakened. Even so, when Botha was at war with the Broederbond in the early eighties, F.W. de Klerk and many other cabinet members maintained close ties with the organisation. Professor T. Dunbar Moodie is of the view that '[o]nce power had been attained, Broederbond informal networks certainly advanced the personal careers of "friends" ... Moreover, it is clear from Broederbond minutes that broers had easy access to "friends in responsible positions" (meaning "broers" who were also members of parliament, civil servants and government ministers).'[14]

De Klerk would have known about the Constitutional Policy Committee's 1986 position paper titled 'Basic political policy conditions for the survival of the Afrikaner'. Gerrit Viljoen and Wimpie de Klerk were permanent members of the committee, and Roelf Meyer and deputy

---

13. Notes by Tony Trew, 'Meeting with people from home – 22–24 February 1988', p. 1.
14. T. Dunbar Moodie, '"Cyril's eyes lit up." Roelf Meyer, Francois Venter, the Afrikaner Broederbond and the decision to abandon "group rights" in favour of a "regstaat" (constitutional state)', unpublished paper, 2012, p. 3.

minister of constitutional development Tertius Delport frequently met with the committee.[15] It is not inconceivable that Kobie Coetsee, Niël Barnard, Willie Willemse and Fanie van der Merwe[16] were also members of the Broederbond. Barnard, at the very least, would have closely followed the Constitutional Policy Committee's discussions.

The committee would have been finalising its position paper when Pieter de Lange, then chairman of the Broederbond, met Thabo Mbeki in New York in May 1986. The Broederbond recognised that government's interactions with black people should extend beyond those serving in the bantustan and local government structures. According to Dunbar Moodie, 'Initially, there was a strong move also for ordinary members to meet with important Coloured and African leaders. Lists of potential contacts, including, for instance, Winnie Mandela, were drawn up ... In the end, however, the Executive Council seems to have decided that the *Staatkundige* Committee's energies were best spent on debating with and informing its own members – whether in the branches or the government.'[17] It appears that the Broederbond at that stage did not think it wise to find itself at loggerheads with Botha.

In February 1987, the Constitutional Policy Committee held a brainstorming session (*dinkskrum*) with about a hundred 'friends'.[18] 'Topics for discussion included constitutional mechanisms, means of identifying "groups" whose rights might be entrenched (sometimes later called "mechanisms for protection of minorities"), party-political structures,

---

15. Ibid. Roelf Meyer became leader of the NP government team at the Convention for a Democratic South Africa (CODESA) after Gerrit Viljoen fell ill.
16. Fanie van der Merwe was one of the joint secretaries of CODESA, the Multi-Party Negotiating Forum that succeeded it, and the Transitional Executive Council.
17. Dunbar Moodie, '"Cyril's eyes lit up."', p. 11.
18. Ibid. 'Afrikaner dignitaries ... including distinguished academics, members of parliament and provincial representatives, pressmen, lawyers, central and local government officials, security officials (including police, military and intelligence officers), businessmen, industrialists (many of those heading up the great parastatals as well as Afrikaner finance and industry), churchmen, teachers (including the director general of education), and a couple of farmers.' The Erfenisstigting, which manages the Broederbond archives, was not prepared to make available the attendance register of the *dinkskrum*.

identifying the policy positions of moderate and radical negotiating partners (*gespreksgenote*), arrangements for negotiations and international opinion.'[19] Dunbar Moodie continues:

[T]he meeting concluded 'the disenfranchised (*buitestaatlik*) black man must be included in the highest political decision-making processes.'

The *dinkskrum* agreed that after negotiations a constitution should be set up and implemented by parliament. There was a growing conviction, however, that there needed to be a place for extra-parliamentary pre-negotiations which would complement parliament and would be free of the government, but would operate with the blessing and funds from the government. Its conclusions would be presented to parliament for confirmation.

The ANC was recognised as 'a multi-ethnic revolutionary movement that operates across the boundaries of race, colour and language,' and as the leader of an effective alliance of various 'freedom movements.' Because it was controlled by the SA Communist Party there could be no conversation/negotiation with the ANC, although contact might be made with nationalistic elements within the organisation.[20]

It is reasonable to assume that this was De Klerk's position at the time of the February 1987 *dinkskrum*. Those present recognised that apartheid had not worked and proposed entrenched group rights as a means of protecting minority rights. They supported pre-negotiations, but not with the ANC. All that De Klerk reveals in his autobiography is that he was aware of the discussions taking place with Mandela and at Mells Park. But, he adds, 'together with most members of the government I was

19. Ibid.
20. Ibid., p. 13.

very wary of such exercises. I felt that when the time came, the government and no one else from our side should determine the timing and direction of the process. We were worried that well-intentioned efforts by businessmen and academics serve only to muddy the waters and complicate government's task.'[21]

One of the hazards of autobiographies is having to cut through the spin to understand the subject's actual views at any given time. According to Esterhuyse, 'De Klerk's idea of power-sharing was the Broederbond's idea of power-sharing. That was not a negotiated deal.'[22]

Professor Paul Williams, in his PhD thesis, gives us insight into the views of Broederbond chair Pieter de Lange:

> What had occurred since the late 1970s was an intense debate over the best means to achieve this goal which eventually saw apartheid lose out to the rather transparent concepts of 'power-sharing' and 'sufficient consensus'. De Lange himself acknowledged as much when he later admitted that *'we never abandoned the idea that whites would have power'*.[23]

The issues discussed with Mandela and with Mbeki coincide with the topics debated inside the Broederbond. This suggests that in some ways the Broederbond remained an influential think tank for De Klerk to tap into.

The *dinkskrum* agreed that any Bill of Rights should apply to individual as well as group rights. How to define groups and what constituted group rights was central to the debates within the Broederbond. Their records indicate that these issues were still unresolved by the beginning of 1990. It is, therefore, reasonable to conclude that by the time

---

21. De Klerk, *The Last Trek – A New Beginning*, pp. 173–4.
22. Patti Waldmeir's interview with Willie Esterhuyse, quoted in Williams, 'Intellectuals and the end of apartheid', p. 154.
23. Paul Williams's interview with Pieter de Lange, Stellenbosch, 7 July 1999, quoted in ibid. (authors' emphasis).

De Klerk made his speech on 2 February 1990, the idea of group rights had become central to the protection of Afrikaner minority rights, but that there was, however, no consensus on who belonged to what group and what the concept of group rights entailed.

In the elections of 6 September 1989, the NP under De Klerk placed six goals before the white electorate. Among them was the promise 'to normalise the political process and to negotiate a new constitutional dispensation'. This clearly meant re-establishing the principle of cabinet rule by dismantling the NSMS, which, incidentally, De Klerk claimed 'played a central role in counteracting the revolutionary threat of the mid-eighties'.[24] This was actioned on 28 November 1989, when De Klerk announced that the NSMS would be disbanded.

In language indistinguishable from that of his predecessor, De Klerk described the outcome of the September elections as a 'clear mandate for the continuation of reform and the creation of a new dispensation'.[25] The crucial questions remained unanswered. Would government abandon the search for black collaborators from within apartheid structures? Would it dispense with the idea that the existing parliament be the locus for finding the 'new dispensation'? Would it abandon the concept of white control under the guise of protecting minority rights? The 'continuation of reform' would have to confront the issues of Mandela's release, the unbanning of the ANC and talks with the ANC as essential steps in the 'creation of a new dispensation'. Until De Klerk grasped the nettle of reform, he would remain paralysed over the way forward. The release of Walter Sisulu and the other Rivonia trialists in October 1989 and the repeal of various pieces of discriminatory legislation suggest that he was getting there.

The parties involved in the various talks up till this point answered

---

24. De Klerk, *The Last Trek – A New Beginning*, p. 152. He takes credit for his membership of the SSC but does not accept responsibility for any of the extra-legal murders we draw attention to in this book.
25. Ibid., p. 148.

the crucial questions before De Klerk held his cabinet bosberaad in early December 1989. This made it possible for the bosberaad to confront the situation and accept 'the full consequence of power-sharing – provided there would be reasonable protection for minority rights' and to agree 'that the ANC would have to be part of the process'. 'This would require a strategy to bring the ANC to the negotiating table,' De Klerk later noted. 'We reached consensus on the need for an approach that would surprise our opponents and give us the early initiative. We would have to ensure that we would, throughout, stay in control of the process, and maintain good government and law and order.'[26]

Which brings us back to the question: Did F.W. de Klerk have a strategy as he claims, or was he flying by the seat of his pants? At this stage, it seems that he and his party were without a plan – at best, they had the bare bones, but were unable to flesh it out. And De Klerk was unclear about the process for negotiations. He was, however, alert to the moment and alive to the tactics required to propel him to centre stage.

In his memo of April 1989 to P.W. Botha, Mandela had succinctly outlined the nub of the matter that negotiations would have to address: how to reconcile the principle of majority rule, which is the foundation of democracy and the necessary condition for peace in South Africa, with the fears and concerns of the white minority, who controlled the levers of power and privilege and who wanted guarantees that majority rule would not mean black domination. De Klerk's historic address did not present a challenge to South Africa. It presented him as the driver of the bus taking South Africa into the future and asserted that he was in full control of the situation.

'We did not wait until the position of power dominance turned against us before we decided to negotiate a peaceful settlement,' De Klerk told *Die Burger* on 31 March 1990. 'The initiative is in our hands. We have

---

26. Ibid., p. 162.

the means to ensure that the process develops peacefully and in an orderly way.'[27] Subsequent events would indicate whether De Klerk was on top of the game or whether this assessment amounted to an effort to convince himself that he could control the flow of the water once the sluice gates were opened.

Tambo had devoted all his energies to ensuring the world presented South Africa with a road map out of apartheid and to democracy. He wanted to ensure that the outcome of negotiations would be a triumph of democracy and not some cooked-up settlement that evaded the precept that all humans are born equal and ought to enjoy equal rights and access to government.

How South Africa found its way forward was the challenge for the period after the Groote Schuur meeting of May 1990. How De Klerk responded would determine his place in history. But it would go beyond F.W. de Klerk. The roles played by all the parties and personalities gathered under the roof of the World Trade Centre in Kempton Park, Johannesburg, where the multiparty talks took place, would be brought into the evaluation. And a place in history would be found for the ordinary people from all walks of life who helped South Africa's march to freedom. They had borne the brunt of an inhuman system, a crime against humanity, and no honours showered on the individual actors should in any way obscure or diminish their role.

---

27. *Die Burger*, 31 March 1990, quoted in Johannes Rantete and Hermann Giliomee, 'Transition to democracy through transaction?: Bilateral negotiations between the ANC and the NP in South Africa', *African Affairs*, 91, 1992, pp. 515–42.

ANNEXURES

ANNEXURE A

Memo from Nelson Mandela to P.W. Botha

Full text of April 1989 memo by Nelson Mandela to P.W. Botha as a prelude to their meeting. It was given to Minister Kobie Coetsee to hand over to Botha sometime in April 1989. Mandela sent a copy to Oliver Tambo, the president of the ANC.

The deepening political crisis in our country has been a matter of grave concern to me for quite some time and I now consider it necessary in the national interest for the African National Congress and the government to meet urgently to negotiate an effective political settlement.

At the outset I must point out that I make this move without consultation with the ANC. I am a loyal and disciplined member of the ANC, my political loyalty is owed, primarily, if not exclusively, to this organisation and particularly to our Lusaka headquarters where the official leadership is stationed and from where our affairs are directed.

The Organisation First

In the normal course of events, I would put my views to the organisation first, and if these views were accepted, the organisation would then decide on who were the best qualified members to handle the matter on its behalf and on exactly when to make the move. But in the current circumstances I cannot follow this course, and this is the only reason why I am acting on my own initiative, in the hope that the organisation will, in due course endorse my action.

I must stress that no prisoner irrespective of his status or influence, can conduct negotiations of this nature from prison. In our special situation negotiation on political matters is literally a matter of life and death which requires to be handled by the organisation itself through its appointed representatives.

The step I am taking should, therefore, not be seen as the beginning of actual negotiations between the government and the ANC. My task is a very limited one, and that is to bring the country's two major political bodies to the negotiating table.

My Release Not the Issue

I must further point out that the question of my release from prison is not an issue, at least at this stage of the discussions, and I am certainly not asking to be freed. But I do hope that the government will, as soon as possible, give me the opportunity from my present quarters to sound the views of my colleagues inside and outside the country on this move. Only if this initiative is formally endorsed by the ANC will it have any significance.

I will touch presently on some of the problems which seem to constitute an obstacle to a meeting between the ANC and the government. But I must emphasise right at this stage that this step is not a response to the call by the government on ANC leaders to declare whether or not they are nationalists and to renounce the South African Communist Party before there can be negotiations. No self-respecting freedom fighter will take orders from the government on how to wage the freedom struggle against that same government and on who his allies in the freedom struggle should be.

To obey such instructions would be a violation of the long-standing and fruitful solidarity which distinguishes our liberation movement, and a betrayal of those who have worked so closely and suffered so much with us for almost seventy years. Far from responding to that call my intervention is influenced by purely domestic issues, by the civil strife and ruin into which the country is now sliding. I am disturbed, as many other South Africans no doubt are, by the spectre of a South Africa split into two hostile camps; blacks (the term 'blacks' is used in a broad sense to include all those who are not whites) on one side and whites on the other, slaughtering one another; by acute tensions which are building up dangerously in practically every sphere of our lives, a situation which, in turn, preshadows more violent clashes in the days ahead. This is the crisis that has freed me to act.

Current Views Among Blacks

I must add that the purpose of this discussion is not only to urge the government to talk to the ANC, but it is also to acquaint you with the views current among blacks, especially those in the Mass Democratic Movement.

If I am unable to express these views frankly and freely, you will never know how the majority of South Africans think on the policy and actions of the government; you will never know how to deal with their grievances and demands. It is perhaps proper to remind you that the media here and abroad has given certain public figures in this country a rather negative image not only in regard to human rights questions, but also in respect to their prescriptive stance when dealing with black leaders generally.

The impression is shared not only by the vast majority of blacks but also by a substantial section of the whites. If I had allowed myself to be influenced by this impression, I would not even have thought of making this move. Nevertheless, I have come here with an open mind and the impression I will carry away from this meeting will be determined almost exclusively by the manner in which you respond to my proposal.

It is in this spirit that I have undertaken this mission, and I sincerely hope that nothing will be done or said here that will force me to revise my views on this aspect.

Obstacles to Negotiation

I have already indicated that I propose to deal with some of the obstacles to a meeting between the government and the ANC. The government gives several reasons why it will not negotiate with us. However, for purposes of this discussion, I will confine myself to only three main demands set by the government as a precondition for negotiations, namely that the ANC must first renounce violence, break with the SACP and abandon its demand for majority rule.

Renunciation of Violence

The position of the ANC on the question of violence is very simple. The organisation has no vested interest in violence. It abhors any action which may cause loss of life, destruction of property and misery to the people. It has worked long and patiently for a South Africa of common values and for an undivided and peaceful non-racial state. But we consider the armed struggle a legitimate form of self-defence against a morally repugnant system of government which will not allow even peaceful forms of protest.

It is more than ironical that it should be the government which demands that we should renounce violence. The government knows only too well that there is not a single political organisation in this country, inside and outside parliament, which can ever compare with the ANC in its total commitment to peaceful change.

Right from the early days of its history, the organisation diligently sought peaceful solutions and, to that extent, it talked patiently to successive South African governments, a policy we tried to follow in dealing with the present government.

Apartheid Violence

Not only did the government ignore our demands for a meeting, instead it took advantage of our commitment to a non-violent struggle and unleashed the most violent form of racial oppression this country has ever seen. It stripped us of all basic human rights, outlawed our organisations and barred all channels of peaceful resistance. It met our demands with force and, despite the grave problems facing the country, it continues to refuse to talk to us. There can only be one answer to this challenge; violent forms of struggle.

Down the years oppressed people have fought for their birthright by peaceful means, where that was possible, and through force where peaceful channels were closed. The history of this country also confirms this vital lesson. Africans as well as Afrikaners were, at one time or other, compelled to take up arms in defence of their freedom against British imperialism. The fact that both were finally defeated by superior arms, and by the vast resources of that empire, does not negate this lesson.

But from what has happened in South Africa during the last forty years, we must conclude that now that the roles are reversed, and the Afrikaner is no longer a freedom fighter, but is in power, the entire lesson of history must be brushed aside. Not even a disciplined non-violent protest will now be tolerated. To the government a black man has neither a just cause to espouse nor freedom rights to defend. The whites must have the monopoly of political power, and of committing violence against innocent and defence-less people. That situation was totally unacceptable to us and the formation of uMkhonto weSizwe was intended to end that monopoly, and to forcibly bring home to the government that the oppressed people of this country were prepared to stand up and defend themselves.

It is significant to note that throughout the past four decades, and more especially over the last twenty-six years, the government has met our demands with force only, and has done hardly anything to create a suitable climate for dialogue. On the contrary, the government continues to govern with a heavy hand, and to incite whites against negotiation with the ANC. The publication of the booklet *Talking with the ANC...* which completely dis-torts the history and policy of the ANC, the extremely offensive language used by government spokesmen against freedom fighters, and the intimi-dation of whites who want to hear the views of the ANC at first hand, are all part of the government's strategy to wreck meaningful dialogue.

Pretoria Not Ready for Talks

It is perfectly clear on the facts that the refusal of the ANC to renounce violence is not the real problem facing the government. The truth is that the government is not yet ready for negotiation and for the sharing of political power with blacks. It is still committed to white domination and, for that reason, it will only tolerate those blacks who are willing to serve on its apartheid structures. Its policy is to remove from the political scene blacks who refuse to conform, who reject white supremacy and its apartheid struc-tures, and who insist on equal rights with whites.

This is the real reason for the government's refusal to talk to us, and for its demand that we should disarm ourselves, while it continues to use violence against our people. This is the reason for its massive propaganda campaign to discredit the ANC, and present it to the public as a communist-dominated organisation bent on murder and destruction. In this situation the reaction of the oppressed people is clearly predictable.

Armed Struggle

White South Africa must accept the plain fact that the ANC will not suspend, to say nothing of abandoning, the armed struggle until the government shows its willingness to surrender the monopoly of political power, and to negotiate directly and in good faith with the acknowledged black leaders. The renunciation of violence by either the government or the ANC should not be a precondition to, but the result of, negotiation.

Moreover, by ignoring credible black leaders, and imposing a succession of still-born negotiation structures, the government is not only squandering the country's precious resources but it is in fact discrediting the negotiation process itself, and prolonging civil strife. The position of the ANC on the question of violence is, therefore, very clear. A government which used violence against blacks many years before we took up arms has no right whatsoever to call on us to lay down arms.

The South African Communist Party

I have already pointed out that no self-respecting freedom fighter will allow the government to prescribe who his allies in the freedom struggle should be, and that to obey such instructions would be a betrayal of those who have suffered repression with us for so long.

We equally reject the charge that the ANC is dominated by the SACP and we regard the accusation as part of the smear campaign the government is waging against us. The accusation has, in effect, also been refuted by two totally independent sources. In January 1987, the American State Department published a report on the activities of the SACP in this country which contrasts very sharply with the subjective picture the government has tried to paint against us over the years.

The essence of that report is that, although the influence of the SACP on the ANC is strong, it is unlikely that the Party will ever dominate the ANC.

The same point is made somewhat differently by Mr. Ismail Omar, member of the President's Council, in his book *Reform in Crisis* published in 1988, in which he gives concrete examples of important issues of the day over which the ANC and the SACP have differed.

He also points out that the ANC enjoys greater popular support than the SACP. He adds that, despite the many years of combined struggle, the two remain distinct organisations with ideological and policy differences which preclude a merger of identity.

These observations go some way towards disproving the accusation. But since the allegation has become the focal point of government propaganda against the ANC, I propose to use this opportunity to give you the correct information, in the hope that this will help you to see the matter in its proper perspective, and to evaluate your strategy afresh.

Co-operation between the ANC and the South African Communist Party goes back to the early 'twenties and has always been, and still is, strictly limited to the struggle against racial oppression and for a just society. At no time has the organisation ever adopted or co-operated with communism itself. Apart from the question of co-operation between the two organisations, members of the SACP have always been free to join the ANC. But once they do so, they become fully bound by the policy of the organisation set out in the Freedom Charter. As members of the ANC engaged in the anti-apartheid struggle, their Marxist ideology is not directly relevant. The SACP has throughout the years accepted the leading role of the ANC, a position which is respected by the SACP members who join the ANC.

Firmly Established Tradition

There is, of course, a firmly established tradition in the ANC in terms of which any attempt is resisted, from whatever quarter, which is intended to undermine co-operation between the two organisations.

Even within the ranks of the ANC there have been, at one time or another, people – and some of them were highly respected and influential individuals – who were against this co-operation and who wanted SACP members expelled from the organisation. Those who persisted in these activities were themselves ultimately expelled or they broke away in despair.

In either case their departure ended their political careers, or they formed other political organisations which, in due course, crumbled into splinter groups. No dedicated ANC member will ever heed a call to break with the SACP. We regard such a demand as a purely divisive government strategy.

It is in fact a call on us to commit suicide. Which man of honour will ever desert a lifelong friend at the instance of a common opponent and still retain a measure of credibility among his people?

Which opponent will ever trust such a treacherous freedom fighter? Yet this is what the government is, in effect, asking us to do – to desert our faithful allies. We will not fall into that trap.

ANC is Non-Aligned

The government also accuses us of being agents of the Soviet Union. The truth is that the ANC is non-aligned, and we welcome support from the East and the West, from the socialist and capitalist countries. The only difference, as we have explained on countless occasions before, is that the socialist countries supply us with weapons, which the West refuses to give us. We have no intention whatsoever of changing our stand on this question.

The government's exaggerated hostility to the SACP and its refusal to have any dealings with that party have a hollow ring. Such an attitude is not only out of step with the growing co-operation between the capitalist and socialist countries in different parts of the world, but it is also inconsistent with the policy of the government itself, when dealing with our neighbouring states.

Not only has South Africa concluded treaties with the Marxist states of Angola and Mozambique – quite rightly in our opinion – but she also wants to strengthen ties with Marxist Zimbabwe. The government will certainly find it difficult, if not altogether impossible, to reconcile its readiness to work with foreign Marxists for the peaceful resolution of mutual problems, with its uncompromising refusal to talk to South African Marxists.

The reason for this inconsistency is obvious. As I have already said, the government is still too deeply committed to the principle of white domination and, despite lip service to reform, it is deadly opposed to the sharing of political power with blacks, and the SACP is merely being used as a smokescreen to retain the monopoly of political power.

The smear campaign against the ANC also helps the government to evade the real issue at stake, namely, the exclusion from political power of the black majority by a white minority, which is the source of all our troubles.

Personal Position

Concerning my own personal position, I have already informed you that I will not respond to the government's demand that ANC members should state whether they are members of the SACP or not. But because much has been said by the media, as well as by government leaders regarding my political beliefs, I propose to use this opportunity to put the record straight. My political beliefs have been explained in the course of several political trials in which I was charged, in the policy documents of the ANC and in my autobiography, *The Struggle is My Life*, which I wrote in prison in 1975.[1] I stated in these trials and publications that I did not belong to any organisation apart from the ANC. In my address to the court which sentenced me to life in prison in June 1964, I said:

'Today I am attracted by the idea of a classless society, an attraction which springs in part from Marxist reading, and in part from my admiration of the structure and organisation of early African societies in this country.

'It is true, as I have already stated, that I have been influenced by Marxist thought. But this is also true of many leaders of the new independent states. Such widely different persons as Gandhi, Nehru, Nkrumah and Nasser all acknowledge this fact. We all accept the need for some form of socialism to enable our people to catch up with the advanced countries of the world, and to overcome their legacy of poverty.'

---

1. Mandela was under the impression that the autobiography which had been smuggled out of prison in 1976 had been published under this title. The autobiography under the title *Long Walk to Freedom* was published only in 1994.

My Views Still the Same

My views are still the same. Equally important is the fact that many ANC leaders who are labeled communists by the government, embrace nothing different from these beliefs. The term 'communist' when used by the government has a totally different meaning from the conventional one. Practically every freedom fighter who receives his military training or education in the socialist countries is, to the government, a communist.

It would appear to be established government policy that, as long as the National Party is in power in this country, there can be no black freedom struggle, and no black freedom fighter. Any black political organisation which, like us, fights for the liberation of its people through armed struggle, must invariably be dominated by the SACP.

This attitude is not only the result of government propaganda. It is a logical consequence of white supremacy. After more than 300 years of racial indoctrination, the country's whites have developed such deep-seated contempt for blacks as to believe that we cannot think for ourselves, that we are incapable of fighting for political rights without incitement by some white agitator.

In accusing the ANC of domination by the SACP, and in calling on ANC members to renounce the Party, the government is deliberately exploiting that contempt.

Majority Rule

The government is equally vehement in condemning the principle of majority rule. The principle is rejected despite the fact that it is a pillar of democratic rule in many countries of the world. It is a principle which is fully accepted in the white politics of this country.

Only now that the stark reality has dawned that apartheid has failed, and that blacks will one day have an effective voice in government, are we told by whites here, and by their Western friends, that majority rule is a disaster to be avoided at all costs. Majority rule is acceptable to whites as long as it is considered within the context of white politics.

If black political aspirations are to be accommodated, then some other formula must be found provided that formula does not raise blacks to a position of equality with whites.

Yet majority rule and internal peace are like the two sides of a single coin, and white South Africa simply has to accept that there will never be peace and stability in this country until the principle is fully applied.

It is precisely because of its denial that the government has become the enemy of practically every black man. It is that denial that has sparked off the current civil strife.

Negotiated Political Settlement

By insisting on compliance with the above-mentioned conditions before there can be talks, the government clearly confirms that it wants no peace in this country but turmoil; no strong and independent ANC, but a weak and servile organisation playing a supportive role to white minority rule, not a non-aligned ANC but one which is a satellite of the West, and which is ready to serve the interests of capitalism.

No worthy leaders of a freedom movement will ever submit to conditions which are essentially terms of surrender dictated by a victorious commander to a beaten enemy, and which are really intended to weaken the organisation and to humiliate its leadership.

The key to the whole situation is a negotiated settlement, and a meeting between the government and the ANC will be the first major step towards lasting peace in the country, better relations with our neighbour states, admission to the Organisation of African Unity, readmission to the United Nations and other world bodies, to international markets and improved international relations generally.

An accord with the ANC, and the introduction of a non-racial society, is the only way in which our rich and beautiful country will be saved from the stigma which repels the world.

Two central issues will have to be addressed at such a meeting; firstly, the demand for majority rule in a unitary state; secondly, the concern of white South Africa over this demand, as well as the insistence of whites on structural guarantees that majority rule will not mean domination of the white minority by blacks.

The most crucial task which will face the government and the ANC will be to reconcile these two positions. Such reconciliation will be achieved only if both parties are willing to compromise. The organisation will determine precisely how negotiations should be conducted. It may well be that this should be done at least in two stages. The first, where the organisation and the government will work out together the preconditions for a proper climate for negotiations. Up to now both parties have been broadcasting their conditions for negotiations without putting them directly to each other.

The second stage would be the actual negotiations themselves when the climate is ripe for doing so. Any other approach would entail the danger of an irresolvable stalemate.

Overcome the Current Deadlock

Lastly, I must point out that the move I have taken provides you with the opportunity to overcome the current deadlock, and to normalise the country's political situation. I hope you will seize it without delay. I believe that the overwhelming majority of South Africans, black and white, hope to see the ANC and the government working closely together to lay the foundations for a new era in our country, in which racial discrimination and prejudice, coercion and confrontation, death and destruction will be forgotten.

Nelson Mandela

ANNEXURE B

Constitutional Guidelines for a Democratic South Africa

Discussion paper published by the ANC in August 1988.

The Freedom Charter, adopted in 1955 by the Congress of the People at Kliptown near Johannesburg, was the first systematic statement in the history of our country of the political and constitutional vision of a free, democratic and non-racial South Africa.

The Freedom Charter remains today unique as the only South African document of its kind that adheres firmly to democratic principles as accepted throughout the world. Amongst South Africans it has become by far the most widely accepted programme for a post-apartheid country. The stage is now approaching where the Freedom Charter must be converted from a vision for the future into a constitutional reality.

We in the African National Congress submit to the people of South Africa, and all those throughout the world who wish to see an end to apartheid, our basic guidelines for the foundations of government in a post-apartheid South Africa. Extensive and democratic debate on these guidelines will mobilise the widest sections of our population to achieve agreement on how to put an end to the tyranny and oppression under which our people live, thus enabling them to lead normal and decent lives as free citizens in a free country.

The immediate aim is to create a just and democratic society that will sweep away the centuries-old legacy of colonial conquest and white domination, and abolish all laws imposing racial oppression and discrimination. The removal of discriminatory laws and eradication of all vestiges of the illegitimate regime are, however, not enough; the structures and institutions of apartheid must be dismantled and be replaced by democratic ones. Steps must be taken to ensure that apartheid ideas and practices are not permitted to appear in old forms or new.

In addition, the effects of centuries of racial discrimination and inequality must be overcome by constitutional provisions for corrective action which guarantees a rapid and irreversible redistribution of wealth and opening up of facilities to all. The constitution must also be such as to promote the habits of non-racial and non-sexist thinking, the practice of anti-racist behaviour and the acquisition of genuinely shared patriotic consciousness.

The constitution must give firm protection to the fundamental human rights of all citizens. There shall be equal rights for all individuals, irrespective of race, colour, sex or creed. In addition, it requires the entrenching of equal cultural, linguistic and religious rights for all.

Under the conditions of contemporary South Africa 87% of the land and 95% of the instruments of production of the country are in the hands of the ruling class, which is solely drawn from the white community. It follows, therefore, that constitutional protection for group rights would perpetuate the status quo and would mean that the mass of the people would continue to be constitutionally trapped in poverty and remain as outsiders in the land of their birth.

Finally, success of the constitution will be, to a large extent, determined by the degree to which it promotes conditions for the active involvement of all sectors of the population and at all levels in government and in the economic and cultural life. Bearing these fundamental objectives in mind, we declare that the elimination of apartheid and the creation of a truly just and democratic South Africa requires a constitution based on the following principles:

The State:

a) South Africa shall be an independent, unitary, democratic and non-racial state.

b) i. Sovereignty shall belong to the people as a whole and shall be exercised through one central legislature, executive and administration.

   ii. Provision shall be made for the delegation of the powers of the central authority to subordinate administrative units for purposes of more efficient administration and democratic participation.

c) The institution of hereditary rulers and chiefs shall be transformed to serve the interests of the people as a whole in conformity with the democratic principles embodied in the constitution.

d) All organs of government including justice, security and armed forces shall be representative of the people as a whole, democratic in their structure and functioning, and dedicated to defending the principles of the constitution.

Franchise

e) In the exercise of their sovereignty, the people shall have the right to vote under a system of universal suffrage based on the principle of one person, one vote.

f) Every voter shall have the right to stand for election and be elected to all legislative bodies.

National Identity

g) It shall be state policy to promote the growth of a single national identity and loyalty binding on all South Africans. At the same time, the state shall recognise the linguistic and cultural diversity of the people and provide facilities for free linguistic and cultural development.

A Bill of Rights and Affirmative Action

h) The constitution shall include a Bill of Rights based on the Freedom Charter. Such a Bill of Rights shall guarantee the fundamental human rights of all citizens irrespective of race, colour, sex or creed, and shall provide appropriate mechanism for their enforcement.

i) The state and all social institutions shall be under a constitutional duty to eradicate racial discrimination in all its forms.

j) The state and all social institutions shall be under a constitutional duty to take active steps to eradicate, speedily, the economic and social inequalities produced by racial discrimination.

k) The advocacy and practice of racism, fascism, nazism or the incitement of regional exclusiveness or hatred shall be outlawed.

l) Subject to clauses (i) and (k) above, the democratic state shall guarantee the basic rights and freedoms, such as freedom of association, expression, thought, worship and the press. Furthermore, the state shall have the duty to protect the right to work, and guarantee education and social security.

m) All parties which conform to the provision of paragraphs (i) to (k) shall have the legal right to exist and to take part in the political life of the country.

Economy

n) The state shall ensure that the entire economy serves the interests and well-being of all sections of the population.

o) The state shall have the right to determine the general context in which economic life takes place and define and limit the rights and obligations attaching to the ownership and use of productive capacity.

p) The private sector of the economy shall be obliged to co-operate with state in realising the objectives of the Freedom Charter in promoting the social well-being.

q) The economy shall be a mixed one, with a public sector, a private sector, a co-operative sector and a small-scale family sector.

r) Co-operative forms of economic enterprise, village industries and small-scale family activities should be supported by the state.

s) The state shall promote the acquisition of managerial, technical and scientific skills among all sections of the population, especially the blacks.

t) Property for personal use and consumption shall be constitutionally protected.

Land

u) The state shall devise and implement a Land Reform Programme that will include and address the following issues:

i. Abolition of all racial restrictions on ownership and use of land.

ii. Implementation of land reforms in conformity with the principle of Affirmative Action, taking into account the status of victims of forced removals.

Workers

v) A charter protecting workers' trade union rights, especially the right to strike and collective bargaining shall be incorporated into the constitution.

Women

w) Women shall have equal rights in all spheres of public and private life and the state shall take affirmative action to eliminate inequalities and discrimination between the sexes.

The Family

x) The family, parenthood and children's rights shall be protected.

International

y) South Africa shall be a non-aligned state committed to the principles of the Charter of the Organisation of African Unity and the Charter of the United Nations and to the achievements of national liberation, world peace and disarmament.

ANNEXURE C
Harare Declaration

Declaration of the Organisation of African Unity Ad-Hoc Committee on Southern Africa on the question of South Africa, Harare, Zimbabwe, 21 August 1989.

I. Preamble

1. The people of Africa, singly, collectively and acting through the OAU, are engaged in serious efforts to establish peace throughout the continent by ending all conflicts through negotiations based on the principle of justice and peace for all.

2. We reaffirm our conviction, which history confirms, that where colonial, racial and apartheid domination exists, there can neither be peace nor justice.

3. Accordingly, we reiterate that while the apartheid system in South Africa persists, the peoples of our continent as a whole cannot achieve the fundamental objectives of justice, human dignity and peace which are both crucial in themselves and fundamental to the stability and development of Africa.

4. With regard to the region of Southern Africa, the entire continent is vitally interested that the processes, in which it is involved, leading to the complete and genuine independence of Namibia, as well as peace in Angola and Mozambique, should succeed in the shortest possible time. Equally, Africa is deeply concerned that the destabilisation by South Africa of all the countries of the region, whether through direct aggression, sponsorship of surrogates, economic subversion and other means, should end immediately.

5. We recognise the reality that permanent peace and stability in Southern Africa can only be achieved when the system of apartheid in South Africa has been liquidated and South Africa transformed into a united, democratic and non-racial country. We therefore reiterate that

all the necessary measures should be adopted now, to bring a speedy end to the apartheid system, in the interest of all the people of Southern Africa, our continent and the world at large.

6. We believe that, as a result of the liberation struggle and international pressure against apartheid, as well as global efforts to liquidate regional conflicts, possibilities exist for further movement towards the resolution of the problems facing the people of South Africa. For these possibilities to lead to fundamental change in South Africa, the Pretoria regime must abandon its abhorrent concepts and practices of racial domination and its record of failure to honour agreements all of which have already resulted in the loss of lives and the destruction of much property in the countries of Southern Africa.

7. We reaffirm our recognition of the rights of all peoples, including those of South Africa, to determine their own destiny, and to work out for themselves the institutions and the system of government under which they will, by general consent, live and work together to build a harmonious society. The Organisation of African Unity remains committed to do everything possible and necessary, to assist the people of South Africa, in such ways as the representatives of the oppressed may determine, to achieve this objective. We are certain that, arising from this duty to help end the criminal apartheid system, the rest of the world community is ready to extend similar assistance to the people of South Africa.

8. We make these commitments because we believe that all people are equal and have equal rights to human dignity and respect, regardless of colour, race, sex or creed. We believe that all men and women have the right and duty to participate in their own government, as equal members of society. No individual or group of individuals has any rights to govern others without their consent. The apartheid system violates all these fundamental and universal principles. Correctly characterised as a crime against humanity, it is responsible for the death of countless numbers of people in South Africa, resulting in untold loss of life, destruction of property and massive displacement

of innocent men, women and children. This scourge and affront to humanity must be fought and eradicated in its totality.

9. We have therefore supported and continue to support all those in South Africa who pursue this noble objective through political, armed and other forms of struggle. We believe this to be our duty, carried out in the interest of all humanity.

10. While extending this support to those who strive for a non-racial and democratic society in South Africa, a point on which no compromise is possible, we have repeatedly expressed our preference to a solution arrived at by peaceful means. We know that the majority of the people of South Africa and their liberation movement, who have been compelled to take up arms, have also upheld this position for many decades and continue to do so.

11. The positions contained in this Declaration are consistent with and are a continuation of those elaborated in the Lusaka Manifesto, two decades ago. They take into account the changes that have taken place in South Africa since that Manifesto was adopted by the OAU and the rest of the international community. They constitute a new challenge to the Pretoria regime to join in the noble effort to end the apartheid system, an objective to which the OAU has been committed from its birth.

12. Consequently, we shall continue to do everything in our power to help intensify the liberation struggle and international pressure against the system of apartheid until this system is ended and South Africa is transformed into a united democratic and non-racial country, with justice and security for all its citizens.

13. In keeping with this solemn resolve, and responding to the wishes of the representatives of the majority of the people of South Africa, we publicly pledge ourselves to the positions contained hereunder. We are convinced that their implementation will lead to the speedy end of the apartheid system and therefore the opening of a new dawn of peace for all the peoples of Africa, in which racism, colonial domination and white minority rule on our continent would be abolished for ever.

II. Statement of Principles

14. We believe that a conjuncture of circumstances exists which, if there is a demonstrable readiness on the part of the Pretoria regime to engage in negotiations genuinely and seriously, could create the possibility to end apartheid through negotiations. Such an eventuality would be an expression of the long-standing preference of the people of South Africa to arrive at a political settlement.

15. We would therefore encourage the people of South Africa, as part of their overall struggle, to get together to negotiate an end to the apartheid system and agree on all the measures that are necessary to transform their country into a non-racial democracy. We support the position held by the majority of the people of South Africa that these objectives and not the amendment or reform of the apartheid system, should be the aims of the negotiations.

16. We are at one with them that the outcome of such a process should be a new constitutional order based on the following principles, among others:

    16.1. South Africa shall become a united, democratic and non-racial state.

    16.2. All its people shall enjoy common and equal citizenship and nationality, regardless of race, colour, sex or creed.

    16.3. All its people shall have the right to participate in the government and administration of the country on the basis of a universal suffrage, exercised through one person one vote, under a common voters roll.

    16.4. All people have the right to form and join any political party of their choice, provided that this is not in the furtherance of racism.

    16.5. All shall enjoy universally recognised human rights, freedoms and civil liberties, protected under an entrenched Bill of Rights.

    16.6. South Africa shall have a new legal system which shall guarantee equality of all before the law.

    16.7. South Africa shall have an independent and non-racial judiciary.

16.8. There shall be created an economic order which shall promote and advance the well-being of all South Africans.

16.9. A democratic South Africa shall respect the rights and sovereignty and territorial integrity of all countries and pursue a policy of peace, friendship and mutually beneficial co-operation with all people.

17. We believe that the agreement on the principles shall continue the foundation for an internationally acceptable solution which shall enable South Africa to take its rightful place as an equal partner among the African and world community of nations.

III. Climate for Negotiations

18. Together with the rest of the world, we believe that it is essential, before any negotiations take place, that the necessary climate for negotiations be created. The apartheid regime has the urgent responsibility to respond positively to this universally acclaimed demand and thus create this climate.

19. Accordingly, the present regime should, at the very least:

19.1. Release all political prisoners and detainees unconditionally and refrain from imposing any restrictions on them.

19.2. Lift all bans and restrictions on all proscribed and restricted organisations and people.

19.3. Remove all troops from the townships.

19.4. End the state of emergency and repeal all legislation, such as, and including, the Internal Security Act, designed to circumscribe political activity.

19.5. Cease all political executions.

20. These measures are necessary to produce the conditions in which free discussion can take place – an essential condition to ensure that the people themselves participate in the process of remaking their country. The measures listed above should therefore precede negotiations.

IV. Guidelines to the Process of Negotiation

21. We support the view of the South African liberation movement that upon the creation of this climate, the process of negotiations should commence along the following lines:

   21.1. Discussions should take place between the liberation movement and the South African regime to achieve the suspension of hostilities on both sides by agreeing to a mutually binding cease fire.

   21.2. Negotiations should then proceed to establish the basis for the adoption of a new Constitution by agreeing on among, others, the Principles enunciated above.

   21.3. Having agreed on these Principles, the parties should then negotiate the necessary mechanism for drawing up the new Constitution.

   21.4. The parties shall define and agree on the role to be played by the international community in ensuring a successful transition to a democratic order.

   21.5. The parties shall agree on the formation of an interim government to supervise the process of the drawing up and adoption of a new constitution; govern and administer the country, as well as effect the transition to a democratic order including the holding of the elections.

   21.6. After the adoption of the new Constitution, all armed hostilities will be deemed to have formally terminated.

   21.7. For its part, the international community would lift the sanctions that have been imposed against apartheid South Africa.

22. The new South Africa shall qualify for the membership of the Organisation of African Unity.

V. Programme of Action

23. In pursuance of the objectives stated in this document, Organisation of African Unity hereby commits itself to:

   23.1. Inform governments and inter-governmental organisations throughout the world, including the Non-Aligned Movement, the United Nations General Assembly, the Security Council, the Commonwealth and others of these perspectives, and solicit their support.

23.2. Mandate the OAU ad-hoc committee on Southern Africa, acting as the representative of the OAU, assisted by the Frontline States, to remain seized of the issue of a political resolution to the South Africa question.

23.3. Step up all-round support for the South African liberation movement and campaign in the rest of the world in pursuance of this objective.

23.4. Intensify the campaign for mandatory and comprehensive sanctions against apartheid South Africa; in this regard, immediately mobilise against the re-scheduling of Pretoria's foreign debts; work for the imposition of a mandatory oil embargo and the full observance by all countries of the arms embargo.

23.5. Ensure that the African continent does not relax existing measures for the total isolation of apartheid South Africa.

23.6. Continue to monitor the situation in Namibia and extend all necessary support to SWAPO in its struggle for a genuinely independent Namibia.

23.7. Extend such assistance as the Governments of Angola and Mozambique may request in order to secure peace for their people.

23.8. Render all possible assistance to the Frontline States to enable them to withstand Pretoria's campaign of aggression and destabilisation and enable them to continue to give their all-round support to the people of Namibia and South Africa.

24. We appeal to all people of goodwill throughout the world to support this Programme of Action as a necessary measure to secure the earliest liquidation of the apartheid system and the transformation of South Africa into a united, democratic and non-racial country.

Bibliography

Books

Barnard, Niël. *Peaceful Revolution: Inside the War Room at the Negotiations.* Cape Town: Tafelberg, 2017.

————. *Secret Revolution: Memoirs of a Spy Boss.* Cape Town: Tafelberg, 2015.

Baskin, Jeremy. *Striking Back: A History of COSATU.* Johannesburg: Ravan Press, 1991.

Bell, Terry, and Dumisa Buhle Ntsebeza. *Unfinished Business: South Africa, Apartheid and Truth.* London: Verso, 2003.

Callinicos, Luli. *Oliver Tambo: Beyond the Engeli Mountains.* Cape Town: David Philip, 2004.

Cooper, Carole, et al. *Survey of Race Relations in South Africa: 1985.* Johannesburg: SAIRR, 1986.

De Klerk, F.W. *The Last Trek – A New Beginning: The Autobiography.* London: Macmillan, 1999.

De Villiers, Riaan, and Stemmet, Jan-Ad. *Prisoner 913 – The Release of Nelson Mandela,* Cape Town: Tafelberg, 2020.

Esterhuyse, Willie. *Endgame: Secret Talks and the End of Apartheid.* Cape Town: Tafelberg, 2012.

————, and Gerhard van Niekerk. *Die Tronkgespreke.* Cape Town: Tafelberg, 2018.

Gerhart, Gail M., and Clive L. Glaser (eds). *From Protest to Challenge: A Documentary History of African Politics in South Africa, 1882–1990,* vol. 6: *Challenge and Victory, 1980–1990.* Bloomington: Indiana University Press, 2010.

207

Gevisser, Mark. *Thabo Mbeki: The Dream Deferred.* Johannesburg: Jonathan Ball, 2007.

Giliomee, Hermann. *The Last Afrikaner Leaders.* Cape Town: Tafelberg, 2012.

Groenink, Evelyn. *Incorruptible: The Story of the Murders of Dulcie September, Anton Lubowski and Chris Hani.* Johannesburg: Jacana, 2018.

Harrison, David. *The White Tribe of Africa: South Africa in Perspective.* Berkeley: University of California Press, 1981.

Jenkin, Tim. *Inside Out: Escape from Pretoria Prison.* Johannesburg: Jacana, 2003.

Jordan, Z. Pallo. *Letters to My Comrades.* Johannesburg: Jacana, 2017.

Karis, Thomas G., and Gail M. Gerhart (eds). *From Protest to Challenge: A Documentary History of African Politics in South Africa 1881–1964*, vol. 2: *Hope and Challenge, 1935–1952.* Stanford: Hoover Institution Press, 1973.

———, *From Protest to Challenge: A Documentary History of African Politics in South Africa, 1882–1990*, vol. 5: *Nadir and Resurgence, 1964–1979.* Bloomington: Indiana University Press, 1997.

Klug, Heinz. *Constituting Democracy: Law, Globalism and South Africa's Political Reconstruction.* Cambridge: Cambridge University Press, 2000.

Lipton, Merle. *Capitalism and Apartheid: South Africa 1910–1986.* New Jersey: Rowman and Allanheld, 1985.

Macmillan, Hugh. *The Lusaka Years: The ANC in Exile in Zambia, 1963 to 1994.* Johannesburg: Jacana, 2013.

Maharaj, Mac (ed.). *Reflections in Prison: Voices from the South African Liberation Struggle.* Cape Town: Zebra Press, 2001.

Mandela, Nelson. *Long Walk to Freedom.* Johannesburg: Macdonald Purnell, 1994.

Matisonn, John. *God, Spies and Lies: Finding South Africa's Future Through its Past.* Vlaeberg: Missing Ink, 2015.

Mzala. *Gatsha Buthelezi: Chief with a Double Agenda.* London: Zed Books, 1988.

Ndlovu, Sifiso Mxolisi, and Miranda Strydom (eds). *The Thabo Mbeki I Know*. Johannesburg: Picador Africa, 2016.

O'Malley, Padraig. *Shades of Difference: Mac Maharaj and the Struggle for South Africa*. New York: Penguin, 2007.

O'Meara, Dan. *Forty Lost Years: The Apartheid State and the Politics of the National Party, 1948–1994*. Johannesburg: Ravan Press, 1996.

Papenfus, Theresa. *Pik Botha and His Times*. Pretoria: Litera, 2010.

Price, Robert M., and Carl Gustav Rosberg (eds). *The Apartheid Regime: Political Power and Racial Domination*. Berkeley: Institute of International Studies, University of California, 1980.

SADET. *The Road to Democracy in South Africa*, vol. 1, *1960–1970*. Pretoria: UNISA Press, 2014.

————. *The Road to Democracy in South Africa*, vol. 2, *1970–1980*. Pretoria: UNISA Press, 2014.

Sampson, Anthony. *Mandela: The Authorised Biography*. London: HarperCollins, 1999.

Seekings, Jeremy, *The UDF: A History of the United Democratic Front in South Africa 1983–1991*. Cape Town: David Philip, 2000.

Shubin, Vladimir. *ANC: A View from Moscow*. Cape Town: Mayibuye Books, UWC, nd.; *The Hot 'Cold War': The USSR in Southern Africa*. London: Pluto Press, 2008.

Sparks, Allister. *Tomorrow Is Another Country: The Inside Story of South Africa's Negotiated Revolution*. Sandton: Struik Book Distributors, 1994.

TRC. *Report of the Truth and Reconciliation Commission*, vol. 2.

Veloso, Jacinto. *Memories at Low Altitude: The Autobiography of a Mozambican Security Chief*. Cape Town: Zebra Press, 2012.

Articles, journals and documents

'A submission on the question of negotiations', 27 November 1985. Document 129 in Gerhart and Glaser (eds), *From Protest to Challenge*, vol. 6: 589.

ANC submissions to the TRC: (1) 'ANC statement to the Truth and Reconciliation Commission', dated August 1996; (2) 'Umkhonto we

Sizwe operations report' in 'Further submissions and responses by the ANC to questions raised by the Commission for Truth and Reconciliation', dated 12 May 1997.

'Basiese staatkundige voorwaardes vir die voortbestaan van die Afrikaner' (Basic political policy conditions for the survival of the Afrikaner), in the Erfenisstigting Archive, ref. AB 10/32/2/1, Voortrekker Monument.

Cherry, Janet. 'No easy road to truth: The TRC in the Eastern Cape'. Paper presented at the Wits History Workshop – The TRC: Commissioning the Past, 11–14 June 1999.

Claiborne, William. 'Prisoners returned in 4-way swap'. *Washington Post*, 8 September 1987.

Clur, Colleen Gaye Ryan. 'From acquiescence to dissent: Beyers Naude 1915–1977'. MA thesis, UNISA, June 1997.

Cowell, Alan. 'South African president warns of further raids'. *New York Times*, 22 May 1986.

Dash, Samuel. 'A rare talk with Nelson Mandela'. *New York Times Magazine*, 7 July 1985.

Diseko, Nozipho T. 'The origins and development of the South African Students' Movement (SASM)'. *Journal of Southern African Studies* 18, no. 1 (March 1992): 40–62.

Dunbar Moodie, T. '"Cyril's eyes lit up." Roelf Meyer, Francois Venter, the Afrikaner Broederbond and the decision to abandon "group rights" in favour of a "regstaat" (constitutional state)'. Unpublished paper, 2012.

Edwards, Karl. 'Three volume study of Mac Maharaj for NIS'. Mayibuye Centre, Cape Town.

'Europeans give Botha a frosty visit'. *New York Times*, 10 June 1984.

Hansard parliamentary records, 31 January 1985.

Harden, Blaine. 'S. African businessmen meet with exiled guerrilla leaders'. *Washington Post*, 14 September 1985.

Haysom, Nicholas. 'Mabangalala: The rise of right-wing vigilantes'. Occasional paper no. 10. Centre for Applied Legal Studies, University of the Witwatersrand, 1986.

Kairos Document, 'Challenge to the church: A theological comment on the political crisis in South Africa', dated 25 September 1985. Available at https://www.sahistory.org.za/archive/challenge-church-theological -comment-political-crisis-south-africa-kairos-document-1985.

Lawrence, Ralph. Review of *Mission to South Africa: The Commonwealth Report – The Findings of the Eminent Persons Group on South Africa*. Harmondsworth: Penguin Books for the Commonwealth Secretariat, 1986.

Leatt, James. 'Fattis and Monis dispute: A case study of the role of pressure groups in labour relations'. First presented at the Unit for Futures Research Seminar, Stellenbosch, September 1980. *Reality* 13, no. 5 (September 1981): 13–17.

'Letter from British Prime Minister Margaret Thatcher to South African President PW Botha, October 31 1985'. Available at https://www.politicsweb.co.za/documents/free-nelson-mandela --margaret-thatcher.

Lewis, David. 'Black workers and trade unions', in Karis and Gerhart, *From Protest to Challenge*, vol. 5: 197.

Mark Gevisser Collection, South African History Archive, AL3284, G.190.

Mbeki, Thabo. 'Steve Biko: 30 years after', in Chris van Wyk (ed.), *We Write What We Like*. Johannesburg: Wits University Press, 2007: 21–41.

'Memorandum to the NEC by the Constitution Committee, September 20, 1986', in the ANC Collection, Lusaka/London, Box 042, Folder 1, University of Fort Hare Archives.

Michael Young Papers, Borthwick Institute for Archives, University of York, ref. UOY.

O'Malley Archive. 'Chronology of some pointers to the history of the media in South Africa'. Available at https://omalley.nelsonmandela .org/omalley/index.php/site/q/03lv02167/04lv02264/05lv02303/06lvo 2329/07lv02330.htm.

Press statement by General Council of SARU, issued after its meeting held in Cape Town on 10 and 11 September 1988. Available at

http://www.historicalpapers.wits.ac.za/inventories/inv_pdf0/AG3403/
    AG3403-A1-2-6-004-jpeg.pdf.

'Report by Commonwealth Eminent Persons Group on meeting with
    ANC representatives in Lusaka, May 17, 1985'. Document 134 in
    Gerhart and Glaser (eds), *From Protest to Challenge*, vol. 6: 599–601.

'Report of the Politico-military Strategy Commission to the ANC NEC',
    1979 (referred to as the Green Book).

Shandler, David. 'Structural crisis and liberalism: A history of the
    Progressive Federal Party 1981–1989'. MA thesis, UCT, 1990.

Simons Papers, UCT.

Smith, Kathryn, Chandré Gould and Brian Rappert (curators). *Poisoned
    Pasts: Legacies of South Africa's Chemical and Biological Warfare
    Programme.* Exhibition at the Nelson Mandela Foundation,
    Johannesburg, November 2016.

South African Labour Bulletin, various issues.

Steinberg, Jonny. 'Poring over Mandela's words, apartheid's apparatchiks
    learnt sweet nothing'. *Business Day,* 29 October 2020.

Tambo, Oliver. "'South Africa at the Crossroads", Canon Collins
    Memorial Lecture by Oliver Tambo, London, 28 May 1987'. Available
    at https://www.sahistory.org.za/archive/south-africa-crossroads-canon
    -collins-memorial-lecture-oliver-tambo-london-28-may-1987. Also
    published in *Review of African Political Economy* 14, no. 40 (1987).

Trew, Tony. Notes of the Mells Park Talks, 1987–1990. Meetings held in
    (1) October/November 1987; (2) February 1988; (3) August 1988;
    (4) August 1988; (5) December 1988; (6) April 1989; (7) September
    1989; (8) February 1990; and (9) June 1990. Copy in possession of
    Mac Maharaj.

Van der Merwe, Hendrik. 'Facilitation and mediation in South Africa: Three
    case studies'. *Emory International Law Review* 11, no. 1 (Spring 1997).

Vula communications, in maharaj/vula comms.

Williams, Paul D. 'Intellectuals and the end of apartheid: Critical security
    studies and the South African transition'. PhD thesis, University of
    Wales, 2001.

About the Authors

Mac Maharaj, born 22 April 1935, has been active in the freedom struggle since 1953. From 1955 to 1957, he served as a reporter for the weekly *New Age* and managed its Durban office in 1957. He joined the SACP in 1958 and was a member of the Central Committee and the Politburo when he left the organisation at the end of 1990.

In the United Kingdom, he was a founding member and subsequently secretary of the South African Freedom Association. He was also a founding member of the Anti-Apartheid Movement. He underwent training in printing and sabotage in the German Democratic Republic from March 1961 to March 1962. He was deployed full-time from 1961 to 1994.

Maharaj was sentenced to twelve years' imprisonment in December 1964, which he served in Robben Island prison. In 1976, he was involved in the writing and smuggling out of prison of the first draft of Nelson Mandela's autobiography. Upon his release from prison, he was banned and placed under house arrest. He went into exile in July 1977 and was appointed secretary of the newly established Internal Political and Reconstruction Department of the ANC in December 1977. He was co-opted to the Revolutionary Council and its successor, the Politico-Military Council.

In 1985, Maharaj was elected to the National Executive Committee of the ANC. The following year, he was appointed by ANC president Oliver Tambo to lead Operation Vula, during the course of which he entered South Africa clandestinely in July 1988. He was arrested in July 1990. In December 1991 he was appointed joint secretary of CODESA, and he served as one of the joint secretaries of the Transitional Executive Council in 1994. He was appointed minister of transport in the first democratic executive led by President Mandela. At the end of its term, in 1999, he retired from active involvement, relinquished all his positions in the ANC and has remained an ordinary member since that time.

In 2011, he was appointed spokesperson for President Jacob Zuma, and retired from this position in April 2015.

In 2001, Maharaj edited *Reflections in Prison*, a collection of essays written in 1976 by several prisoners in the single cells section of Robben Island prison. His biography, *Shades of Difference: Mac Maharaj and the Struggle for South Africa*, by Padraig O'Malley, was published in 2007. He has participated in several publications, including *Mandela: The Authorised Portrait*.

Zweledinga Pallo Jordan was born on 22 May 1942 in Kroonstad in the Orange Free State and grew up in Cape Town. He became active in politics, selling movement newspapers at an early age, and became a member of the Cape Peninsula Students' Union and later the Modern Youth Society as a teenager.

After being inducted into uMkhonto weSizwe in 1972, he was deployed as a political instructor for MK in 1976 and took the MK oath at Funda Special Operations Camp outside Luanda in January 1979. From 1975 he also served in the ANC's Department of Information and Publicity as head of research on a full-time basis.

He was appointed head of Radio Freedom in 1977 and director of the ANC's first internal mass propaganda campaign, 'The Year of the Spear', in 1979, marking the centenary of the 1879 Battle of Isandlwana.

Elected to the ANC National Executive Committee in 1985, he served as administrative secretary of the NEC secretariat from 1985 to 1988; as convenor of the NEC's Strategy and Tactics Committee; and on the NEC's subcommittees on Negotiations and Constitutional Guidelines. In 1989, he was deployed as director of information and publicity.

Jordan accompanied Oliver Tambo, Mac Maharaj, Chris Hani, Thabo Mbeki and James Stuart to the meeting between white business leaders and the ANC at the Luangwa game reserve, Zambia, in 1986. He also formed part of the ANC's delegations to the IDASA-sponsored Dakar (1987) and Paris (1989) conferences.

He returned to South Africa in June 1990 and was re-elected to the NEC in 1991, at the ANC's first national conference held inside the country in thirty years, and again in 1996, 2002, 2007 and 2012.

He served as a minister in South Africa's democratic government from 1994 until 2009.

Index

Ackerman, Raymond 106
African Americans 23, 35, 60–61
'African Claims in South Africa' 98
African National Congress *see* ANC
Afrikaner Broederbond *see* Broederbond
Afrikaner business sector 11, 26, 32–33
Afrikaners 5, 32, 73, 81
Agnew, Rudolph 126–127
All-in African Conference 3–4
Al-Qalam 149
alternative facts *see* misinformation
AmaAfrika National Front 56 n9
America *see* USA
ANC
    All-in African Conference 3–4
    Angola and 18–19
    annual January 8 statements 45–47, 133
    armed struggle 2–5, 8–10, 15–16, 19, 36,
        48, 85–87, 107–110, 113–117, 152, 158,
        162, 167–169
    Black Consciousness Movement and
        38 n5, 45
    Conference Towards a Democratic
        South Africa 162
    Congress of the People 3
    Constitutional Commission 99–101,
        132–134, 137, 163, 193–197
    democratic practice in 135
    dynamics within 78, 134–135, 138–139,
        141
    in exile 7–8, 39–40, 135, 142
    'four pillars of struggle' 15–16, 37
    'Green Book' 37 n3, 45–46
    Groote Schuur talks 1, 4
    Harare Declaration 59, 126, 160–165,
        167–168, 199–205
    Inkatha and 36, 78

    international community and 48, 60–61,
        76, 110, 112–114, 117, 135–136, 145, 161
    IPRD 45–46
    Kabwe Conference (1985) 75–76, 90–91,
        102–103
    Lusaka Manifesto 10
    media coverage 159
    misinformation about 51, 135
    Morogoro Conference (1969) 44–45
    Mozambique and 18–19
    National Convention Alliance and 106
    National Forum conference 38
    NEC 23, 45, 100–101, 132–134, 136–137,
        140
    'New face of counter-revolution, The'
        (paper) 98–99, 132
    Nkomati Accord 58, 71, 97
    NSC and 151
    NWC (National Working Committee)
        81–82, 100–101, 109, 112–113, 132, 135,
        140–141, 144, 162
    OAU and 23
    political prisoners 168
    protests 15, 40, 157
    'Question of Negotiations, The'
        136–137
    Revolutionary Council 45, 139–140
    SACP and 78, 174
    sports boycotts 141–146
    Swaziland and 57
    'talks about talks' 67–68, 74–76, 78–82,
        101–105, 107–108, 116–118, 121, 129–131,
        152, 155–156, 168–170, 177
    TRC 8, 30 n6, 52
    see also MK
Anglo American 11, 67, 104
Angola 17–19, 57–59, 72, 75, 155–156

anti-apartheid movements 23, 60–61, 71, 150
apartheid 4, 7, 11–14, 22
APCs (Area Political Committees) 139–140
armed struggle 2–5, 8–10, 15–16, 19, 36, 48, 85–87, 90–91, 107–110, 113–117, 152, 158, 162, 167–169
arms trade 23
Art of Counter-Revolutionary War, The 28
assassinations 51–56
Association of European Parliamentarians with Africa 60
Ayob, Ismail 88
Azanian People's Organisation see AZAPO
Azanian Students' Organisation 35–36
AZAPO 35, 38

Ball, Chris 106
Bantu Education system 20–21
bantustans (homelands) 16–17, 31, 39, 50, 55, 57, 67–69, 77–78, 148
Barayi, Elijah 44
Barclays Bank 158
Barnard, Niël 72 n2, 74, 82–83, 116, 123–124, 127–131, 139, 151–154, 158, 167–169, 171, 173
'Basic political policy conditions for the survival of the Afrikaner' 127
Basson, Wouter 53–55
Beaufré, Andre 28
Bedford, Tommy 141–142
Beeld 79–80, 139, 159
Bethell, Lord 85–87
Bhengu, Sibusiso 67
Biko, Steve 21, 23, 25, 38 n5, 45, 52
Bill of Rights 69, 98–99, 164, 175
biological weapons see chemical and biological weapons
Bizos, George 120
Black Allied Workers' Union 43
Black Community Programmes 21
Black Consciousness Movement 15, 20–22, 35–36, 38, 43, 45, 61
'black-on-black' violence 21 n10, 56
Black People's Convention see BPC
Bloom, Tony 70, 78 n9, 104, 106

Boesak, Allan 38, 150, 161
bomb explosions 47–49, 52, 90
Boraine, Alex 107
Boshoff, Carel 64
BOSS 19, 74
Botha, Pik 1, 5, 73, 93–94, 116–117
Botha, P.W.
    Angola and 19, 155–156
    Broederbond and 64, 73
    business sector and 32–33
    chemical and biological weapons 53
    Commonwealth of Nations 110–111
    EPG and 114–115, 117
    Europe, tour of 73, 76
    labour relations 27
    as leader 28, 70
    Nelson Mandela and 76–78, 82–84, 87–89, 151–157, 163, 177, 181–192
    Nkomati Accord 58, 73–75
    NSC 148
    nuclear weapons programme 51
    reforms to apartheid system 31, 64–65, 69–70, 94–95, 148–151
    resignations of 154, 157
    SSC 29–30
    strategies of 16–17, 28–31, 44, 50–51, 71, 75–76, 78–81, 90, 107, 120, 147–148, 154–155, 159
    'talks about talks' 70, 79, 116, 123–124, 127–130, 151–152, 155–156
Botswana 49–50, 91–92
boycotts 39, 42–43, 60, 71–72, 90, 138, 144–146
    see also sports boycotts
BPC 21, 38 n5
Braam, Conny 55
Britain see UK
Broederbond 11–14, 16 n3, 25–26, 32, 63–65, 73, 79, 120–121, 127, 142, 172–175
Brutus, Dennis 146
Bureau of State Security see BOSS
Burger, Die 177–178
business sector 11, 14, 26, 32–33, 64, 66–70, 73, 104–106, 108, 126–127
Buthelezi Commission 69–70
Buthelezi, Mangosuthu Gatsha 36, 67–70, 77–78, 105–106, 151

cabinet bosberaad, December 1989
170–171, 176–177
Calata, Fort 52
Cape Action League 37
Cape Times 108–110
Cape Town Municipal Workers'
Association 42
Carolus, Cheryl 1
Chase Manhattan Bank 93–94
chemical and biological weapons 53–55
Chikane, Frank 55, 150
Chissano, Joaquim 155
Christian Institute of Southern Africa
12, 21
churches 40–41, 90, 150
cinema, attack on 52
Ciskei 77, 156
Citizen, The 27
Civil Cooperation Bureau 52
Claasen, Jonathan 92
Coetsee, Kobie 1, 77, 84–85, 89, 114, 116,
119–124, 137, 151–154, 157–158, 167–169,
171, 173
Coetzee, Dirk 54
Cohen, Hank 161
Cold War 75
colonialism 7
Coloured community 25–26, 31, 50, 63–64,
71–72, 147
Commonwealth of Nations 24, 110–114, 157
communication 138, 164
Comprehensive Anti-Apartheid Act (USA)
61, 94–95, 117
compulsory military service
see conscription
Conference for a Democratic Future 169
Conference Towards a Democratic South
Africa 162
conglomerates 26, 32–33, 64
Congress Alliance 44–45
Congress of South African Students 35
Congress of South African Trade Unions
see COSATU
Congress of the People 3
Conscientious Objectors Campaign 90
conscription 19, 92–93
Conservative Party 64–65, 73 n3, 157

Consolidated Gold Fields 127–129
Constellation of Southern African States 32
Constitutional Commission, ANC 99–101,
132–134
'Constitutional Guidelines for a
Democratic South Africa' 132–134, 137,
163, 193–197
Constitutional Policy Committee,
Broederbond 172–175
Consultative Conference of African
Leaders 3
'contact group' 59
co-option strategy 15, 17, 25, 31, 50, 67, 122,
137, 147, 159
Coordinating Intelligence Committee
115–116
Coovadia, Jerry 106
Coronation Brick and Tile factory 16
COSATU 17, 35, 44, 90, 132, 150, 157,
162
Council of Unions of South Africa
see CUSA
'Cradock Four' 52
Craven, Danie 141–143
cricket 13
Crisis News 149
Crocker, Chester 112
Cuba 18, 61, 72
Culture in Another South Africa arts
festival 145
CUSA 43

Dakar Conference 81, 139, 142
Dar es Salaam Declaration 23
Dash, Samuel 85, 86–87
deaths in detention 7, 10, 21
De Beer, Zach 104, 106
Defiance Campaign 2–3
De Jonge, Klaas 55, 90, 155–156
De Klerk, F.W. 1–2, 4–6, 51, 116, 131, 149,
154–157, 167–178
De Klerk, Jan 2
De Klerk, Wimpie 172
De Lange, Jan Pieter 65, 73, 120–121, 173,
175
Delport, Tertius 173
democracy 5, 133–135, 163, 177–178

Democratic Party 157
Department of Home Affairs 80–81
Detainees' Parents Support Committee 36, 90
détente, policy of 10–11, 19, 74
detention facilities, ANC 75
detention without trial 7, 10, 21, 51, 149
De Villiers, Dawie 1
De Villiers, Fleur 127
Dhlakama, Afonso 57
Dippenaar, Möller 127
disinformation 25, 75–76, 83
divide and rule, tactic of 25, 31, 159
'division of power' 28, 70
divisions 12, 17, 78, 138–139, 141
Dlamini, Enoch 55
Dlamini, Peter 54
Duduza activists, attack on 91
Dunbar Moodie, T. 172, 173–174
Du Plessis, Barend 1, 93
Du Preez, Jan 54
Durban Housing Action Committee 37
Durban-Pinetown industrial complex 15–16
Dutch Reformed Church 12
Du Toit, Wynand 82, 155

ECC 90, 92–93, 149
economic growth 14, 16–17, 31–32, 71
education 15, 20–21
Eglin, Colin 66, 67, 68, 69
elections 11, 25–26, 39–40, 148–151, 155, 157, 176
Eminent Persons Group *see* EPG
End Conscription Campaign *see* ECC
Endgame 128
EPG 111–117, 120–121, 135–136, 137, 147
Esterhuyse, Willie 79, 116, 123, 127–131, 152, 175
Eximbank loans 24

false information *see* misinformation
Fatti's & Moni's 42–43
Federation of South African Trade Unions *see* FOSATU
Federation of South African Women 36
First, Ruth 52

FLS (Frontline States) 59, 71, 97, 112, 126, 161–162
FNLA 18
Food and Canning Workers' Union 42
FOSATU 41–43
'four pillars of struggle' 15–16, 37
France 59, 73–74, 156
Fraser, Malcolm 116–117
Freedom Charter 3, 35, 44, 98, 100
Free Mandela Campaign 76–77
front companies 51, 53
Frontline States (FLS) 59, 71, 97, 112, 126, 161–162
funerals of activists 40

Gaborone, raid on 91
Gazankulu bantustan 68
General and Allied Workers Union 43
General Law Amendment Act 9
General Mining Corporation 11
General Workers Union 42
Gerhart, Gail 150, 153
Germany 59, 71
Giliomee, Hermann 95
Glaser, Clive 150, 153
Gleneagles Agreement 24
Goniwe, Matthew 52
Good Hope Conference 32
government debt 93
Gqabi, Joe 48–49, 52
Graaff, Sir De Villiers 4
'Green Book' 37 n3, 45–46
Groenewald, Tienie 115–116
Groote Schuur talks 1–2, 4–5, 172
group rights 133, 158, 175–176
'Gugulethu Seven' 92
Gumede, Archie 1, 39
Gwala, Harry 122, 160

Hadebe, Moffat 8
Hani, Chris 140–141
Harare Declaration 59, 126, 160–165, 167–168, 199–205
Heard, Tony 11, 108–110
Heunis, Chris 56, 70
Heyns, Johan 162
Home Guards 55

homelands *see* bantustans
hospitals, protests in 157
Houston, Gregory 8–9, 10
Howe, Geoffrey 158
human rights 133
Huntington, Samuel 28, 30

IDASA 138, 142
India 61
Indian community 25–26, 31, 37, 50,
    63–64, 71–72, 147
industrial relations 16, 27
Information Scandal 27
Ingwavuma district 57
Inkatha 36, 52 n2, 67–68, 77–78
Institute for Contextual Theology 40–41
Institute for Democratic Alternatives in
    South Africa *see* IDASA
International Campaign Against Apartheid
    Sport 146
international community 17, 22–23, 27,
    35, 72–73, 85–87, 93–95, 135–136,
    157–158, 161
International Confederation of Free Trade
    Unions 22
International Olympic Committee 13
International Solidarity Conference 145
Ismail, Aboobaker (aka Rashid) 48
Italy 60, 61, 73–74

Jenkin, Tim 9
JMCs (Joint Management Centres) 29–30,
    51–52
Joint Rent Action Committee 37
Jordan, Pallo 97–100, 132

'Kairos Document' 40–41
KaNgwane bantustan 57
Kathrada, Ahmed 1, 84–85, 167
Kaunda, Kenneth 104, 155, 157, 162–163
Kissinger, Henry 94
kitskonstabels ('special constables') 56
Koeberg nuclear power station 49
Kohl, Helmut 71, 155
Kruger, Koos 127
KwaMakhutha massacre 52
KwaZulu bantustan 68–69, 77

labour 26–27, 31–32
Labour Party 68, 148
Lancaster House talks 112
Last Afrikaner Leaders, The 95
Lawrence, Ralph 116–117
Lebowa bantustan 68
Lee, Stephen 9
Le Grange, Louis 77
Lesotho 49–50, 92
Liberal Party 3 n4, 66
Lombard report 69–70
Loots, Hermanus (aka James Stuart)
    97–98
Louw, Mike 123, 169
Lubane, Petrus 54
Lusaka Accord 72
Lusaka Manifesto 10
Luthuli, Albert 8
Luyt, Louis 27, 141–144

Machel, Samora 57–58, 71, 92 n44, 97
Madaka, Topsy 54
Magmoed, Shaun 92
Maharaj, Mac 160–161, 164
Mail on Sunday 85
majority rule 67, 125–126, 153, 177
Makana, Simon (aka Nkokheli) 97–98
Makatini, Johnny 112–113
Malan, D.F. 2–3
Malan, Magnus 28
Malan, Wynand 78–79
Mamasela, Joe 54–55, 91
'Mandela document' 124–126, 163, 177,
    181–192
Mandela, Nelson
    on armed struggle 3–4, 22, 87–89, 110,
        167
    P.W. Botha and 76–78, 82–84, 87–89,
        151–157, 163, 177, 181–192
    EPG and 114
    Groote Schuur talks 1, 4–5
    Harare Declaration 126
    hospitalisation 119
    MDM and 164, 168
    memo to P.W. Botha 124–126, 163, 177,
        181–192
    NUM and 44

Operation Vula 159–160, 162
in Pollsmoor Prison 84–87, 119–120
as president 2
release 2, 60, 76–78, 84, 137, 147, 167
'talks about talks' 79, 116, 119–126,
    152–154, 157–158, 167–169, 171, 174
Mandela, Winnie 9, 88, 137
Mandela, Zindzi 88
manufacturing industry 26
Māori rugby players and spectators 13, 73 n3
Marais, Kowie 66
Masemola, Jafta 167
mass arrests 21–22
Mass Democratic Movement see MDM
mass mobilisation 15–16, 20–21, 36–37,
    45–46, 139–140, 157
Matola Raid 49
Mavuso, Selby 54
Mbeki, Govan 84–85, 122, 152, 158, 160
Mbeki, Thabo 1, 78–80, 97–98, 103–105,
    108, 112–113, 116, 129–130, 140–142, 152,
    159, 173
McCuen, J.J. 28
MDM 17, 106, 150–151, 157, 160, 162, 164,
    168–169
media coverage 9, 33, 52, 56, 75, 94–95, 132,
    149, 159 n16
Mells Park talks 116, 126–132, 137, 151–152,
    158, 163, 169, 171–172, 174
Mennell, Clive 70
Meyer, Roelf 1, 172–173
Mhlaba, Raymond 84–85, 167
Mhlauli, Sicelo 52
migrant labour 16, 26
military raids see raids, cross-border
mining sector 11, 26
minority rights 158, 170, 177
Miranda, Michael 92
misinformation 25, 51, 139
MK 1, 4, 7–10, 18–19, 40, 47–50, 53, 61,
    90–91, 147
    see also ANC
Mkhatshwa, Smangaliso 150
Mkonto, Sparrow 52
Mkwayi, Wilton 167
Mlangeni, Andrew 84–85, 167
Mnyele, Thami 91

Modise, Joe 1
Mogoba, Stanley 106
Mokgabudi, Montsho (aka Obadi) 48
Moloise, Malesela Benjamin 90
Mompati, Ruth 1
Mondlane, Gibson (aka Gibson Ncube) 54
monopolies 26, 32–33, 64
Moroka, James 2–3
Motau, Peter Sello (aka Paul Dikeledi) 52
Motlatsi, James 43
Motsoaledi, Elias 84–85, 167
Motsuenyane, Sam 106
Moumbaris, Alex 9
Mozambican National Resistance
    see RENAMO
Mozambique 17–19, 49–50, 57–59, 71,
    73–75, 156
Mpetha, Oscar 39, 167
MPLA 17–18, 59
Mthimkhulu, Siphiwo 54
Mulder, Connie 16, 27
Muller, Piet 79–81, 139
multiparty democracy 99, 133–134
Murray, Hugh 103–105
Myburgh, Tertius 104

Naidoo, Jay 44
Nair, Billy 164
Namibia 18, 24, 59, 112, 160–161
Natal Indian Congress 35, 37
Natal Sugar Association 69
National Association of Democratic
    Lawyers 133
National Convention Alliance 105, 106
National Council of Trade Unions 150
National Forum conference 38–39
National Front for the Liberation of Angola
    see FNLA
National Intelligence Service see NIS
National Party see NP
National Security Management System
    see NSMS
National Sports Congress 146
National Statutory Council see NSC
National Union for the Total Independence
    of Angola see UNITA
National Union of Mineworkers see NUM

Naudé, Beyers 1, 12, 106, 150
Ndou, Samson 9
'necklacing' 91
Netherlands 61, 145, 156
Neto, Agostinho 18
'New face of counter-revolution, The'
    (paper) 98–99, 132
New Nation 149
New York Times 73
New York Times Magazine 86–87
New Zealand 13, 60, 73 n3
Ngesi, Themba 53–54
Nieuwoudt, Jan Anton 55
NIS 74, 79–81, 83, 122, 127–131, 151–154,
    168–169
Nkomati Accord 58, 71, 73–75, 97, 147
Non-Aligned Movement 164
NP 1–7, 11–14, 25–26, 32, 63–64, 73, 102,
    108, 154–157, 172, 176
NSC 137, 148, 151, 153, 158
NSMS 28–30, 64–65, 148, 176
nuclear weapons programme 51
NUM 43–44
Nyanda, Siphiwe 161
Nyawose, Patrick and Jabu 52
Nyembe, Dorothy 9
Nzo, Alfred 1, 78, 103, 142, 144

OAU 10–11, 23, 60, 126, 161, 164
Obasanjo, Olusegun 112–113, 116–117
oil embargo 23–24
Olympics (1968) 13
O'Malley, Padraig 140, 163
Operation Askari 72
Operation Marion 52
Operation Savannah 17–18
Operation Vula (Vulindlela) 140, 159–163
Oppenheimer, Harry 66, 70, 104
Organisation de l'Armée Secrète 28
Organisation of African Unity see OAU

PAC 10, 15, 38
Pahad, Essop and Aziz 142
Pakendorf, Harald 104
Pan Africanist Congress see PAC
Pan African Youth Movement 23
pass laws 23, 31 n9

Patel, Ebrahim 141–142
Paton, Alan 66
People's Liberation Army of Namibia
    see PLAN
People's Movement for the Liberation of
    Angola see MPLA
PFP 66–70, 78 n9, 105–108, 151, 157
Phina, Samuel 53–54
Pieterson, Zolile Hector 20
PLAN 18
poison 53–55
Polaroid Corporation 23
police see SAP
political prisoners 76–78, 82–84, 88–89,
    152, 165, 167–168
Pollsmoor Prison 84–85, 119–120
Portugal 17–19, 73–74, 155
power-sharing 28, 30–31, 69–70, 170,
    175, 177
power stations, attacks on 48
'pre-emptive' strikes 57, 92
    see also raids, cross-border
'Pretoria Six', trial of 9
Price, Robert M. 13
prisoner exchange, Angola and South
    Africa 155–156
Progressive Federal Party see PFP
Progressive Party 66
Progressive Reform Party 66
Project Coast 53
propaganda 10, 25, 27, 45–46, 75–76
protests and strikes 13–16, 19–27, 33, 39–45,
    60, 63, 67, 72, 90, 149
Pro Veritate 12
Pyramid Detachment 8

Qoboza, Percy 76
'Question of Negotiations, The' 136–137

Radio Deutsche Welle 161
Radio Freedom 40, 45, 46
raids, cross-border 49, 58–59, 91–92, 115,
    117, 120
Ramaphosa, Cyril 43, 44
Ramsamy, Sam 146
Rapport 139
Reagan, Ronald 71, 117, 162

recordings of conversations 82–84, 107
referendum (1960) 3
referendum (1983) 31, 32–33, 65–66, 70
Reform Party 66
reforms to apartheid system 17, 25–26, 30–31, 63–64
see also tricameral system
Release Mandela Campaign 36
Release Mandela Committee 35
Relly, Gavin 104–105, 107
RENAMO 57–59
'Report of the Politico-Military Strategy Commission to the ANC NEC' ('Green Book') 37n3, 45–46
republic, South Africa as 3, 26
Resolution 435 59, 161
Reuters 157
Rhodesia 7–8, 17–19
see also Zimbabwe
Rhoodie, Eschel 27
Riekert Commission 27, 31
Rivonia trial 10
Robben Island prison 84–85, 89
Robins, Chris 18
rock concert at Wembley Stadium, London 60
Rosberg, Carl Gustav 13
Rosholt, Mike 106
Roux, Jannie 82
'Rubicon' speech 94–95, 147
rugby 13, 60, 73n3, 141–146
rural constituencies 26

SACC 40–41, 149–150
Sachs, Albie 100
SACOS 42, 145–146
SACP 40, 45, 78, 174
SACTU 44–45
SADCC 59
SADF 17–19, 48–49, 51–52, 54, 57–59, 72
sanctions against apartheid South Africa 22–24, 27, 35–36, 58–59, 72–73, 76, 93–95, 110–111, 157–158
SANROC 146
SAP 19, 92, 167
SARB 141–146
SARU 142–146

Sasol, attacks on 47–48
Saunders, Chris 106
Scandinavian countries 61, 73
Schreiner, Deneys 69
Schwarz, Harry 66, 67
Secret Revolution 82–83
Security Branch 7, 19, 51, 54–55, 79–81, 90–92, 148
September, Dulcie 52
Sestigers 12
Sharpeville massacre 10, 14, 20
Shultz, George 158
Simons, Jack 100
Sipolilo Campaign 8, 15
Sisulu, Albertina 39
Sisulu, Walter 1, 84–85, 101–102, 167–168, 176
Sisulu, Zwelakhe 149
Skosana, Maki 91
Slabbert, Frederik van Zyl 67–70, 78n9, 105–108, 114, 142
Slovo, Joe 1, 48, 140, 162
Smith, Ian 17
Sobhuza II, King 57n11
'soft' vs 'hard' targets 90–91
Solomon Mahlangu Freedom College 61
Sorour, Peter 104
South African Air Force 49
South African Allied Workers Union 43
South African Bureau of Racial Affairs 64
South African Communist Party see SACP
South African Congress of Trade Unions see SACTU
South African Council of Churches see SACC
South African Council on Sport see SACOS
South African Defence Force see SADF
South African Indian Council 35, 68
South African Law Commission 120
South African Medical Service 53–55
South African National Convention (1908–9) 26
South African Non-Racial Olympic Committee see SANROC
South African Police see SAP
South African Railways Police 91–92

South African Rugby Board *see* SARB
South African Rugby Union *see* SARU
Southern African Catholic Bishops'
  Conference 150
Southern African Development
  Coordination Conference *see* SADCC
South West Africa People's Organisation
  see SWAPO
Soviet Union 61, 74
Soweto Civic Association 36
Soweto Uprising of 1976 19–23, 25–27, 33,
  45, 63, 67
'special constables' (*kitskonstabels*) 56
sports boycotts 13, 22, 24, 60, 73 n3, 138,
  141–146
SSC (State Security Council) 29–30, 82,
  153–154, 172
states of emergency 30, 44, 93, 119–120,
  148–151, 157
Steinberg, Jonny 85
STRATCOM (Strategic Communications)
  29
Strauss, Franz Josef 76, 77
strikes *see* protests and strikes
Sullivan Code 23–24
Sunday Post 76
Suppression of Communism Act 8, 9
surveillance *see* recordings of
  conversations
SWAPO 18, 54, 57, 72
Swaziland 19, 50, 57, 71
Sweden 24, 61
Switzerland 73–74, 131

Tabane, Job Shimankana (aka Cassius
  Make) 52
Tambo, Oliver
  annual January 8 statements 46–47
  on armed struggle 108–110, 162
  Black Consciousness Movement and
    38 n5
  Constitutional Commission 99–101
  democracy 163, 178
  dynamics within ANC 141
  Groote Schuur talks 1
  Harare Declaration 126, 161–163, 178
  health 126, 163
  international community and 112–114,
    135–136, 158, 162
  Nelson Mandela and 88–89, 120,
    159–160
  'Mandela document' 124–125
  Mells Park talks 126–127
  MK 8, 48–49, 90–91
  'New face of counter-revolution, The'
    (paper) 98–99
  Nkomati Accord 97
  Operation Vula 140, 159–162
  PFP and 107–108
  'Rubicon' speech 94
  sports boycotts 144–145
Tanzania 59, 61
Terreblanche, Sampie 79, 127, 152
Terrorism Act 7, 8, 9
Thabo Mbeki I Know, The 129
Thatcher, Margaret 71, 73–74, 76, 110–112,
  130, 155, 160–161, 167
Theron, Johan 54
Time 94
torture 7, 10, 21
'total onslaught' strategy 28–30, 44, 56
trade unions 16, 27, 35, 41–44, 46, 52, 90,
  150
Transkei 17, 77
Transvaal Indian Congress 37
TRC 8, 52, 91
Treason Trial 3
Treaty of Vereeniging 26
Treurnicht, Andries 64–65
Trew, Tony 130, 131, 151
tricameral system 31, 39–40, 50, 65–66,
  70–72, 106, 147–148, 171
Trojan Horse Massacre 91–92
'Troops out of the Townships' campaign
  92–93
Truth and Reconciliation Commission
  see TRC
Tshwete, Steve 144
Tutu, Desmond 88, 106, 150, 161

UDF 35, 38–40, 42, 50–52, 72, 90, 106, 132,
  146, 148–150, 157, 162
UK 13, 24, 59, 71, 73–74, 76, 100, 110–111,
  126–127, 130, 158

uMkhonto weSizwe *see* MK
UN 17 n4, 23–24, 59–60, 126, 164
unemployment 71
unions *see* trade unions
UNITA 18–19, 57, 59, 72, 156
United Democratic Front *see* UDF
United Kingdom *see* UK
United Nations *see* UN
United Party 4, 66
United States of America *see* USA
United Women's Organisation 36
unity 37–38, 65
Unity Movement 37, 38
Unlawful Organisations Act 8
UN Security Council 23, 59, 76, 160–161
Urban Bantu Councils 20, 31, 40, 148–151
urbanisation 16–17
USA 17–18, 23–24, 27, 35, 59–61, 71, 94–95,
    100, 112, 117, 155, 158, 161–162

Vaal Uprising of 1984 39, 43, 90
Van den Bergh, Hendrik 27
Van der Merwe, Hendrik W. 78–82, 103
Van der Merwe, S.S. 'Fanie' 123, 173
Van der Merwe, Stoffel 1
Van Greunen, Maurice 80–81
Van Niekerk, Gerhard 123
Van Rensburg, Nic 54
verkramptes 63–65, 159
verligtes 63–65, 73, 81
Verwoerd, Hendrik 4, 12
Vietnam 48
vigilantes 55, 148
Viljoen, Constand 57
Viljoen, Gerrit 1, 26, 63–64, 167–168, 172
Vlakplaas, Security Branch unit at 52, 54, 91
Vlok, Adriaan 1, 91

Von Hirschberg, Carl 94
Vorster, John 10–11, 13, 17, 19, 25–27, 51,
    63–64

Waddell, Gordon 70
Wankie (Hwange) Campaign 7–9, 15
Washington Star 27
Wessels, Leon 78–79
Western Cape Traders Association 42
Western powers 10, 14, 135–136, 150
Wiehahn Commission 17, 27, 31, 41
Willemse, W.H. 84–86, 121, 123
Williams, Paul 175
Winter, Gordon 159 n16
women, role of 36
Women's International Democratic
    Federation 23
World Council of Churches 12, 60
World Federation of Democratic Youth 23
World Federation of Trade Unions 22
World Peace Council 23
World, The 21

Young, Michael 126–128, 130, 151
young people 19, 35, 54–55, 91–92, 149

Zambia 59, 92
ZANLA (Zimbabwe African National
    Liberation Army) 18–19, 112
ZANU (Zimbabwe African National
    Union) 18, 112
ZAPU (Zimbabwe African People's Union)
    7–8, 18
Zimbabwe 50, 57, 58–59, 92
    see also Rhodesia
ZIPRA (Zimbabwe People's Revolutionary
    Army) 8